THE LANAHAN READINGS IN *Media and Politics*

—— Including Pivotal Rulings from the Supreme Court

THE LANAHAN READINGS IN *Media and Politics*

— Including Pivotal Rulings from the Supreme Court

Edited by

Lewis S. Ringel

CALIFORNIA STATE UNIVERSITY—LONG BEACH

LANAHAN PUBLISHERS, INC.   *Baltimore*

COPYRIGHT © 2009 by LANAHAN PUBLISHERS, INC.

All Rights Reserved
Printed in the United States of America

Since this page could not legibly accommodate all copyright notices, pages 279 through 282 constitute a continuation of this copyright page.

The text of this book was composed in Baskerville with display type in Caslon.
Composition by BYTHEWAY PUBLISHING SERVICES
Manufacturing by VICTOR GRAPHICS, INC.

ISBN-10 1-930398-11-5
ISBN-13 978-1-930398-11-5

LANAHAN PUBLISHERS, INC.
324 Hawthorne Road, Baltimore, MD 21210
1-866-345-1949 [Toll Free]
WWW.LANAHANPUBLISHERS.COM

1 2 3 4 5 6 7 8 9 0

In Loving Memory of

ROBERT LEWIS RINGEL

Philanthropist, Professional Mentor, Wise and Learned Counsel, Fellow Yankee Fan, Devoted Uncle

Dedicated to

My Big Boy, BENJAMIN,
and My Girls, JEANNE, JACQUELINE, and GINGER

CONTENTS

PREFACE   xii

INTRODUCTION—The Modern Media   1

PART ONE   The Framers of the First Amendment and the Free Press   5

1   THOMAS EMERSON   *Toward a General Theory of the First Amendment*
[A legendary Yale University Law Professor collapses arguments for having freedom of expression into four general lines of thought.]   7

2   VINCENT BLASI   *The Checking Value in the First Amendment*
[The Framers of the First Amendment expected the media to act as a kind of 4th branch of government designed for the purpose of checking and balancing the political branches.]   18

3   NORMAN ROSENBERG   *Protecting the Best Men: An Interpretive History of the Law of Libel*
[While they favored a free press that would check the government,

the Founders favored defamation laws that were designed to
protect society's political elite from media criticism.] 25

PART TWO   The Media and Politicians 31

4   CARL BERNSTEIN and BOB WOODWARD   *All the President's Men*
[The media often employs a double-standard where high-ranking public officials are involved.] 34

5   PAUL TAYLOR   *See How They Run*
[The media is sometimes susceptible to being used by politicians for their agenda.] 38

6   LARRY SABATO   *Feeding Frenzy*
[The modern media is too hungry for and consumed by scandals involving public officials.] 45

7   BENJAMIN BRADLEE   *A Good Life: Newspapering and Other Adventures*
[A defense of press coverage of public officials' personal lives in the modern era.] 54

8   STEPHEN FRANTZICH   *September 11th and the Bush Presidency: Rally Around the Rubble*
[An examination of news coverage of presidential approval ratings.] 58

PART THREE   The Media and Campaigns 65

9   DANIEL SHEA and JOHN MICHAEL BURTON   *Campaign Craft*
[All the things needed for a successful modern media campaign.] 68

10   KATHERINE Q. SEELYE   *Making of the Digital Press Corps, 2004*
[How changes in communication technologies affected the 2004 presidential election.] 79

11   RICHARD DAVIS   *Electing Justice: Fixing the Supreme Court Nomination Process*
[How the process of confirming federal judges has come to involve media-based political campaigns.] 84

CONTENTS — ix

PART FOUR Media Coverage of War, Foreign Affairs, and National Security 91

12   BENJAMIN BRADLEE   *A Good Life: Newspapering and Other Adventures*
[A legendary newspaperman discusses why America needs a media that covers matters of war and national security in a vigorous and exacting manner.]   94

13   DANNY SCHECHTER   *Information Warriors: From the News Dissector's Weblog*
[How the Pentagon operates to limit news coverage of wars.]   101

14   JAKE LYNCH   *Tips for Covering Conflict*
[A "peace journalist" offers advice for how to cover conflict.]   106

PART FIVE Entertainment Media and Politics   111

15   IRWIN SONNY FOX   *Using Soap Operas to Confront the World's Population Problem*
[A case study of how an interest group sought to spread its message by getting the world's soap operas to incorporate its viewpoint.]   113

16   EMILY NUSSBAUM   *When a TV Network Could Be Cynical About a War*
[An examination of CBS's decision to air a controversial episode of the sitcom, M*A*S*H, during the Vietnam War.]   119

17   ELIZABETH JENSEN   *Public Broadcasting and Political Balance: A New Twist*
[Should the government seek to fund *only* politically balanced television?]   123

18   CÉSAR G. SORIANO   *Politics Creates a Disturbance in the Force*
[Movies, even fanciful ones, are frequently far more political than many realize or even want.]   127

19   DAVID ROBB   *Operation Hollywood: How the Pentagon Shapes and Censors the Movies*
[Concern about its image in American films has led the Pentagon to seek to alter or even control how it is portrayed on the silver-screen.]   130

20   RAY BRADBURY   *Fahrenheit 451*
[Famed author Ray Bradbury's *coda* to his novel, *Fahrenheit 451*, in which he discusses his view of and response to those who have tried to censor his works over the years.]   137

PART SIX   The "New Media"   141

21   ALESSANDRA STANLEY   *No Jokes or Spin. It's Time (Gasp) to Talk*
[Some musings on an unusual interview with Jon Stewart, host of Comedy Central's *Daily Show*, by CNN's *Crossfire* co-hosts Tucker Carlson and Paul Bagala. Is a parody of a news show real news—or just funny?]   145

22   SHERYL GAY STOLBERG   *Laugh and the Voters Laugh with You, or at Least at You*
[*The Colbert Report's* quest to interview all members of Congress.]   148

23   JOHN BORLAND   *Bloggers Drive Hoax Probe into Bush Memos*
[Increasingly, it is alternative media outlets, such as blogs or online news sources, that are breaking the nation's biggest stories.]   152

24   JIM VANDEHEI   *Blogs Attack From Left as Democrats Reach for Center*
[Bloggers are working to reshape the American political landscape.]   155

25   EUGENE VOLOKH   *You Can Blog, But You Can't Hide*
[Should bloggers be treated as journalists and afforded the same rights as any reporter?]   159

PART SEVEN   Assessing the Media   163

26   MICHAEL PARENTI   *Inventing Reality: The Politics of News Media*
[The media is biased in favor of its corporate ownership.]   165

27   W. LANCE BENNETT   *News: The Politics of Illusion*
[Forget ideological biases: The real news biases are of an organizational and professional nature.]   173

28   TED KOPPEL   *And Now, a Word for our Demographic*
[How the business end of journalism may be affecting the media.]   185

29   MICHAEL SCHUDSON   *The Social Origins of Press Cynicism*
[In light of their professional ethics and sense of professional purpose, journalists are in reality quite optimistic.]   189

30   CARL BERNSTEIN and BOB WOODWARD   *All the President's Men*
[Two reporters question their own ethics in covering America's greatest political scandal.]   197

31   DAVID BRINKLEY   *On Being an Anchorman*
[Some closing thoughts from one of television's most famous network news anchors.]   205

PART EIGHT   The Media and the Law: Private Efforts to Restrict the Free Press   209

32   *New York Times v. Sullivan (1964)*
[The United States Supreme Court federalizes defamation law.]   211

33   *Time Inc. v. Hill (1967)*
[The Court expands the *Sullivan* doctrine of Actual Malice to defamation suits involving public figures.]   218

34   *Gertz v. Welch Inc. (1974)*
[The Court refuses to expand the *Sullivan* doctrine of Actual Malice to defamation suits involving private citizens.]   221

35   *Hustler Magazine v. Falwell (1988)*
[The Court recognizes the right of the media to engage in outrageous speech about public figures—in effect, refusing to anoint itself keeper of the nation's taste.]   229

36   *Cohen v. Cowles Media Co. (1991)*
[The Court rules that journalists can be sued for revealing the identity of their sources.]   234

PART NINE   The Media and the Law: Public Efforts to Restrict or Regulate the Free Press   239

37   *Grosjean v. American Press Co. (1936)*
[The Court protects the print media from unfair taxes.]   241

38 *Red Lion Broadcasting Co. v. FCC (1969)*
[The Court upholds the Fairness Doctrine as applied to the electronic media.]   246

39 *New York Times v. United States (1971)*
[The Court restricts the ability of the federal government to levy prior restraints on the media.]   251

40 *Branzburg v. Hayes (1972)*
[The Court rules that journalists can be compelled to reveal the identity of their sources.]   263

41 *Miami Herald v. Tornillo (1974)*
[The Court holds that the state cannot fashion Fairness Doctrines and apply them to the print media.]   258

42 *Richmond Newspapers, Inc. v. Virginia (1980)*
[The Court rules in favor of media access to trials.]   270

CREDITS AND COPYRIGHTS   279

PREFACE

Overwhelmed. That is the word I would choose to describe how I felt the first time I set out to produce a reading list for a class I had been tapped to teach on media and politics. It was overwhelming because there was (and is) so much good material from which to choose and only so much time to cover it in class and on exams and papers. As the years have past, it remains overwhelming if only because of how quickly the modern media changes. Topics such as shield laws, infotainment, and coverage of the private lives of candidates for political office come into and go out of fashion to be replaced by the next hot issue. Also in constant flux is the technology that the modern media employs and the subjects that comprise the hot news stories of the day.

This collection of readings is designed to ease the selection process and alleviate any doubts that faculty may have about the class suitability and/or the attractiveness to students of the readings that they choose to assign. With a few exceptions, all of the materials found in this reader have been classroom tested and in several cases the reading subject, if not the actual reading, was suggested by students themselves. I have selected for inclusion media law cases and commentaries that are not only favorites of students but have proven themselves well-suited for drawing students into class discussions. To that end, I have included an end-of-reading discussion points aimed at guiding and stimulating student thinking as well as triggering good class discussions. Again, nearly all of these discussion points have been used in classes, and while every class is different in its makeup and interests, in sum, these have proven successful topics to raise when seeking to guide or provoke student discussion of issues related to media and politics.

The readings excerpted in the pages to follow reflect an eclectic approach to the study of media and politics. I define media rather broadly to include more than just news gathering and disseminating institutions. Films, literature, songs, and sitcoms can all be used to spread information or make points related to public issues. Consequently, there is a concerted effort to include readings that analyze and describe more than just the standard media outlets. Further, within the traditional concept of the news gathering media, there has been such change in what constitutes a journalist and in theories of how they should or actually do perform their roles as journalists, that this text includes readings on an array of traditional and nontraditional topics.

This reader brings together some of the biggest names in American journalism history along with relative unknowns—a healthy mix of media establishment and non-establishment authors. Some faculty will find that their students may be more familiar with the non-establishment authors. The same can be said of topics. Traditional media issues of organizational pressures, media bias, and concerns relating to press coverage of national security appear side-by-side with readings examining less traditional topics such as peace journalism, the digital press, the value of public affairs programming, and the issue of whether bloggers are journalists.

It is my belief that any exploration of the media in American society and politics must begin with the First Amendment. Part One, therefore, examines the historical record of the First Amendment and focuses on the Founders' likely (if discernable) intentions. Thomas Emerson offers his summary of why Americans have free expression rights. This is followed by Vincent Blasi's examination of the intellectual influences on the founding generation when it came to freedom of the press. This part concludes with a passage from Norman Rosenberg's comprehensive study of American defamation law and how successive generations of American leaders have relied on the law of libel and slander to silence critics and their belief that without a strong law of defamation the "best men" in society would shrink from public service.

Part Two examines the often complicated relationship between the media and politicians. All but one selection in this part are anecdotal in nature and all but two are written by media professionals. Bob Woodward and Carl Bernstein paint a picture of a press engaging in double-standards—one that offers certain key senior government officials such as Secretaries of State considerably greater deference than is afforded to lower profile or less powerful government officials. Next,

Paul Taylor finds that the press is susceptible to being used by politicians to achieve a particular agenda. Larry Sabato then details the media's tendency to engage in feeding frenzies at the expense of wounded politicians. A selection from the memoir of Benjamin Bradlee details his experiences with a number of famed politicians, most famously President John Kennedy. Concluding this part, Stephen Frantzich addresses the question of whether presidential approval ratings are or ought to be news.

Part Three includes readings on a subject near and dear to politicians: their elections. The first selection comes from Daniel Shea and John Michael Burton's *Campaign Craft*. Shea and Burton offer a kind of "how to run" guide for aspiring politicians that students contemplating a career in the electoral arena or in political journalism will find useful. This piece is followed by a newspaper article by Katherine Seeyle that highlights key technological changes in the electronic media and how such changes affected media coverage of the 2004 presidential election. This part concludes with an excerpt from Richard Davis's *Electing Justice*. Davis traces the politicization of the judicial nomination process, calling our attention to the fact that White Houses have come to treat judicial appointments as electoral campaigns to be waged through the media for the purpose of influencing how Senators (and the public) view judicial nominees.

In Part Four I turn to a popular topic—the media and its coverage of war, foreign policy, and national security. Three readings are included: the first, by Benjamin Bradlee, addresses criticism of how the press covers war and national security. The succeeding readings, both of which originate in Danny Schechter's *Media Wars*, criticize the media for not being aggressive enough in its coverage of American policies abroad. Students will be exposed to government efforts to spin the press as well as arguments in favor of peace journalism.*

Part Five examines the entertainment media and politics. The basic theme of this part is that the entertainment media can be used to shape public opinion whether it be through films or television shows intended to entertain audiences. Irwin Sonny Fox shows how an interest group sought to get a message across to the public by including its view in a soap opera. Emily Nussbaum examines the decision by CBS to air a controversial episode of *M*A*S*H* during the Vietnam War. Next, Elizabeth Jensen looks at government funding of public broadcasting. César Soriano takes students out to Hollywood, and muses on political messages in movies. David Robb keeps students in Hollywood

---

* Peace journalism is the idea that journalists should not be neutral when it comes to covering stories about war or how a nation's foreign policies adversely affect the chances of world peace.

and discusses how the Pentagon has influenced the film industry. Finally, famed author, Ray Bradbury, closes this part with some incisive comments on the dangers of censorship.

Building on several of the themes developed in the preceding part, Part Six looks at the rise of the new media, among them, parodies of news programs and blogs. Alessandra Stanley begins with a piece on a very unusual, but telling, interview with Jon Stewart of *The Daily Show* by CNN *Crossfire* co-hosts Tucker Carlson and Paul Bagala. Then, Sheryl Gay Stolberg takes a look at *The Colbert Report* and the show's interviews with members of Congress. In separate articles, John Borland, Jim VandeHei, and Eugene Volokh dissect the new news reporters, bloggers: how they are breaking some big news stories, how they might reshape the political landscape, and whether they should be treated as journalists.

Part Seven assesses the state of the modern American media. The six selections included in this part examine four important issues essential to such an assessment. The first two readings, by Michael Parenti and by W. Lance Bennett, examine media bias. Parenti focuses on corporate ownership while Bennett looks at more organizational bases of bias. Next, Ted Koppel and Michael Schudson separately assess the nature of the modern media. Koppel raises red flags about the quality of a media driven to please specific demographic groups. In contrast, Schudson is more sanguine about the modern media and its capacity to serve the public. Bob Woodward and Carl Bernstein explore ethical dilemmas that arose during their coverage of the political scandal known as Watergate. This part concludes with David Brinkley's reflections on his legendary career as a pioneering network anchor. In the course of doing so, Brinkley addresses issues such as the trust that viewers place in anchors and the responsibilities and powers that come with that trust.

The final two parts of the book concern media law. Both parts include judicial opinions issued by the U.S. Supreme Court. Part Eight focuses on private efforts to restrict the press, while Part Nine examines public efforts to restrict the press. Among the issues raised are defamation, the protections offered to outrageous speech, suing the press for breach of contract, the power of the state to compel journalists to reveal sources to a grand jury, taxation of the media, prior restraint, the fairness doctrine, and restricting press access to judicial trials. These parts form a fitting bookend to Part One on the First Amendment and our free press—essential reading for any aspiring journalist, politician, or student of the media.

Acknowledgments

I remember it like it was yesterday. I was down in my office looking at email when a message from LANAHAN's Don Fusting came in asking me if I would be interested in editing a reader on media and politics. The idea had been mine—about two years earlier I had suggested such a book during our only face-to-face meeting. How Don remembered such and what made him approach me subsequently I will never know—but I am so thankful that he did and even more appreciative of his efforts on behalf of our project together.

I do not think I would be so fortunate as to be in this position if it had not been for Professor Charles Noble. Chuck's recommendation that I develop and teach a course in media and politics was one of the best things that has happened to me professionally. I thank him for the confidence and faith that he has exhibited in me and for leading me to explore in greater detail a subject in which I had long had considerable interest but had never taught.

I thank the many fine students at California State University, Long Beach, who have taken my class on media and politics. Professors like myself need good students—we feed off of their enthusiasm and creativity, we come to think more clearly as a result of their questions and observations, and we prosper from their suggestions and feedback. In particular, I would like to thank Abe Flores and Scott Godfrey for challenging me and for their efforts toward helping me to improve my media and politics class.

The support staff at the Department of Political Science at California State University, Long Beach, helped me tremendously with this project. In particular, Amelia Marquez, Nancy St. Martin, and our former student-assistant, Briana Barcelo. In addition, my teaching assistants during the time when I produced this book, Sekou Banks, Shelagh Hoffman, Katie Kruger, Shaun Metcalfe, Grant Raupp, and Pan Zunggeemoge, made it possible for me to get my professional work done and stay on schedule.

Much of what I know first-hand about the media comes from my experience working for the State of Maryland Government. I would like to thank the public servants for whom I was honored to work and my supervisors, in particular Amanda Stakum-Conn, Lieutenant Governor Melvin "Mickey" Steinberg, Delegate Joan Pitkin, and the late A. Frank Carven, for affording me immeasurable opportunities to observe and participate in the political process with them or on their behalf.

My parents, Leonard and Harriet Ringel afforded me a good upbringing and instilled in me the values of hard work and a curiosity about and interest in public affairs. I credit my mother, whose interest in journalism, and my father, whose interest in the role of the press in the Watergate investigation, with much of my interest in the media and politics in general.

If there is one thing that I know it is that I married over my head—way over my head. I am forever in debt to my wife, Jeanne, for so many things. Among them, are our children Benjamin Brennan and Jacqueline Renee, and our "first baby," our dog Ginger. Jeanne, Ben, Jacqueline, and Ginger are my life and inspiration. Whenever I would get bogged down or frustrated by some aspect of the book process I would turn to them for support and diversion (something that comes by kids and dogs quite naturally). I thank them for adding so much to my life.

I thank my Uncle Bob and my Aunt Esty for all that they have done for me. It was with considerable pride that I informed my uncle about my book contract. It is with even greater sadness that I find myself writing a memorial section to the man who helped me in my career and life so much. I can only hope that in his final weeks he took some pride in and satisfaction from knowing that he had helped me immensely and that he appreciated the depth to which as a fellow academic I respected and stood in awe of his many professional achievements and talents.

Finally, I would like to thank the various publishers for granting us copyright permissions, my colleagues in academia and the news professionals who wrote testimonials for the book, everyone who suggested readings, and LANAHAN for its good work in making this book possible.

I, of course, am responsible for this work, and any errors that may exist.

INTRODUCTION—The Modern Media

This book examines the modern American media. Particular attention is paid to the media's coverage of and involvement in American politics. A variety of reading materials concerning a host of issues and topics have been selected. To emphasize the eclectic nature of the modern media, a conscious effort has been made to select readings from across a wide universe. In the pages to follow there are excerpts from academic texts, autobiographies, newspapers, the Internet, works of fiction, speeches, and court cases. The topics and form may vary but if there is one thing that each has in common it is that each has something to say about today's media as we know it.

Before proceeding to identify and outline the modern media, a few words are in order about two important terms. The first is media. It can be hazardous to superimpose a single definition on a large body of readings composed by a number of different individuals. But in practice, the term media is almost universally used to connote entities and persons in the profession of gathering, disseminating, and commenting upon news. Traditionally, these functions have been performed by journalists who together comprised the media. The modern media, however, has expanded to include a growing number of traditionally entertainment-oriented films, television shows, web-sites, works of literature, and popular songs that comment on public issues. That such creative vehicles have commented on public issues is not novel. What is new is that so many people receive so much of their information from these untraditional media sources rather than from more traditional sources such as newspapers or news broadcasts. Consider, for instance, a film such as *Fahrenheit 9/11* or a television show such as *The Daily Show*. These are two examples of creative vehicles that comment on politicians and public issues, yet, neither gather nor disseminate news in the traditional sense of the word. Rather, they are in the business of commenting upon what others have gathered and disseminated. They do so in a manner that is informative and entertaining (infotainment, it is called) and, to the likely chagrin of many professional journalists, they appear to have an impact on public opinion about or on public awareness of public issues. The same might be said of the many web-sites that feature politically charged songs or videos which provide the public information about issues important to the host. The modern American is increasingly becoming a visual person who is quite comfortable with and reliant upon untraditional sources of public information through which their public commentaries have affected what Americans know or think they know about the world around them. For our purposes, therefore, reading selections about the media try to reflect the changes in the modern media's form and functions when it comes to informing us about politics.

The second term in need of defining is politics. Politics, as it will be used in this text, is meant to describe the use of influence to achieve some desired end. It is typically understood, or at least expected, that the American media, at least the traditional media, has an obligation to inform its audience about who is engaging in politics, how and why this politics is occurring, and how the audience will be affected. Increasingly, politicians use the media as a means for achieving some objective. When this happens, the medium intended to check up on and monitor politics as practiced by politicians becomes part of the political process itself. When such occurs, terms such as media and politics take on a whole new importance as the camera or microphone changes hands (figuratively) and a whole new subject emerges. The term politics, in conjunction with media, therefore, is meant to convey both how the media covers political issues as well as how the media is involved in political actions.

The fact that terms such as media and politics would require revision is indicative of the fact that the American media of the 21st century has gone through and remains in a period of tremendous change. Much of what had once been true or fact has been altered or even vanguished by forces unforeseen ten or twenty years ago. The media has long had corporate ownership, however, the number of corporations owning television and radio stations has shrunk so that most media outlets and public airwaves licenses are in the hands of a precious few conglomerates. As a result, the media with which we are left is leaner and perhaps more driven by bottom-lines than before. Information is reported on now in more venues, by more outlets, and at a faster pace than in the past. The days when the three broadcast network newscasts dominated the airwaves are gone. So too is the era when news consumers would have to wait for the morning paper or hours in between broadcasts to learn about an evening's events. News consumers now choose from a dizzying array of news providers that come in forms and from places unimaginable to past generations. For instance, consumers can now get the news through a cell phone or on-line. Simply put, the modern news consumer can access news in any number of ways anyplace, anytime, anywhere. Compared with the past, the media that provides the news is better educated, less respectful of the personal lives of its subjects, and more representative of many traditionally disadvantaged groups such as women or minorities. The new media has reduced the role of the journalist while raising the level to which it will go to entertain its audience. As technology once in the hand of a privileged few has become more widespread, a growing number of individuals have sought to add their own commentary about public affairs to the national discourse. The result, is that the media of the early 21st century is an eclectic one blending a variety of media and technologies; it speaks about politics in many different voices and comes in an assortment of forms such as documentaries, web-blogs, public access cable channels, independent newspapers and films, talk radio, and even mainstream, big-budget entertainment films or television shows.

For all the many ways that the media has changed, there is much that remains constant, changing only in appearances rather than substance. Members of the media are still cynical about their subjects, often scoffing at efforts by politicians to stoke the media or curry its favor. Members of the media are human and their work is still affected by a variety of rivalries or jealousies. The media is still driven to discover the truth and many within it (as well as within the larger society) are still obsessed with scandals, especially those involving public officials. The public, while it has greater choices when it decides whom to watch or what to read, remains largely dependent on the media for information about public affairs. In order to serve that public, the media, for all of its high-tech advances, still needs the same basic thing it has always needed: good, honest, and accurate sources for its stories. There are ethical considerations or dilemmas that continue to gnaw at the media's collective conscious and there is still the need for members of the media to struggle to rise above their own biases. Furthermore, the media is still affected by the law and the nation's courts and other lawmakers. The legal doctrines and the exact legal controversies may change, but at a basic level the nation's conflicts involving the media and its laws of expression are still typically settled by its courts.

PART ONE

The Framers of the First Amendment and the Free Press

PART OF THE FIRST AMENDMENT to the Constitution of the United States affirms that "Congress shall make no law . . . abridging the freedom of speech, or of the press; or the right of the people peaceably to assemble, and to petition the Government for a redress of grievances." With these few words, the authors of the First Amendment set the nation on a path toward a system of free expression. Why did they do so? What did they have in mind when they did so? What are the benefits of their efforts? What did their countrymen think of what the authors of the First Amendment had done? What have subsequent generations thought of or done about the First Amendment? These are questions that have long intrigued, and presumably will continue to intrigue, students of the First Amendment. The reading selections included in this section examine these questions, and more, from different sets of perspectives. The following offers a glimpse into what to expect in the readings that comprise this chapter.

First up is Thomas Emerson's "Toward a General Theory of the First Amendment." Emerson examines a plethora of justifications for having a system of free expression. These include legal treaties, judicial opinions, and academic texts. His focus takes us as far back as the 17th century and as recent as Supreme Court decisions of the 20th century. In all, Emerson discovers four basic justifications for why societies adopt and maintain systems of free expression.

Following Emerson is Vincent Blasi's "The Checking Value in the

First Amendment." Where Emerson examined justifications for free expression across time, Blasi focuses exclusively on what or who led the authors of the First Amendment to draft and ratify the text itself. Blasi identified four main intellectual influences and ultimately concludes that it was a desire to provide a check on government vice that explains the Framer's decision to provide for a system of free expression.

What did the Framers' contemporaries think of the Framers' intentions when it came to establishing a free press? In particular, what did they think of the power of the state and/or private citizens to punish the press for defamatory publications or statements? Norman Rosenberg explores these issues in this excerpt from his book, *Protecting the Best Men: An Interpretive History of the Law of Libel*. According to Rosenberg, the first few generations of Americans, while expressing support for freedom of the press, did not take quite as broad a view of the right of, or the advisability of allowing, the press to defame society's most elite citizens. Such findings suggest that the Framers, or at least the first few generations to succeed them, did not view freedom of the press quite as broadly as we often think or expect.

1

Toward a General Theory of the First Amendement

THOMAS EMERSON

Ever wonder why America has a system of free expression? In a classic law review article, Professor Thomas Emerson gleans four justifications to support America's system of free expression. He does so after reviewing a wide historical record that includes court opinions, political theory, newspaper articles, letters to newspaper editors, speeches, diary entries, and personal letters. Note just how far back Emerson looks and that his examination of the historical record reaches as far back as the British thinkers, John Locke and John Stuart Mill.

The Function of Freedom of Expression in a Democratic Society

The right of the individual to freedom of expression has deep roots in our history. But the concept as we know it now is essentially a product of the development of the liberal constitutional state. It is an integral part of the great intellectual and social movement beginning with the Renaissance which transformed the Western world from a feudal and authoritarian society to one whose faith rested upon the dignity, the reason and the freedom of the individual. The theory in its modern form has thus evolved over a period of more than three centuries, being applied under different circumstances and seeking to deal with different problems. It is sufficient for our purposes to restate it in its final, composite form, as it comes to us today.

The values sought by society in protecting the right to freedom of expression may be grouped into four broad categories. Maintenance of a system of free expression is necessary (1) as assuring individual self-fulfillment, (2) as a means of attaining the truth, (3) as a method of securing participation by the members of the society in social, including political, decision-making, and (4) as maintaining the balance between stability and change in the society. We consider these in their affirmative aspects, without regard at this time to the problems of limitation or reconciliation with other values.

Individual Self-Fulfillment

The right to freedom of expression is justified first of all as the right of an individual purely in his capacity as an individual. It derives from the widely accepted premise of Western thought that the proper end of man is the realization of his character and potentialities as a human being. Man is distinguished from other animals principally by the qualities of his mind. He has powers to reason and to feel in ways that are unique in degree if not in kind. He has the capacity to think in abstract terms, to use language, to communicate his thoughts and emotions, to build a culture. He has powers of imagination, insight and feeling. It is through development of these powers that man finds his meaning and his place in the world.

The achievement of self-realization commences with development of the mind. But the process of conscious thought by its very nature can have no limits. An individual cannot tell where it may lead nor anticipate its end. Moreover, it is an *individual* process. Every man is influenced by his fellows, dead and living, but his mind is his own and its functioning is necessarily an individual affair.

From this it follows that every man—in the development of his own personality—has the right to form his own beliefs and opinions. And, it also follows, that he has the right to express these beliefs and opinions. Otherwise they are of little account. For expression is an integral part of the development of ideas, of mental exploration and of the affirmation of self. The power to realize his potentiality as a human being begins at this point and must extend at least this far if the whole nature of man is not to be thwarted.

Hence suppression of belief, opinion and expression is an affront to the dignity of man, a negation of man's essential nature. What [John] Milton said of licensing of the press is equally true of any form of restraint over expression: it is "the greatest displeasure and indignity to a free and knowing spirit that can be put upon him."

The right to freedom of expression derives, secondly, from basic Western notions of the role of the individual in his capacity as a member of society. Man is a social animal, necessarily and probably willingly so. He lives in company with his fellow men; he joins with them in creating a common culture; he is subject to the necessary controls of society and particularly of the state. His right to express his beliefs and opinions, in this role as a member of his community, follows from two fundamental principles. One is that the purpose of society, and of its more formal aspect the state, is to promote the welfare of the individual. Society and the state are not ends in themselves; they exist to serve the individual. The second is the principle of equality, formulated as the proposition that every individual is entitled to equal opportunity to share in common decisions which affect him.

From these concepts there follows the right of the individual to access to knowledge; to shape his own views; to communicate his needs, preferences and judgments; in short, to participate in formulating the aims and achievements of his society and his state. To cut off his search for truth, or his expression of it, is thus to elevate society and the state to a despotic command and to reduce the individual to the arbitrary control of others. The individual, in short, owes an obligation to cooperate with his fellow men, but that responsibility carries with it the right to freedom in expressing himself.

Two basic implications of the theory need to be emphasized. The first is that it is not a general measure of the individual's right to freedom of expression that any particular exercise of the right may be thought to promote or retard other goals of the society. The theory asserts that freedom of expression, while not the sole or sufficient end of society, is a good in itself, or at least an essential element in a good society. The society may seek to achieve other or more inclusive ends—such as virtue, justice, equality, or the maximum realization of the potentialities of its members. These problems are not necessarily solved by accepting the rules for freedom of expression. But, as a general proposition, the society may not seek to solve them by suppressing the beliefs or opinions of individual members. To achieve these other goals it must rely upon other methods: the use of counter-expression and the regulation or control of conduct which is not expression. Hence the right to control individual expression, on the ground that it is judged to promote good or evil, justice or injustice, equality or inequality, is not, speaking generally, within the competence of the good society.

The second implication, in a sense a corollary of the first, is that the theory rests upon a fundamental distinction between belief, opinion and communication of ideas on the one hand, and different forms of conduct on the other. For shorthand purposes we refer to this distinction hereafter as one between "expression" and "action." As just observed, in order to achieve its desired goals, a society or the state is entitled to exercise control over action—whether by prohibiting or compelling it—on an entirely different and vastly more extensive basis. But expression occupies a specially protected position. In this sector of human conduct, the social right of suppression or compulsion is at its lowest point, in most respects non-existent.

This marking off of the special area of expression is a crucial ingredient of the basic theory for several reasons. In the first place thought and communication are the fountainhead of all expression of the individual personality. To cut off the flow at the source is to dry up the whole stream. Freedom at this point is essential to all other freedoms. Hence society must withhold its right of suppression until the stage of action is reached. Secondly, expression is normally conceived as doing less injury to other social goals than action. It generally has less immediate consequences, is less irremediable in its impact. Thirdly, the power of society and the state over the individual is so pervasive, and construction of doctrines, institutions and administrative practices to limit this power so difficult, that only by drawing such a protective line between expression and action is it possible to strike a safe balance between authority and freedom.

Attainment of Truth

In the traditional theory, freedom of expression is not only an individual but a social good. It is, to begin with, the best process for advancing knowledge and discovering truth.

Considered in this aspect, the theory starts with the premise that the soundest and most rational judgment is arrived at by considering all facts and arguments which can be put forth in behalf of or against any proposition. Human judgment is a frail thing. It may err in being subject to emotion, prejudice or personal interest. It suffers from lack of information, insight, or inadequate thinking. It can seldom rest at the point any single person carries it, but must always remain incomplete and subject to further extension, refinement, rejection or modification. Hence an individual who seeks knowledge and truth must hear all sides of the question, especially as presented by those who feel strongly and argue militantly for a different view. He must consider all alternatives, test his judgment by exposing it to opposition, make full use of different minds to sift the true from the false. Conversely, suppression of information, discussion, or the clash of opinion prevents one from reaching the most rational judgment, blocks the generation of new ideas, and tends to perpetuate error. This is the method of the Socratic dialogue, employed on a universal scale.

The process is a continuous one. As further knowledge becomes available, as conditions change, as new insights are revealed, the judgment is open to reappraisal, improvement or abandonment.

The theory demands that discussion must be kept open no matter how certainly true an accepted opinion may seem to be. Many of the most widely acknowledged truths have turned out to be erroneous. Many of the most significant advances in human knowledge—from Copernicus to Einstein—have resulted from challenging hitherto unquestioned assumptions. No opinion can be immune from challenge.

The process also applies regardless of how false or pernicious the new opinion appears to be. For the unaccepted opinion may be true or partially true. And there is no way of suppressing the false without suppressing the true. Furthermore, even if the new opinion is wholly false, its presentation and open discussion serves a vital social purpose. It compels a rethinking and retesting of the accepted opinion. It results in a deeper understanding of the reasons for holding the opinion and a fuller appreciation of its meaning.

The only justification for suppressing an opinion is that those who seek to suppress it are infallible in their judgment of the truth. But no individual or group can be infallible, particularly in a constantly changing world.

It is essential to note that the theory contemplates more than a process for arriving at an individual judgment. It asserts that the process is also the best method for reaching a general or social judgment. This is true in part because a social judgment is made up of individual judgments. It will therefore be vitally conditioned by the quality of the individual judgments which compose it. More importantly, the same reasons which make open discussion essential for an intelligent individual judgment make it imperative for rational social judgments. Through the acquisition of new knowledge, the toleration of new ideas, the testing of opinion in open competition, the discipline of rethinking its assumptions, a society will be better able to reach common decisions that will meet the needs and aspirations of its members.

Participation in Decision-Making

The third main function of a system of freedom of expression is to provide for participation in decision-making through a process of open discussion which is available to all members of the community. Conceivably the technique of reaching the best common judgment could be limited to an elite, or could be extended to most members of the society excluding only those who were felt to be clearly unworthy. In its earlier forms the theory was often so restricted. But as the nineteenth century progressed it came to be accepted that all men were entitled to participate in the process of formulating the common decisions.

This development was partly due to acceptance of the concept that freedom of expression was a right of the individual, as discussed previously. But it was also inherent in the logic of free expression as a social good. In order for the process to operate at its best, every relevant fact must be brought out, every opinion and every insight must be available for consideration. Since facts are discovered and opinions formed only by the individual, the system demands that all persons participate. As John Stuart Mill expressed it, "If all mankind minus one, were of one opinion, and only one person were of the contrary opinion, mankind would be no more justified in silencing that one person, than he, if he had the power, would be justified in silencing mankind."

But in addition to these reasons, the right of all members of society to form their own beliefs and communicate them freely to others must be regarded as an essential principle of a democratically-organized society. The growing pressures for democracy and equality reinforced the logical implications of the theory and demanded opportunity for all persons to share in making social decisions. This is, of course, especially true of political decisions. But the basic theory carried beyond the political realm. It embraced the right to participate in the building of the whole culture, and included freedom of expression in religion, literature, art, science and all areas of human learning and knowledge.

In the field of political action, as just mentioned, the theory of freedom of expression has particular significance. It is through the political process that most of the immediate decisions on the survival, welfare and progress of a society are made. It is here that the state has a special incentive to repress opposition and often wields a more effective power of suppression. Freedom of expression in the political realm is usually a necessary condition for securing freedom elsewhere. It is in the political sector, therefore, that the crucial battles over free expression are most often fought.

As the general theory makes clear, freedom of discussion in public affairs serves an important function regardless of whether the political structure of a nation is democratic or not. Every government must have some process for feeding back to it information concerning the attitudes, needs and wishes of its citizens. It must, therefore, afford some degree of freedom at least to some of its citizens, to make known their wants and desires. Indeed in a more formal aspect—as a petition for redress of grievances—this right of communicating to the government in power was one of the earliest forms of political expression. The Magna Carta and the Bill of Rights of 1689, for instance, were promulgated in response to such petitions. In general, the greater the degree of political discussion allowed, the more responsive is the government, the closer is it brought to the will of its people, and the harder must it strive to be worthy of their support.

The crucial point, however, is not that freedom of expression is politically useful, but that it is indispensable to the operation of a democratic form of government. Once one accepts the premise of the Declaration of Independence—that governments derive "their just powers from the consent of the governed"—it follows that the governed must, in order to exercise their right of consent, have full freedom of expression both in forming individual judgments and in forming the common judgment. Together with the argument for freedom of religious belief, this proposition was the one most frequently and most insistently urged in support of freedom of expression.

The proponents of freedom of political expression often addressed themselves to the question whether the people were competent to perform the functions entrusted to them, whether they could acquire sufficient information or possessed sufficient capacity for judgment. The men of the eighteenth century, with their implicit faith in the power of reason and the perfectibility of man, entertained few doubts on this score. Political theorists of the nineteenth and twentieth centuries have been more cautious. And there was some disagreement as to whether the right of political expression could safely be extended to societies which had not reached a certain point in the development of education and culture. But these problems were actually questions concerning the viability of democracy itself. And once a society was committed to democratic procedures, or rather in the process of committing itself, it necessarily embraced the principle of open political discussion.

Balance Between Stability and Change

The traditional doctrine of freedom of expression, finally, embodies a theory of social control. The principle of open discussion is a method of achieving a more adaptable and at the same time more stable community, of maintaining the precarious balance between healthy cleavage and necessary consensus. This may not always have been true, and may not be true of many existing societies. But where men have learned how to function within the law, an open society will be the stronger and more cohesive one.

The reasons supporting this proposition can only be stated here in summary form. In the first place, suppression of discussion makes a rational judgment impossible. In effect it substitutes force for logic. Moreover, coercion of expression is likely to be ineffective. While it may prevent social change, at least for a time, it cannot eradicate thought or belief; nor can it promote loyalty or unity. As [Walter] Bagehot observed, "Persecution in intellectual countries produces a superficial conformity, but also underneath an intense, incessant, implacable doubt."

Furthermore, suppression promotes inflexibility and stultification, preventing the society from adjusting to changing circumstances or developing new ideas. Any society, and any institution in society, naturally tends toward rigidity. Attitudes and ideas become stereotyped; institutions lose their vitality. The result is mechanical or arbitrary application of outworn principles, mounting grievances unacknowledged, inability to conceive new approaches, and general stagnation. Opposition serves a vital social function in offsetting or ameliorating this normal process of bureaucratic decay.

Again, suppression of expression conceals the real problems confronting a society and diverts public attention from the critical issues. It is likely to result in neglect of the grievances which are the actual basis of the unrest, and thus prevent their correction. For it both hides the extent of opposition and hardens the position of all sides, thus making a rational compromise difficult or impossible. Further, suppression drives opposition underground, leaving those suppressed either apathetic or desperate. It thus saps the vitality of the society or makes resort to force more likely. And finally it weakens and debilitates the majority whose support for the common decision is necessary. For it hinders an intelligent understanding of the reasons for adopting the decision and, as [John Stuart] Mill observed, "beliefs not grounded on conviction are likely to give way before the slightest semblance of an argument." In short, suppression of opposition may well mean that when change is finally forced on the community it will come in more violent and radical form.

The argument that the process of open discussion, far from causing society to fly apart, stimulates forces that lead to greater cohesion, also rests upon the concept of political legitimation. Stated in narrower and perhaps cruder terms, the position is that allowing dissidents to expound their views enables them "to let off steam." The classic example is the Hyde Park meeting where any person is permitted to say anything he wishes to whatever audience he can assemble. This results in a release of energy, a lessening of frustration, and a channeling of resistance into courses consistent with law and order. It operates, in short, as a catharsis throughout the body politic.

The principle of political legitimation, however, is more broadly fundamental. It asserts that persons who have had full freedom to state their position and to persuade others to adopt it will, when the decision goes against them, be more ready to accept the common judgment. They will recognize that they have been treated fairly, in accordance with rational rules for social living. They will feel that they have done all within their power, and will understand that the only remaining alternative is to abandon the ground rules altogether through resort to force, a course of action upon which most individuals in a healthy society are unwilling to embark. In many circumstances, they will retain the opportunity to try again and will hope in the end to persuade a majority to their position. Just as in a judicial proceeding where due process has been observed, they will feel that the resulting decision, even though not to their liking, is the legitimate one.

In dealing with the problem of social control, supporters of free expression likewise emphasize that the issue must be considered in the total context of forces operating to promote or diminish cohesion in a society. By and large, they theorize, a society is more likely to be subject to general inertia than to volatile change. Hence resistance to the political order is unlikely to reach the stage of disorder unless a substantial section of the population is living under seriously adverse or discriminatory conditions. Only a government which consistently fails to relieve valid grievances need fear the outbreak of violent opposition. Thus, given the inertia which so often characterizes a society, freedom of expression, far from causing upheaval, is more properly viewed as a leavening process, facilitating necessary social and political change and keeping a society from stultification and decay.

Moreover, the state retains adequate powers to promote political unity and suppress resort to force. For one thing it shares the right to freedom of expression with its citizens. While there may be some limits on this power, the state is normally in a much better position to obtain information and in a much more authoritative position from which to communicate its official views than the ordinary citizen or group of citizens. More importantly, the state possesses the authority to restrict or compel action. The right with which we are concerned, as already noted, extends only to expression; when the stage of action is reached the great power of the state becomes available for regulation or prohibition. And finally the state has not only the power but the obligation to control the conditions under which freedom of expression can function for the general welfare. This includes not only responsibility for eliminating grievances which may give rise to disorder but also a responsibility for maintaining economic and social conditions under which the ground rules of democracy can operate.

Proponents of the theory acknowledge that the process of full discussion, open to all, involves some risks to the society that practices it. At times there may be substantial delay in the working out of critical problems. There can be no ironclad guarantee that in the end a decision beneficial to society will be reached. The process, by encouraging diversity and dissent, does at times tend to loosen the common bonds that hold society together and may threaten to bring about its dissolution. The answer given is that the stakes are high and that the risks must be run. No society can expect to achieve absolute security.

Change is inevitable; the only question is the rate and the method. The theory of freedom of expression offers greater possibilities for rational, orderly adjustment than a system of suppression. Moreover, they urge, as the lesson of experience, that the dangers are usually imaginary; that suppression is invoked more often to the prejudice of the general welfare than for its advancement. To this they add that the risks are the lesser evil, that the alternatives are worse, that the only security worth having is that based on freedom.

Thus, the theory of freedom of expression involves more than a technique for arriving at better social judgments through democratic procedures. It comprehends a vision of society, a faith and a whole way of life. The theory grew out of an age that was awakened and invigorated by the idea of a new society in which man's mind was free, his fate determined by his own powers of reason, and his prospects of creating a rational and enlightened civilization virtually unlimited. It is put forward as a prescription for attaining a creative, progressive, exciting and intellectually robust community. It contemplates a mode of life that, through encouraging toleration, skepticism, reason and initiative, will allow man to realize his full potentialities. It spurns the alternative of a society that is tyrannical, conformist, irrational and stagnant. It is this concept of society that was embodied in the first amendment.

It is not within the scope of this article to demonstrate the soundness of the traditional theory underlying freedom of expression, or its viability under modern conditions. The writer believes that such a demonstration can be made. But the significant point here is that we as a nation are presently committed to the theory, that alternative principles have no substantial support, and that our system of freedom of expression must be based upon and designed for the realization of the fundamental propositions embodied in the traditional theory.

The Dynamics of Limitation

In constructing and maintaining a system of freedom of expression, the principal problems and major controversies have arisen when the attempt is made to fit the affirmative theory—that is, the affirmative functions served by the system—into a more comprehensive scheme of social values and social goals. The crucial issues have revolved around the question of what limitations, if any, ought to be imposed upon freedom of expression in order to reconcile that interest with other individual and social interests sought by the good society. Most of our efforts in the past to formulate rules for limiting freedom of expression have been seriously defective through failure to take into consideration the realistic context in which such limitations are administered. The crux of the problem is that the limitations, whatever they may be, must be applied by one group of human beings to other human beings. In order to take adequate account of this factor it is necessary to have some understanding of the forces in conflict, the practical difficulties in formulating limitations, the state apparatus necessary to enforce them, the possibility of distorting them to attain ulterior purposes, and the impact of the whole process upon achieving an effective system of free expression.

The starting point is a recognition of the powerful forces that impel men toward the elimination of unorthodox expression. Most men have a strong inclination to suppress opposition even where differences in viewpoint are comparatively slight. But a system of free expression must be framed to withstand far greater stress. The test of any such system is not whether it tolerates minor deviations but whether it permits criticism of the fundamental beliefs and practices of the society. And in this area the drives to repress, both irrational and rational, tend to become overwhelming.

The human propensity to curb unwanted criticism has long been noted by the theorists of freedom of expression. Thus John Stuart Mill, early in his essay *On Liberty*, remarked:

> The disposition of mankind, whether as rulers or as fellow-citizens, to impose their own opinions and inclinations as a rule of conduct on others, is so energetically supported by some of the best and by some of the worst feelings incident to human nature, that it is hardly ever kept under restraint by anything but want of power.

The strong innate drive to suppress deviant opinion has also been stressed in modern studies of the authoritarian personality. An attack upon cherished premises tends to create anxiety, especially in those who have a strong inner need for certainty. The deviant opinion is felt as a threat to personal security. And the response tends to be fear, hatred or a similar emotion, from which springs a compulsion to eliminate the source of the danger. In such circumstances it is natural to turn to the state for protection against the supposed evil. Such factors play a prominent part in the formulation of restrictions upon expression and, equally important, in their administration.

DISCUSSION POINTS

1   What four justifications for having a system of free expression does Emerson identify?

2   Which of these four justifications do you find most and/or least persuasive and why?

3   Can you think of any additional, or new, justifications that you would add to these four?

2

The Checking Value in the First Amendment

VINCENT BLASI

The authors of both the American Constitution and the Bill of Rights were typically quite concerned with the potential for misuse of power by the state. Consequently, they built into the American system of government a variety of institutional devices aimed at limiting or checking the powers of the state and its leaders. According to Vincent Blasi, one of these devices was a free press. The press, he argues, was intended to serve a "check" on the government by exposing such governmental sins as bad decision making, ineffectiveness, inefficiency, corruption, and/or mistruths. In tracing the history that led up to the drafting and ratification of the First Amendment, Blasi illustrates the impact that a number of British thinkers had on this process and its ultimate product. Take note of how united many of the leading and most influential Americans of the day, men such as James Madison, Thomas Jefferson, and Alexander Hamilton, were in their belief in the need for a free press as well as in the righteousness of the "checking value."

Throughout the analysis, one must keep in mind that the checking value is to be viewed as a possible supplement to, not a substitute for, the values that have been at the center of twentieth-century thinking about the First Amendment. . . . I do not purport to offer a comprehensive ordering of First Amendment values or to suggest that the checking value should form the cornerstone of all First Amendment analysis. My only purpose is to further the understanding of one basic value which has been underemphasized in this century and which, I believe, should be a significant component in any general theory of the First Amendment.

The Checking Value: Sources and Premises

. . .

The tendency of officials to abuse their public trust is a theme that has permeated political thought from classical times to the present. John Locke devoted much of his *Second Treatise on Civil Government*, first published in 1690, to this specific problem. But although Locke set forth an influential theory that the general citizenry has a right to overthrow rulers who abuse the public trust, he did not emphasize the role of the press in the process of checking governmental authority. In the decades immediately after Locke wrote, however, two institutions—the newspaper and the opposition party—developed into major forces in the politics of the times; partly as a result, the idea that free expression serves as a check on the behavior of incumbents assumed a prominent place in the political discourse of eighteenth-century England.

Among the English essayists of this period who were read by the colonists, four deserve special mention. The most important was "Cato," the pen name of coauthors John Trenchard and Thomas Gordon, who in the 1720s published a series of essays attacking the overbearing and manipulative administration of Sir Robert Walpole. The essays were widely read and discussed in both England and the colonies. . . .

Cato's discussion of the values underlying free expression is contained primarily in his Letter Number 15, entitled "Of Freedom of Speech." Cato's emphasis is on the need for popular recourse against evil officials:

> Whoever would overthrow the Liberty of a Nation must begin by subduing the Freeness of Speech; a Thing terrible to publick Traytors.
>
> . . . .
>
> That Men ought to speak well of their Governours, is true, while their Governours deserve to be well spoken of, but to do publick Mischief without Hearing of it is only the Prerogative and Felicity of Tyranny . . .

The essay next proceeds to a didactic review of ancient Roman and English history to make the point that while free expression poses no threat to enlightened rulers, it helps to check abuses of official power by "Traytors and Oppressors." The concluding portion of the essay mentions in passing the value of free expression in nurturing "excellent

Writers" and "Men of Genius" but rests its argument ultimately on the checking value . . .

While Cato probably was the English political writer most influential among the American colonists, the English political figure who most excited their admiration was the flamboyant John Wilkes. In 1763 Wilkes published the forty-fifth issue of his journal, the *North Briton*, which included a stinging attack on a speech given by George III. This prompted the king's ministers to file an information for seditious libel and to issue general warrants for the arrest and search of some 200 persons involved in the publication and dissemination of Number 45. Wilkes's private study was ransacked, his papers were seized, and Number 45 was ordered burned. A member of Parliament at the time, Wilkes was expelled from the House of Commons and prosecuted for seditious libel. He fled to France from whence he sent back to London numerous tracts and letters defending his cause and setting himself up as a martyr.

Wilkes['s] . . . discussion of freedom of the press, contained in the first issue of the *North Briton*, follows Cato in emphasizing the checking value of free expression:

> The liberty of the press is the birth-right of a Briton, and is justly esteemed the firmest bulwark of the liberties of this country. It has been the terror of all bad ministers; for their dark and dangerous designs, or their weakness, inability, and duplicity, have thus been detected and shewn to the public, generally in too strong and just colours for them long to bear up against the odium of mankind. . . . A wicked and corrupt administration must naturally dread this appeal to the world; and will be for keeping all the means of information equally from the prince, parliament and people.

The controversy over the prosecution and expulsion of Wilkes produced a lively debate among pamphleteers. Probably the two most important defenders of Wilkes's freedom of expression were "Father of Candor" and "Junius," anonymous writers whose identities have yet to be conclusively established. Father of Candor . . . presented a detailed criticism of the doctrine of seditious libel. He conceded that "libels on particular persons in their private capacities" should be punishable, but contended that "the case is totally different with respect to an administration; for the country in general is always the better or worse for its conduct, and therefore every man has a right to know, to consider and to reflect upon it." He based his argument directly on the checking value: "The liberty of exposing and opposing a bad administration by the pen is among the necessary privileges of a free people, and is perhaps the greatest benefit that can be derived from the liberty of the press."

The *Letters of Junius* are renowned not only for their contribution to political thought but also for the litigation that ensued over crown efforts to suppress them. To the chagrin of Lord Mansfield, the prosecutions of various publishers of the *Letters* were aborted by rebellious verdicts, which are now celebrated as leading examples of the practice of jury nullification. Several parliamentary leaders, including Lord Camden, Edmund Burke, and John Glynn, emerged during the controversy as prominent critics of the traditional law of seditious libel. The dispute was closely followed in the colonies. As Professor Chafee puts it, "The First Amendment was written by men to whom Wilkes and Junius were household words . . . ."

. . . the *Letters of Junius* were more concerned with immediate political issues than with abstract theories of government and liberty. But Junius did present one general discussion of liberty of press and in it he emphasized the checking value:

> A considerable latitude must be allowed in the discussion of public affairs, or the liberty of the press will be of no benefit to society. As the indulgence of private malice and personal slander should be checked and resisted by every legal means, so a constant examination into the characters and conduct of ministers and magistrates should be equally promoted and encouraged. They, who conceive that our newspapers are no restraint upon bad men, or impediment to the execution of bad measures, know nothing of this country. In that state of abandoned servility and prostitution, to which the undue influence of the crown has reduced the other branches of the legislature, our ministers and magistrates have in reality little punishment to fear, and few difficulties to contend with, beyond the censure of the press, and the spirit of resistance which it excites among the people.

Cato and Wilkes and Father of Candor and Junius probably did not represent the thinking of most Englishmen. They were opposition figures. But according to Bernard Bailyn's luminous book *The Ideological Origins of the American Revolution*:

> To say simply that this tradition of opposition thought was quickly transmitted to America and widely appreciated there is to understate the fact. Opposition thought, in the form it acquired at the turn of the seventeenth century and in the early eighteenth century, was devoured by the colonists. From the earliest years of the century it nourished their political thought and sensibilities. There seems never to have been a time

after the Hanoverian succession when these writings were not central to American political expression or absent from polemical politics.

From his study of the pamphlets of the American revolution, Bailyn concludes that the colonists were preoccupied with the fragility of constitutional government.... [T]he allocation of political power was a central concern to the colonists, and "[m]ost commonly the discussion of power centered on its essential characteristic of aggressiveness: its endlessly propulsive tendency to expand itself beyond legitimate boundaries."

Thus, the colonial pamphleteers, like the opposition leaders in England whom they so admired, organized much of their political thought around the need they perceived to check the abuse of governmental power. The First Amendment was an outgrowth of this body of thought, . . .

. . . In the 1770s and 1780s, however, as the colonists consummated their revolution and set about the task of implementing their political principles, proponents of press freedom began to mention additional values such as general enlightenment and popular participation in decision making. Even so, the value of checking misconduct by public officials remained one of the central concerns in virtually every discussion of freedom of the press. . . .

The draftsman of the First Amendment was James Madison. His most fully developed discussion of freedom of the press is contained in the Virginia Report of 1799–1800, a document he prepared for the Virginia House of Delegates in criticism of the federal Alien and Sedition Acts. Elaborating on a theory he had sketched out ten years earlier in presenting his proposed draft of the Bill of Rights to the United States House of Representatives, Madison argued that the British legal doctrine of freedom of the press, which consisted mainly in the prohibition of prior restraints and permitted criminal punishment for seditious libel, represented a narrow conception of liberty inapplicable to the American system of government. For in England, he observed, "[t]he representatives of the people in the legislature are not only exempt themselves from distrust, but are considered as sufficient guardians of the rights of their constituents against the danger from the executive." In contrast, "[i]n the United States, the executive magistrates are not held to be infallible, nor the legislatures to be omnipotent; and both being elective, are both responsible." "Is it not natural and necessary," asked Madison, "under such different circumstances, that a different degree of freedom in the use of the press should be contemplated?"

Madison proceeded to explain why the federal Sedition Act claimed "a power which, more than any other, ought to produce universal alarm." His principal argument was that the freedom to criticize government officials is essential to the process by which the electorate turns out of office those who fail to discharge their trusts. When public officials fail in this respect, said Madison, "it is natural and proper, that, according to the cause and degree of their faults, they should be brought into contempt or disrepute, and incur the hatred of the people." Whether and to what extent the public trust has been breached "can only be determined by a free examination thereof, and a free communication among the people thereon." Madison placed more emphasis than earlier theorists on the role of the electorate in the checking process, and also on the need to check errors of judgment as well as illegal or despotic actions by government officials. Nonetheless, the Virginia Report constitutes a detailed argument by the author of the First Amendment that one of the principal purposes of freedom of the press is to permit intensive scrutiny of the behavior of public officials.

Thomas Jefferson also tended to view liberty of the press in terms of the checking value. In a 1790 letter to Noah Webster, Jefferson distinguished between rights that individuals retain because their enjoyment is not inconsistent with the purposes of government, and other rights that constitute "certain fences which experience has proved peculiarly efficacious against wrong." He then gave examples: "Of the first kind, for instance, is freedom of religion; of the second, trial by jury, habeas corpus laws, free presses." Thirty-three years later, in a letter to Adamantios Coray, Jefferson once again stressed the checking value in explaining his commitment to freedom of the press: "This formidable censor of the public functionaries, by arraigning them at the tribunal of public opinion, produces reform peaceably, which must otherwise be done by revolution." He added, almost as an afterthought, "It is also the best instrument for enlightening the mind of man and improving him as a rational, moral, and social being . . . ."

Examples could be proliferated: the exchange of letters in 1789 between Chief Justice William Cushing of Massachusetts and John Adams, the commentary to a widely read 1803 edition of Blackstone by the respected judge and law professor St. George Tucker, the comprehensive *Treatise Concerning Political Enquiry and the Liberty of the Press* by Tunis Wortman, Alexander Hamilton's argument in 1804 before the New York Supreme Court in the case of *People v. Croswell*. These authorities, and those discussed above, do not establish that the generation of Americans which enacted the First Amendment built its whole philosophy of freedom of the press around the checking value. Then, as now, the commitment to free expression embodied a complex of values. There can be no doubt, however, that one of the most important values attributed to a free press by eighteenth-century political thinkers was that of checking the inherent tendency of government officials to abuse the power entrusted to them. Insofar as the views prevalent at the time of adoption have relevance to contemporary interpretation, the checking value rests on a most impressive foundation

DISCUSSION POINTS

1   Seldom will one find a person who does not agree with or accept the need for a free press to check the government. Equally seldom, perhaps, is finding two people who agree on what checking the government should mean. Put simply, do you think that there should be limits on what the press can do in reporting on the government? If so, what are they and how do you reconcile them with the language of the First Amendment which states: "Congress shall make no law . . . abridging the freedom of speech or of the press?"

2   There has been much furor over the press's occasional exposure of the certain classified aspects of the United States's war on terrorism both at home and abroad as well as its coverage of the wars in Afghanistan and Iraq. What do you make of this criticism of the press in light of Blasi's findings relating to how many prominent 18th century Americans viewed the free press in its relation to the state?

3   Who or what should or does check the press to ensure that it does not abuse or that it lives up to its public trust and obligations as a watchdog on the government?

3

Protecting the Best Men: An Interpretive History of the Law of Libel

NORMAN ROSENBERG

Although the founding generation of Americans favored and appreciated a free press, they were not without concerns about its impact on American society and its political system. Paramount among these concerns was the widespread fear if the press was too free to report on the public lives of elites and/or if its reporting on elite lives was so penetrating and so vociferous that it might discourage society's best citizens from performing public service. If this occurred, society would not be governed by its very best citizens but instead by the "rabble" that formed the less privileged classes. Norman Rosenberg, in this selection from his 1974 book Protecting the Best Men, *examines how this concern developed and how it affected the American media and politics for nearly 200 years.*

Historically, Anglo-American law had always proscribed some kinds of political speech. The elites who dominated Britain's old authoritarian state, of course, assumed that mere words could be so corrosive to both social order and political authority that strict legal controls were needed to restrict dangerous discussions. The Star Chamber law of seditious libel, which extended to all political criticism, epitomized this approach. In theory, Britain's liberal revolutions of the seventeenth century overthrew the authoritarian state and its view of political expression. Yet even though the new liberal order traced ultimate authority back to an act of popular will (the Lockean contract), both theory and practice placed substantial limits on political insurgency in general and critical speech in particular.

The basic boundaries, as English historian Christopher Hill argues, were drawn in the seventeenth century. The victorious political coalitions "established the sacred rights of property (abolition of feudal tenures, no arbitrary taxation), gave political power to the propertied (sovereignty of Parliament and the common law, abolition of prerogative courts), and removed all impediments to the triumph of the ideology of the men of property—the protestant ethic." The revolution that according to Hill "might have established communal property, and a far wider democracy in political and legal institutions" only threatened to happen. Similarly, in North America, where radical republican ideas seeped more deeply into the general political culture than in England, the ideal of blended, constitutional government still dominated political imaginations. This meant that constitutionally sanctioned government tempered the desires of the populace, including the desire to criticize governmental and public officials, by the reason of the common law and statutory restrictions.

Drawing the precise legal lines between legitimate and illegitimate political criticism proved a difficult task. Some Anglo-American constitutionalists, such as Sir William Blackstone, argued that common law reason dictated that all libelous criticism of governmental and public officials—regardless of accuracy, motives, and intentions—should be subject to postpublication criminal penalties. But this restatement of Star Chamber law always faced challenges. As Andrew Hamilton's argument in the *Zenger* case suggested, belief in a real, though ill-defined, liberty to "complain" about a "bad" administration described the eighteenth-century realities of libel and free speech more accurately than any generalization derived from the views of political and legal elites. Certainly the British officials trying to deal with the "seditious" speeches and writings of their colonial opponents understood this to be the case. . . .

By the mid-1790s, however, Federalists like Hamilton and Alexander Addison came to fear the impact of popular political criticism, and the rise of the Jeffersonian opposition intensified their misgivings. The Sedition Act of 1798 represented their legal response. It marked not only the first attempt in post-Revolutionary America to use systematic criminal libel prosecutions as a part of political conflict, but also one of the first legislative efforts to respond to criticism of Blackstonian libel doctrines by accepting the Zengerian principles—truth as a defense and jury determination of the "law of the case"—as formal additions to defamation doctrines.

The Sedition Act was part of more than a decade of debate over how a republican society should determine the legitimate limits upon free speech, and libel law provided the focus. Differences generally centered upon the proper forums for legal adjudication (state or federal courts), the appropriate kind of legal action (criminal or civil), and the precise legal-constitutional standards (the Zengerian or the more restrictive Hamiltonian position). Prominent Jeffersonians rejected, with a few notable exceptions, the elitist notion that libel law should protect public leaders from all defamatory criticism; nevertheless, they joined Federalists in agreeing that the law should proscribe certain libelous attacks and in fearing that defamatory criticism could drive the best men from public life and corrupt the whole process of political discussion. In fact, Jeffersonians like George Hay and Thomas McKean urged augmenting libel law through prepublication good-behavior bonds. Most important, even the Jeffersonian libertarians agreed that the law of libel, when bounded by certain legal-constitutional safeguards, did not clash with the basic liberal idea of what constituted liberty of political expression. Although a full-blown justification for constitutional boundary drawing and for judicial protection of freespeech rights would not emerge until later in the century, debates of the early nineteenth century did enshrine the proposition that trained legal minds could separate legitimate political speech, the kind that bolstered a republican society's basic goals, from expression that undermined its fundamental values and essential political mechanisms. To most members of the early nineteenth century's legal and political establishments, the Hamiltonian emphasis upon truth, good motives, and justifiable ends seemed a wise and legitimate accommodation between the need for protecting political criticism and the necessity for protecting the reputations of the best men and for safeguarding the integrity of public debate.

In addition to sparking the first extensive American debates over judicially drawn boundaries for expression, events of the late eighteenth and early nineteenth centuries also prompted the first serious discussions in North America of the dominant liberal image of free expression: the marketplace of ideas. The basic metaphor could be traced back to the seventeenth century, especially to John Milton, but the Jeffersonian opponents of the Sedition Act first gave it an important place in American legal discussions. During the Jacksonian era, especially in justifications for tolerating the party and popular presses, and for accepting their *de facto* immunity from most libel suits, marketplace imagery dominated both legal and popular discussions.

The model of a free marketplace for expression and the task of common law boundary drawing came together in the writings of Thomas Cooley. Cooley's theory of political libel clearly bore the imprint of mid–nineteenth-century political realities. Reared in the political culture of the antebellum North, Cooley rejected the antipress policy arguments of earlier libel law theorists and incorporated a positive view of the party and popular presses into his overall approach to libel and free expression. He praised the press for giving citizens useful information on a wide variety of public issues, and he criticized outdated defamation laws for blocking the free flow of knowledge and opinion. Mindful of popular opposition to political libel suits, confident of the progressive impact of market mechanisms, and fearful of overbearing governmental authority, Cooley insisted that the state should not unnecessarily interfere with political discussion, . . . Although it stopped short of protecting all libelous political falsehoods, Cooley's view of conditional privilege built a new libertarian legal theory by linking common law doctrines and marketplace imagery to constitutional guarantees of free expression.

By the 1880s, however, even Cooley began to back away from a faith in an essentially self-regulating intellectual marketplace. . . . Although Cooley's own judicial opinions never openly repudiated his libertarian principles, the vast majority of state and federal court decisions and the bulk of legal writing ultimately did. Cooley's earlier writings . . . came to represent doctrinal and policy positions that were to be rejected in favor of more restrictive ones.

In the late nineteenth century, discussions about defamation law returned to an essentially Hamiltonian framework. Reviving older policy arguments, most members of the legal and political establishments proposed that libel law should draw the boundaries of free speech at libelous falsehoods, even when statements related to the conduct and character of political figures or to issues of general public concern. Although a dissenting minority position persisted . . . on the eve of World War I, a neo-Hamiltonian view of libel and free expression generally prevailed.

Meanwhile, by the early twentieth century, libel law was ceasing to be the central focus for legal discussions of free expression. World War I, which brought the beginnings of a national surveillance state, roughly marks the time in which libel law receded into the background of what was now becoming known as First-Amendment constitutional theory. Yet this new constitutional thought actually grew, in large part, out of assumptions about the nature of political communication and the role of law that had been shaped in earlier debates over the law of libel.

For about the next fifty years, discussions over libel law took place at the periphery of First-Amendment debates, and libel law became the primary concern of those interested in the mass media and of specialists in tort law. The 1934 debates of the American Law Institute and the black-letter law in most jurisdictions suggested that libel rules should reach most defamatory falsehoods, even ones that involved public affairs. But, as the realist scholars of the twenties and thirties stressed, there was a considerable gap between neo-Hamiltonian doctrines and the actual process of public discussion. Countless judicial precedents and statutory changes threw up counterdoctrines and offered libel defendants, especially those in the media, alternative legal courses. Moreover, the realities of the tort litigation process raised numerous practical obstacles for plaintiffs, although they generally allowed defendants to take advantage of the well-known inertia of the legal system. And politicians who filed libel suits always had to overcome popular suspicions about the virtue of those public officials who took their detractors to court. Libel suits, including ones involving political figures and public issues, did not disappear; but for those who had to fight them, especially members of the mass media, and for those who had to explain them, prominent members of the legal community, the law of libel seemed to pose few problems that could not be managed within the confines of traditional common law battlegrounds.

When a changing social and political milieu ultimately forced the United States Supreme Court to constitutionalize defamation law in 1964, it adopted a set of policy arguments about political dissent and free markets and an approach to boundary drawing that resembled those advanced a century earlier by Thomas Cooley. At first glance, it seemed that the libertarian legacy—one that brought together the marketplace vision of Anglo-American liberalism, the common law traditions of liberal legalism, and the newer currents of cold-war liberal thought—had reached its mature development. According to supporters of *New York Times v. Sullivan* and its progeny, the law of libel had been transformed into the law of free speech.

DISCUSSION POINTS

1 Is the fear that a free press would drive many of society's best citizens to not perform public service valid or is it a quaint one that is too dated to be of continued concern?

2 Many of the leading American political figures of the period that Rosenberg examines viewed themselves as part of the privileged class of citizens that a defamation standard favoring plaintiffs would protect. How much of their views on this subject do you think were the product of self-interest? Does the fact that there may have been some self-interest involved make their concerns any less valid?

3 Having read this article, read the defamation cases included in the chapters of this text on media law. Do these rulings provide an effective counter-argument to those who advanced the view that the press must be limited so as to not drive the best people out of public life?

PART TWO

The Media and Politicians

THE READINGS SELECTED FOR Part Two offer insight into the relationship between politicians and the media. Like most political relationships, the one between the media and politicians is complex. There is a kind of symbiotic nature to their relationship. On the one hand, they both often need something from each other and, consequently, often work well with one another. The media, for instance, needs news to report, quotes to pass along, and information to verify. The media is especially interested in exclusives which often can only be obtained from politicians. Politicians need name recognition and the appearance of expertise and of working hard; they can obtain such through good and regular press coverage. Politicians may also wish to gauge public reaction to pending nominations or policy questions. Such reaction can be obtained as the result of a good press leak or from members of the media who are willing to engage in trading favors with politicians such as information. At the same time, however, there is animosity between the two that boils over when the media and politicians find their interests in collision. This is especially true if one believes that the other has been less than straight or honest in their dealings. It is also often the result of press coverage that offends or wounds a politician's pride or career. Many politicians, perhaps most famously former President Lyndon Johnson, encouraged members of the media to be "team players" and exhorted them to cover (or not) stories as "your president would want or as the nation would need." When the media would invariably fail or refuse to do so, President Johnson would be angry and at times take the rejection personally.

The relationship between the media and politicians is further complicated by the fact that the two are increasingly coming from the same schools and backgrounds and have much more in common as far as professional, educational, socio-economic, and culture experiences than ever before. Also complicating matters is the fact that many journalists have some prior political experience and some politicians have prior experience in journalism. These shared values and life or professional experiences mean that politicians and members of the media are likely to know each other personally and in informal settings (e.g. some may be former college roommates, they may worship together, or they may have mutual friends). This is especially true at the highest echelons of journalism and political life. In fact, in terms of matters such as demographics and live experiences, members of the media have a great deal in common with members of Congress, especially with the senators. For members of the media, it may be difficult to be objective about the actions and expectations of men and women who are so much like them. This is especially true where genuine friendships have formed or where a critical story about one politician may require the journalist to examine and even criticize his or her own beliefs or background (e.g., stories about how much a politician is affected by religious convictions or about how a candidate for public office, like the journalist, attended a club or school that discriminated against women or minorities).

Bob Woodward and Carl Bernstein, two *Washington Post* reporters, begin this section with a selection from their book, *All the President's Men*. The two offer insight into the direct personal dealings that occur between reporters and their sources or the subjects of their stories. At the time that *All the President's Men* was published, Woodward and Bernstein were young, inexperienced reporters. They appear surprised to discover that a kind of double-standard exists between the most senior members of the government and of the media which provides certain public officials with special privileges that the media would not afford to most members of the government.

Politicians can use the media to turn a negative public image around. At times their actions may be spontaneous, at other times it may be pre-meditated. Paul Taylor, a veteran reporter, tells us about one politician, publically labeled a "wimp" by the mainstream media, who went looking for a fight and got one, and rode it all the way to the White House.

Relations between the media and politicians frequently sour when media coverage focuses on scandals. Media scholar and analyst Larry Sabato relies upon largely anecdotal evidence culled from interviews with politicians and journalists alike to paint a picture of the modern media and political scandals. The resulting image is not a pretty one; in fact, Sabato likens reporters to sharks or piranhas blinded by desire in a feeding frenzy directed at wounded prey (the politicians) and brought on by the scent of blood in the water. Sabato's portrayal of the media is largely negative and potentially devastating. In the interest of fair play and balance, Benjamin Bradlee, a veteran newspaperman, is offered a chance to provide a defense of the media especially where scandals that concern an office-holder's or office-seeker's private life.

The modern media sometimes focuses on certain topics whose classification as a news story some may question. This is true of some stories about presidential popularity or approval. Stephen Frantzich examines the history and implications of such reporting especially as they relate to President George W. Bush in the post-September 11, 2001, world.

4

All the President's Men

CARL BERNSTEIN
BOB WOODWARD

Washington Post *reporters Bob Woodward and Carl Bernstein wrote about their experiences and the lessons that they learned while participating in the media's investigation of the most famous American political scandal of all time: Watergate. At the heart of this scandal was President Richard Nixon's efforts to (often illegally) coverup illegal actions that he or his aides had committed. In an effort to determine where newspapers investigating Watergate were getting their information, the Administration illegally wiretapped the phones of several journalists as well as of several administration officials. In this passage, Woodward and Bernstein tell how then Secretary of State Henry Kissinger admitted to ordering the wiretaps himself and how their editors, out of respect for the Secretary's position, allowed the Secretary to retract his confession. This episode describes a kind of double standards that favors high-ranking officials. Pay attention to the importance of precise language. Note the involvement of editors, such as Howard Simons and Benjamin Bradlee, in the discussion and ultimate decision not to publish.*

May 14, [acting FBI director William] Ruckelshaus announced that, as part of the [Nixon] administration's search for news leaks, 17 wiretaps in all had been ordered in 1969–71.... Ruckelshaus did not disclose the names of the 13 government officials and four reporters whose phones had been tapped. The question was—who had authorized it?

Woodward placed a direct call to a top FBI official. The official was not oblique: some of the wiretap authorizations had come to the FBI either orally or by letter from Henry Kissinger.

Incredulous, Woodward called a former FBI man.

"I know Kissinger gave some authorizations," he said.

The White House switchboard put Woodward directly through to Kissinger's office. It was about 6:00 P.M.

"Hello," the familiar voice said in a heavy German accent.

Woodward explained that they had information from two FBI sources that Kissinger had authorized the taps on his own aides.

Kissinger paused. "It could be Mr. Haldeman who authorized the taps," he said.

How about Kissinger? Woodward asked.

"I don't believe it was true," he stated.

Is that a denial?

A pause. "I frankly don't remember." He might have provided the FBI with the names of individuals who had seen or handled various documents which had been leaked. "It is quite possible that they [the FBI] construed this as an authorization. . . . In possible individual cases it is possible that I pointed out who handled what document to my deputy [General Alexander Haig], who in turn would have passed on the information to the FBI."

Woodward said that two sources had specified that Kissinger had *personally* authorized the taps.

A brief pause. "Almost never," he said.

Woodward suggested that "almost never" meant "sometimes." Was Kissinger then confirming the story?

Kissinger raised his voice angrily. "I don't have to submit to police interrogation about this," he said. Calming down, he went on, "If it is possible, and if it happened, then I have to take responsibility for it. . . . I'm responsible for this office."

Did you do it? Woodward asked.

"You aren't quoting me?" Kissinger asked.

Sure he was, Woodward said.

"What!" Kissinger shouted. "I'm telling you what I said was for background."

Woodward said they had made no such agreement.

"I've tried to be honest and now you're going to penalize me," Kissinger said.

No penalty intended, Woodward said, but he could not accept retroactive background.

"In five years in Washington," Kissinger said sharply, "I've never been trapped into talking like this."

Woodward wondered what kind of treatment Kissinger was accustomed to get from reporters.

Kissinger had an effective way of moving back and forth from anger to tranquility. "I talked in order to be helpful," he said next. And then, angrily, "What conceivable motive would I have had in granting you an interview?"

Woodward said that he would check with the *Post*'s diplomatic reporters to see if different rules about background and on-the-record conversations were observed.

"You've totally violated any procedure I've ever had with any reporter," Kissinger announced, and said goodbye.

Woodward consulted Murrey Marder, the *Post*'s chief diplomatic reporter. Did reporters usually allow Kissinger to determine, after an interview, whether it was going to be on the record, off the record or only for background.

Well, yes and no. Marder said. Technically, Woodward was right, but most reporters who covered Kissinger regularly let "Henry" place statements on background after the conversation. Half an hour later, Marder came by Woodward's desk to say that Henry had called him to complain bitterly about his interview with Woodward. Marder, Bernstein and Woodward went into Howard Simons' office to discuss what had happened. . . .

Simons' phone rang. He picked it up, gave a few grunts and switched the call to the speaker phone so everyone could hear.

"Tell the assembled multitude, Bennie," Simons said.

It was Bradlee, speaking from his home in a stiff German accent. "What are you guys doing?" he asked. "I just got a call from Henry. He's mad."

Simons explained

"You decide what to do," Bradlee said. "I'll play reporter and read you what Henry said and you can use it if it will help."

Simons smiled. "Is it on background?"

Kissinger, moving up the line from Marder to Bradlee, was doing what is known in diplomatic circles as "hardening your position." His statement to Bradlee was that it was "almost inconceivable" that he could have authorized the wiretapping.

"Almost inconceivable" is not a denial, Woodward noted, and argued for the story.

But it was nearly eight, too late for the first editions. Simons decided to hold it a day.

Woodward was angry. He felt the editors had waffled on the story because of Kissinger's position. Bernstein disagreed. The information from the FBI sources had come so easily—perhaps they were part of an effort to shift responsibility from Haldeman and Ehrlichman to Kissinger. It was worth waiting a day to find out.

As it turned out, though, the story could not wait a day. Sy Hersh had it. A day later, he wrote in the *Times* that Kissinger had played a role in fingering some of his aides as possible leaks. Marder did the story for the *Post* a day after that.

DISCUSSION POINTS

1   What is the double-standard that Woodward and Bernstein describe? Is it appropriate?

2   *The Washington Post*'s distrust of unnamed government sources seems to have led it to hold off on running the story (which was accurate) out of fear that it was being set up by the Nixon Administration (which it was not in this instance). Does this suggest that the media can be too skeptical and suspicious when it comes to its investigations of public officials? Can you conceive of a scenario in which public officials could manipulate such skepticism or suspicions?

3   Consider the importance of precise language to situations such as this. What can be learned from the close scrutiny that Woodward applied to Secretary Kissinger's carefully chosen words?

4   Often, as this episode reveals, the decision to publish or to not publish rests with persons other than reporters. Where should it reside? Consider this episode in conjunction with other reading selections about editors and reporters.

5

See How They Run

PAUL TAYLOR

Politicians frequently acquire public personas that emphasize certain perceived character attributes or traits. At times, these personas can be negative. The media frequently plays a major role in influencing these personas and through them public perceptions of individual politicians. Then Vice President George H. W. Bush, a candidate for the Republican Party's presidential nomination, had been branded a "wimp" both by the media and by many in the public. Reporter Paul Taylor, in this excerpt from his diary of the 1988 presidential race, describes how two of Bush's top campaign advisors, Lee Atwater and Roger Ailes, encouraged the Vice President to go on the air and, in essence, pick a fight with CBS news anchor Dan Rather. Rather, while an old Bush friend, was famous for being tough on politicians and was despised by Republicans who believed him biased against them and their party.

... For years, the press had been making it abundantly clear that if front-runner George Bush was ever going to be elected President, he'd first have to prove he was man enough. The word that crystallized the doubts about him was "wimp." In 1987, it began working its way out of the Washington press corps' echo chamber and into their stories. It wasn't merely an invention of the press. Many voters used that word, or some variant, to describe their uncertainty about Bush's basic strength of character, depth of conviction, independence of mind....

This skepticism was weakly felt by most voters, for they didn't know enough about Bush to have worked up deep feelings. It was different with the Washington press corps. Many political reporters had watched Bush at close range over a long haul, and had come to doubt his backbone.... During the campaign pre-season leading up to 1988, pundits of every ideological leaning, from Garry Trudeau (Bush "put his manhood in a blind trust") to George Will (Bush "emits the tinny arf of a lapdog"), seemed to go out of their way to advertise their naked contempt for the Vice President.

In October 1987, on the eve of Bush's formal announcement for the presidency, *Newsweek* ran his picture on its cover, alongside the headline: "Fighting the 'Wimp Factor.'" The Bush forces were outraged. "The first campaign school I went to . . . said there's only one day that you're going to have good press in a campaign—that's the day you announce," recalled Lee Atwater, Bush's campaign manager. "Well, here's a guy announcing for President of the United States, and a national news magazine creates a prop. The net effect was that for the next ten days all we got at press conferences and on television talk shows and nightly news shows were reporters waving the *Newsweek* magazine cover at us. I think it was an example of something that happened this year more than I've ever seen in my twenty years of involvement. It was as if the media became a participant in the process." . . .

Atwater and Ailes had a theory that Bush's good manners were misconstrued by voters as a lack of spine. They knew he had a fiercely competitive streak that he didn't like to show, and they were determined to tease it to the surface. The best way to do that, they figured, was to make sure Bush mastered the "defining moments" of the campaign—those two or three memorable confrontations that seem to occur in every presidential race and get taken by the voters as parables about character. These moments capture the public's imagination precisely because they seem spontaneous. Ailes and Atwater thought they were too important to be left to chance. . . .

In 1988, the first defining moment for Bush came in a live interview with CBS's Dan Rather—and there was nothing spontaneous about it. Atwater and Ailes had been leery about the interview from the moment it had been proposed by CBS in early January. They counseled Bush against doing it. "I just smelled setup," said Atwater. "Rather was a middle-aged guy with a sagging career who remembered what the Kennedy interview did for Roger Mudd." Bush would hear nothing of it. "I feel comfortable with Rather," he scribbled on the letter from CBS producer Richard Cohen proposing the interview as part of a series of political profiles that Rather was doing on the *CBS Evening News*. . . .

In the weeks leading up to the interview, Tom Bettag, executive producer of the *CBS Evening News*, made it clear to the Bush camp that the focus of Rather's questions would be on the Iran–contra issue.

Atwater's concerns mounted. "By the Friday before the [Monday, January 25, 1988] interview, we were hearing all kinds of rumors that CBS was out to do a number on Bush," he said. "I had been warning the Vice President to stay away, and he said, 'Lee, I know you're looking out for my best interests, but Dan has been a friend of mine for twenty-five years.' In fact, he sort of scolded me, in a friendly way, for being so paranoid."

On the Sunday before the interview, Ailes received a phone call at home from Peter Teeley, the campaign press secretary at the time. Ailes recalled: "He said, 'I think this CBS thing is going to be worse than we thought. You had better get down to Washington.' I started checking around. I had a source inside CBS News who went outside to a pay phone and called me and said, 'I'm sorry to have to tell you this, but they're running around the CBS newsroom saying they're going to take George Bush out of the race tonight. They have hired a Democratic consultant [Thomas Donilon, a strategist for Carter, Mondale and Biden] to work with Rather. They have created a five-minute [lead-in] segment which is going to indict him by putting him on the screen with some sorry characters who have some problems. Then they're going to hand him a blindfold and Rather is going to execute him. So you guys better be ready.'"

At Ailes's insistence, CBS had agreed to conduct the interview live. That would give Bush an edge: he could evade or filibuster secure in the knowledge that no amount of pasting and editing could give his words meanings he did not intend. Moreover, if the tightly wound Rather came on too strong, Bush could play the counterpuncher. Ailes coaches his clients to view every human contact as an instant size-up, in which a person has just a few seconds to absorb a given situation and then control the atmosphere by projecting calm self-assurance. He's also a great believer in what he calls the "man in the pit" theory of political confrontation. "If a reporter is bullying you, the viewers at home may start to root for you," Ailes wrote in a book, *You Are the Message*. "The more inflammatory the journalist, the cooler you should be." . . .

When Atwater heard about the phone call Ailes had gotten Sunday from his friend at CBS, he called up Bush. "I said, 'Mr. Vice President, I know how you feel about this interview, but just in case I'm right and you're wrong, I've asked Roger to come out and meet you at the airport to go over a few things,'" he recalled.

"And he said, 'God, Lee, you just don't give up.'"

On the drive in from Andrews Air Force Base to Bush's vice-presidential office, Ailes told Bush what he'd heard and fed him some lines to use. "He didn't believe it was going to be a political execution or an attempt at a political execution," Ailes recalled. "I said, 'Why don't we plan for it just in case?' Basically, we decided we weren't going to take it lying down."

The interview was conducted with Rather at his New York anchor desk and Bush in his Capitol Hill office. As Bush watched the taped five-minute introductory report on Iran-contra on a television monitor, he grew upset. "If that's all this is going to be about," Bush snapped to the CBS technicians in his office just before he went on the air live, "they're going to find themselves with a seven-minute walkout on their hands." Ailes stood a few paces away, off-camera, happily stoking his client's fire. Several times during the ensuing interview, he wrote out key words in big letters on a yellow pad to remind Bush what to say.

Rather's first question was on Iran-contra, and Bush started blazing away: "I find this to be a rehash and a little bit, if you'll excuse me, of a misrepresentation on the part of CBS, who said you're doing political profiles of all the candidates." He summarized the contents of the Cohen letter.

What happened over the next nine minutes was the spectacle of two ambushes colliding. Rather had anticipated a counterattack ("We knew it was going to be a brawl," recalled CBS's Cohen) and did not back off. The interview was all sparks.

Bush: "May I answer that?"
Rather: "That wasn't a question. It was a statement."
Bush: "It was a statement and I'll answer it."
Rather: "Let me ask the question, if I may, first."
And later:
Rather: "I don't want to be argumentative, Mr. Vice President."
Bush: "You do, Dan."

Two-thirds of the way through the firefight, Ailes scribbled the words "Not fair to judge career" on his legal pad to remind Bush of what they'd planned in the car ride in from Andrews.

"It's not fair to judge my whole career by a rehash on Iran," Bush immediately told Rather. "How would you like it if I judged your whole career by those seven minutes when you walked off the set in New York?" The reference was to an incident the previous September, when Rather had lost his temper and walked off the set because the start of his evening news broadcast had been delayed a few minutes by CBS's coverage of a match at the U.S. Open tennis tournament. The network was forced to go black for six minutes while producers frantically coaxed Rather back to his anchor desk. It was a breach of professionalism that some in the industry, including Rather's sainted predecessor, Walter Cronkite, considered a firing offense.

When Bush landed that blow, Rather initially was too stunned to respond. For the remainder of the interview, his questions took on a more biting tone, and his composure seemed shot. "Mr. Vice President," he hectored moments later, "you've made us hypocrites in the face of the world! How could you, how could you sign on to such a policy?"

The close of the interview was even more ragged. With a producer shouting into his earphone to bring the overlong segment to a close, Rather said: "I appreciate the straightforward way in which you've engaged in this exchange. There are clearly some unanswered questions. Are you willing to go to a news conference before the Iowa caucuses, answer questions from all . . ."

Bush: "I've been to eighty-six news conferences since March, eighty-six of 'em since March . . ."

Rather: "I gather the answer is no. Thank you very much for being with us, Mr. Vice President. We'll be back with more news in a moment." . . .

Though Rather came under a great deal of criticism from viewers and station owners, his line of questioning had been much sounder in substance than in tone. For more than a year, Bush had been evasive about his role in the Iran–contra episode, using the claim of executive privilege to refrain from disclosing what advice he had given President Reagan. . . .

Had Rather been one of his own network correspondents, and had he posed his questions at a regular campaign press conference, hardly an eyebrow would have been raised. Reporters frequently badger politicians; it's part of the job description. Network anchors are different. Someone once described them as the secular equivalent of deities, for they come into everyone's home each night and explain the mysteries of the world Rather got pounded not just by viewers but by colleagues in the media. "There was no excuse for him assuming the roles of judge and jury in a newscast," wrote Los Angeles *Times* TV critic Howard Rosenberg. "Who appointed him America's shrieking ayatollah of truth?" ABC's Ted Koppel observed more shrewdly a few days later that the problem was not that Rather had asked tough questions, but that he'd allowed himself to be maneuvered into serving as "a high priest in the ceremonial de-wimping of George Bush."

Bush was exhilarated by the exchange—if also a bit discombobulated. Over the next few days, he seemed so excited that he stepped on his newly acquired macho-man plumage a couple of times—gushing to an audience in Cody, Wyoming, that he deserved "combat pay" for the encounter and confiding to a group in Pierre, South Dakota, that it had been "Tension City" going head to head with Rather.

Ailes and Atwater were ecstatic. "I think it was the most important event of the entire primary campaign," said Atwater. "It was stronger than grits in the South. Rather is a guy people love to hate down there. I think it sealed Super Tuesday for us, and I think it was one of the reasons we were able to come back strong in New Hampshire after we took the hit in Iowa. It solidified our base." There is no polling to support Atwater's contention—in fact, the polls taken immediately after the encounter showed that most viewers disapproved of the way both men handled themselves. But that doesn't make Atwater wrong. The most significant political journey of 1988 was Bush's escape from the wimp image, and his dustup with Rather was one of its milestones. It helped in another way, too: after the fireworks of January 25, 1988, the media's curiosity about Iran-contra waned, and the issue never became a factor in the primaries or the general election.

DISCUSSION POINTS

1 What does this passage reveal about how politicians and journalists might use each other?

2 How or why are news anchors viewed differently by the public when compared to news reporters out in the field? Is this a double standard? How does it affect the media and politics?

3 What is the "'man in the pit' theory of political confrontation?" Is it an accurate theory?

6

Feeding Frenzy

LARRY SABATO

Larry Sabato relies largely on anecdotal evidence culled from interviews with journalists and politicians alike to paint a picture of the American media at the turn of the 21st century. According to Sabato, the modern American media is: consumed by an appetite for political scandals, prone to engaging in behaviors that he refers to as feeding frenzies and pack journalism, and too interested in setting the nation's political agenda rather than simply in reporting the facts as they occur.

It has become a spectacle without equal in modern American politics: The news media, print and broadcast, go after a wounded politician like sharks in a feeding frenzy. The wounds may have been self-inflicted, and the politician may richly deserve his or her fate, but the journalists now take center stage in the process, creating the news as much as reporting it, changing both the shape of election-year politics and the contours of government. Having replaced the political parties as the screening committee for candidates and officeholders, the media propel some politicians toward power and unceremoniously eliminate others. Unavoidably, this enormously influential role—and the news practices employed in exercising it—has provided rich fodder for a multitude of press critics.

These critics' charges against the press cascade down with the fury of rain in a summer squall. Public officials and many other observers see journalists as rude, arrogant, and cynical, given to exaggeration, harassment, sensationalism, and gross insensitivity. From the conservative perspective, their reporting is, more often than not, viewed as evidence of blatant liberal bias, with the facts being fitted to preconceived notions. At the same time, the left indicts the media for being too hesitant to find fault with the status quo and too close to the very establishment they are supposed to check. Moreover, critics of all stripes see journalists as hypercritical of others yet vengeful when criticized themselves, quick to accuse yet slow to correct error, willing to violate the constitutional values of due process and fair trial in the Fifth and Sixth Amendments by acting as judge and jury, yet insistent on wrapping themselves in the First Amendment when challenged on virtually anything. Especially in the post-Watergate era of institutionalized investigative reporting and "star journalism," the press is perceived as being far more interested in finding sleaze and achieving fame and fortune than in serving as an honest broker of information between citizens and government....

Anyone who has ever worked in the news media, or studied the subject dispassionately, knows full well that the conspiracy theorists are wrong. "The media" constitute no monolith, and news organizations are too disorganized and too competitive for much plotting to occur, much less succeed. Feeding frenzies are certainly not the result of intentionally coordinated action, and the chaos surrounding press coverage of most of them surely proves it. Rather, frenzies are a product of other conditions and forces both internal and external to the media, some that have fermented for many years, some of relatively recent vintage....

Growing Intensity and Declining Civility in Coverage

Conditions are always ripe for the spawning of a frenzy in the brave new world of omnipresent journalism. Advances in media technology have revolutionized campaign coverage. Handheld miniature cameras (minicams) and satellite broadcasting have enabled television to go live anywhere, anytime, with ease. Instantaneous transmission (by broadcast and fax) to all corners of the country has dramatically increased the velocity of campaign developments today, accelerating events to their conclusion at breakneck speed. Gary Hart, for example, went from front-runner to ex-candidate in less than a week in May 1987. Continuous public-affairs programming, such as C-SPAN and CNN, helps put more of a politician's utterances on the record, as Senator Joseph Biden discovered to his chagrin when C-SPAN unobtrusively taped Biden's exaggeration of his résumé at a New Hampshire kaffeeklatsch in 1987. (This became a contributing piece of the frenzy that brought Biden down.) C-SPAN, CNN, and satellite broadcasting capability also contribute to the phenomenon called "the news cycle without end," which creates a voracious news appetite demanding to be fed constantly, increasing the pressure to include marginal bits of information and gossip and producing novel if distorting "angles" on the same news to differentiate one report from another. The extraordinary number of local stations covering national politics today—up to several hundred at major political events—creates an echo chamber producing seemingly endless repetitions of essentially the same news stories. This local contingent also swells the corps traveling the campaign trail. Reporters not infrequently outnumber participants at meetings and whistlestops. . . .

Oddly enough, just as the coverage of major political events is expanding with the increased number of media outlets on the campaign trail, the quality is simultaneously declining. Superficial "horserace" reporting—a focus on who's ahead, who's behind, and who's gaining—is now the norm. Of seven thousand print news stories surveyed between Labor Day and Election Day 1988, 57 percent were horserace items and only 10 percent concentrated on real policy issues. On television network news shows during the 1988 primary campaign, two and a half times more horserace pieces aired than did policy-issue ones. . . . [T]he horserace fits many reporters' rather cynical view of politics: Elections are but a game, not a contest of the power of competing ideas. And a focus on the horserace is partisanly unbiased, far more "objective" and disinterested than is the construction of an issue agenda for coverage. . . . [T]his gamesmanship coverage of politics aids in developing frenzies by discouraging sober discussion of policy choices while fostering personal conflict, controversy, and confrontation.

Competitive Pressures

The first lady of Ohio had a succinct explanation for the Cleveland *Plain Dealer*'s front-page focus on her husband, Governor Richard Celeste, and his alleged extramarital affairs. "They're not in the business to promote Dick Celeste. They're in the business to sell papers. And this sells papers." Scandal and sex do indeed sell well—a great deal better than dispassionate discussion of policy issues. . . .

While it has ever been so, today there are added inducements for scandal coverage. First and foremost, contemporary corporate managers of broadcast and print media are closely attuned to the contribution each outlet makes to the overall profit or loss of the company. . . .

Nor are individual reporters oblivious to the reward system in the age of "star journalism." . . .

The competitive philosophy governing this new generation of go-getters can be summed up by their fevered adherence to journalism's two ultimate imperatives: "Don't get beaten to a story by another media outlet," and "If we don't break this, someone else will." Both axioms, and especially the second one, serve to encourage bad judgment and premature decisions to publish or air stories. As the *Washington Post*'s managing editor, Len Downie, concedes, "A lot of half-baked things get into newspapers including ours because people begin writing too much before they have enough facts." Some of the worst situations occur when competing media outlets become dueling entrepreneurs.

Competitive pressures also propel each newspaper and network to try to make a contribution, no matter how small and insignificant, to the unfolding frenzy. Each new fact merits a new story, complete with a recapitulation of the entire saga. This press pile-on by means of minor, "wiggle" disclosures is an ordeal akin to water torture (drip, drip, drip, day after day after day) and well known to many frenzy victims. . . .

Good judgment can be impaired and high standards lowered in the heat of competitive battle. What is becoming more common, and more disturbing, is the domino effect of a kind of "lowest-common-denominator" journalism: If one newspaper prints or one broadcaster airs a story, however questionable or poorly documented it may be, other media outlets will then publish or broadcast the news without independently verifying it. This abdication of journalistic responsibility encourages the purveyors of campaign smut to search out the weak media link. Many newsmen cited experiences similar to those of ABC News's Hal Bruno, who received a series of telephone calls in the summer of 1987 about a major presidential campaign rumor:

> I got calls from people saying, "The *New York Times* is gonna break the story on the weekend." And every week it would be a different news organization you were told had pictures and was gonna break the story. At one time a person called me and said he understood that ABC is gonna break this story. And I said to this person, "You're talking to ABC," and the person said, "Oh, I meant NBC," and hung up.

"All you need anymore is to get to the right reporter and the right paper, which is to say the wrong reporter and the wrong paper, to get a rumor published," notes the *Washington Post*'s Benjamin Weiser. Some journalists, such as the *New York Times*'s Michael Oreskes, bemoan the loss of vigilant gatekeeping by many in the media:

> When we refuse to publish it, someone else publishes it. Then the fact that they published it becomes a story, so it still gets into our paper even

though we originally decided it wasn't worth publishing. So you really lose control over your role as the gatekeeper.... On account of this some people begin to weaken their standards and say, "Well, it's going to get published anyway, so I'll go ahead and publish it first."

In good part then, a feeding frenzy is a manifestation of an adrenaline-charged news competition, with the initial contest won by the outlet breaking the story, the middle-round honors captured by the worst dramatic and sensational revelations, and the endgame trophy captured by the organization that checkmates the candidate and thereby takes him or her out of the race.

Pack Journalism

Oddly enough, the intense competitive pressures we have just discussed cause reporters (and editors and producers) to move forward together in essentially the same story direction, rather than on different story tracks. It is called "pack journalism," a condition former U.S. Senator Eugene McCarthy (D., Minn.) once likened to blackbirds on a telephone wire: When one moves to another wire, they all move. Timothy Crouse, in his delightful book *The Boys on the Bus*, described pack journalism by comparing the press to "a pack of hounds sicked on a fox." A third animal metaphor, fish schooling, may be even more telling. Fish in schools keep close tabs on each other and copy every school movement reflexively. The reason for the behavior is obvious: Any fish out of school loses the safety of numbers and is vulnerable prey....

It is remarkable to observe just how quickly even the heavyweights fall into line with the pack when a frenzy begins. In retrospect, when one weighs the real importance of Gerald Ford's "free Poland" remark* in his October 1976 debate with Jimmy Carter compared to the other vital subjects covered that night, the *Washington Post*'s decision not to mention the "gaffe" until the thirty-third paragraph of its story was commendable and balanced. It was also clearly an independent one, since virtually every other major paper had placed the so-called slip of the tongue front and center. Yet within twenty-four hours the *Post* had capitulated and headlined the comment as well.

Whether on the rise or not, the unfortunate effects of pack journalism are apparent to both news reporters and news consumers: conformity, homogeneity, and formulaic reporting. Innovation is discouraged, and the checks and balances supposedly provided by competition

---

* Republican presidential candidate Gerald Ford mistakenly referred to Poland as being free at a time when it was under communist control of the former Soviet Union.—Ed.

evaporate. Press energies are devoted to finding mere variations on a theme (new angles and wiggle disclosures), while a mob psychology catches hold that allows little mercy for the frenzy victim. CNN's Frank Sesno captures the pack mood perfectly:

> I've been in that group psychology; I know what it's like. You think you're on to something, you've got somebody on the run. How dare they not come clean? How dare they not tell the full story? What are they trying to hide? Why are they hiding it? And you become a crusader for the truth. Goddammit, you're going to get the truth!

Watergate's Watermark on the Media

Sesno's crusader spirit can be traced directly to the lingering effects of the Watergate scandal, which had the most profound impact of any modern event on the manner and substance of the press's conduct. In many respects Watergate began the press's open season on politicians in a chain reaction that today allows for scrutiny of even the most private sanctums of public officials' lives. Moreover, coupled with Vietnam and the civil rights movement, Watergate shifted the orientation of journalism away from mere description—providing an accurate account of happenings—and toward prescription—helping to set the campaign's (and society's) agendas by focusing attention on the candidates' shortcomings as well as certain social problems.

A new breed and a new generation of reporters were attracted to journalism, and particularly its investigative arm. As a group they were idealistic, though aggressively mistrustful of all authority, and they shared a contempt for "politics as usual." Critics called them do-gooders and purists who wanted the world to stand at moral attention for them....

Of course, many of those who found journalism newly attractive in the wake of Watergate were not completely altruistic. The ambitious saw the happy fate of the *Washington Post*'s young Watergate sleuths Bob Woodward and Carl Bernstein, who gained fame and fortune, not to mention big-screen portrayals by Robert Redford and Dustin Hoffman in the movie *All the President's Men*....

The young were attracted not just to journalism but to a particular *kind* of journalism. The role models were not respected, established reporters but two unknowns who refused to play by the rules their seniors had accepted. "Youngsters learned that deductive techniques, all guesswork, and lots of unattributed information [were] the royal road to fame, even if it wasn't being terribly responsible," says Robert Novak....

In the post-Watergate press there is also a volatile mix of guilt and fear at work. The guilt stems from regret that experienced Washington reporters failed to detect the telltale signs of the Watergate scandal early on; that even after the story broke, most journalists underplayed the unfolding disaster until forced to take it more seriously by two wet-behind-the-ears *Post* cubs; that over the years journalism's leading lights had gotten too close to the politicians they were supposed to check and thus for too long failed to tell the public about JFK's and LBJ's dangerous excesses, the government's lies about Vietnam, and the corruption in the Nixon administration and in Congress. The press's ongoing fear is deep seated and complements the guilt. Every journalist is apprehensive about missing the next "big one," of being left on the platform when the next scandal train leaves Union Station. The everlasting press search for another Watergate has produced one oversize "-gate" after another. . . .

. . . Ever since Watergate, most investigative journalists' goal has been not just sensational revelation but the downfall of their target, a trophy head for their wall that is the (im)moral equivalent of Richard Nixon. . . . The sizable financial and personnel investments many major news organizations have made in investigative units almost guarantee that greater attention will be given to scandals and that probably more of them—pseudo and real—will be uncovered. The healthy adversarial relationship that naturally exists between the press and politicians has been sharpened to a razor's edge in the process. Many in the press are not merely skeptical of the pols, they are contemptuous of and corrosively cynical about them, and some reverse the usual presumption of innocence into "guilty unless proven otherwise." . . . [T]he resulting cynicism . . . worries thoughtful veterans. "At times we're too adversarial," says *Los Angeles Times* Washington bureau chief Jack Nelson. "You shouldn't just assume politicians are lying." NBC News commentator John Chancellor somewhat wistfully recounts the days when he could "win an argument by citing U.S. government statistics" because they were considered the unquestionable "final word." Then came Vietnam, Watergate, and "hero worship for Woodward and Bernstein. Skepticism turned to cynicism, and in the White House press corps old-fashioned comity dissolved into a pack of attack dogs," notes Chancellor, regretfully. The Watergate-fed dogs are now used to red meat, and the pack is deeply addicted to the "-gate" scenario.

The Character Issue Takes Hold

A clear consequence of Watergate and other recent historical events was the increasing emphasis placed by the press on the character of candidates. As journalists reviewed the three tragic but exceptionally capable figures who had held the presidency since 1960, they saw that the failures of Kennedy, Johnson, and Nixon were not those of intellect but of ethos. . . .

"We in the press learned from experience that character flaws could have very large costs," says David Broder, "and we couldn't afford to ignore them if we were going to meet our responsibility." . . .

This focus on character is undergirded by certain assumptions—some valid and others dubious. First, the press correctly perceives that it has mainly replaced the political parties as the "screening committee" that winnows the field of candidates and filters out the weaker or more unlucky contenders. Second, many journalists, again correctly, recognize their mistakes under the old Rooseveltian rule* and see the need to tell people about candidate foibles that affect public performance. . . .

The press's third realistic presupposition is that it is giving the public what it wants and expects, more or less. . . .

Less convincing, however, are a number of other assumptions made by the press about elections and the character issue. Some journalists insist that they have an obligation to reveal everything of significance discovered about a candidate's private habits; to do otherwise, they say, is antidemocratic and elitist. Such arguments ignore the press's unavoidable professional obligation to exercise reasonable judgment about what is fit to print and air as well as what is most important for a busy and inattentive public to absorb. Other reporters claim that character matters so much because policy issues matter so little. The issues change frequently, they say, and the pollsters and consultants determine the candidate's policy stands anyway. . . .

Perhaps most troubling is the nearly universally accepted belief that private conduct is a road map to public action. Unquestionably, private behavior can have public consequences, as the review of recent history suggested. However, it is a far-from-settled matter whether private vice inevitably leads to corrupt, immoral leadership or whether private virtue produces public good. An argument can be made that many lives run on two separate tracks (one public, one private) that ought to be judged independently. . . .

More Women in the Press Corps

Instrumental in the emergence of the character issue were women journalists, who have broken the "good ol' boy" mentality—and morality—

---

* The Rooseveltian rule of thumb for press coverage refers to the pre-Watergate era when journalists typically kept the private lives of politicians private unless their private behavior impinged their public performance in a very serious way.—Ed.

prevalent in the press corps for decades. Right on target in her analysis is Cokie Roberts of National Public Radio and ABC News:

> Until a lot of women came into the press corps, the unwritten rule was that the guys worked together during the day and caroused together at night, and nobody reported on anybody. And on the bus, they pretended there were no marriages. We women all started arriving on the bus and we sort of pruded it up. There we were, friends of their wives, not that any of us were gonna run home and tell tales—but they couldn't be sure of it.

. . . As the boys on the bus—or plane—have gone coed, and as the press fraternity has made room for a sorority, the journalistic consensus about character has been profoundly influenced by feminism. In 1979, when *Washington Monthly*'s Charles Peters published a watershed article on Ted Kennedy's personal problems, he was much criticized for broaching the subject. The author of the piece, Suzannah Lessard, had difficulty getting on-the-record comments from committed feminists who were nonetheless deeply disturbed by Kennedy's behavior and found it abhorrent and disrespectful to women. . . . As Lessard later noted, those concerns had dissolved in time for Gary Hart to reap the whirlwind in 1987. This new-wave thinking has "raised collective consciousness in the press corps," according to Schieffer. The most significant effect has been to reinforce the character issue and prepare the way for more feeding frenzies based on private vices.

Loosening of the Libel Law

In the old days, a reporter would think twice about filing a story critical of a politician's character, and his editors probably would have killed it had he been foolish enough to do so. The reason is clear: fear of a libel suit. Veteran journalist Jerry terHorst recalls the first question his supervisors asked about even an ambiguous, suggestive phrase about a congressman: "If we're sued, can you prove beyond a doubt what you just wrote?" The chilling effect of libel laws tilted the press-politician relationship firmly in the direction of the pols, reinforcing the Rooseveltian rule that governed coverage of elected officials.

Such inhibitions were ostensibly lifted in 1964, when the Supreme Court ruled in *New York Times Co.* v. *Sullivan* that simply publishing a defamatory falsehood was not enough to incur a libel judgment. Henceforth a public official would have to prove "actual malice," a requirement extended three years later to all public figures, such as Hollywood stars and prominent athletes. The Supreme Court declared that the First Amendment requires elected officials and candidates to prove that the publisher either believed the challenged statement was false or at least entertained serious doubts about its truth and acted recklessly in publishing it in the face of those doubts. The "actual malice" rule has made it very difficult for a politician to prevail in a libel case. The most comprehensive empirical study on the subject suggests that the *Sullivan* standard has reduced public plaintiffs' success rate in libel cases by as much as 60 percent, with only about one in ten "public person" libel plaintiffs winning against the press....

[T]he loosening of libel law has provided journalists with a safer harbor from liability in their reporting on elected officials and candidates.... [A]t least for the wealthy newspapers and networks, the libel laws are no longer as severe a restraint on "character" or private-life reporting about public officials, and this once-formidable barrier to certain types of feeding frenzies has been lowered considerably.

DISCUSSION POINTS

1   Define feeding frenzy as Sabato uses the term. Provide a current example. What are the implications of this tendency on the part of the media?

2   Define pack journalism as Sabato uses the term. Provide a current example. What are the implications of this tendency on the part of the media?

3   Is the media behavior described by Sabato harmful or helpful to a system that democratically elects its leaders? Why is this your opinion?

7

A Good Life: Newspapering and Other Adventures

BENJAMIN BRADLEE

Benjamin Bradlee is one of the most important and influential newspaper editors in American history. His career in journalist stretched nearly half a century. During that time, both as an editor and as a reporter, he made many judgment calls about what to include in stories and what to leave out when it came to the personal lives of public figures. Looking back at these decisions, in particular those made during the 1988 presidential race with respect to democratic candidate Senator Gary Hart's personal life, Bradlee criticizes the media's performance but defends its responsibility to investigate and report on the private lives of public officials.

In matters of privacy, the question is this: Is there some sacred public right to know that overcomes an equally sacred right to privacy? There is no easy answer to that one....

... At the *Post* we developed a rule about matters of privacy: The private lives of public officials are their own business—unless and until their private behavior encroaches on performance of public duties. We had many shorthand versions of this policy. My favorite was "Drunk at home, your business; drunk on the floor of the U.S. Senate, our business."

But, not all privacy matters fit comfortably within that rule. Especially when and where privacy and sex collide, and they collide a lot in Washington,...

No story in the endless public-or-private debate gave me more difficulty than Gary Hart's extracurricular activities during the 1988 campaign for president.

Hart had arrived on the national scene sixteen years earlier as George McGovern's campaign manager, a new incarnation of the idealistic, anti-establishment intellectual. The press found him more interesting and more fun than McGovern, and he emerged from McGovern's defeat accepted by reporters as a friend and as a man to be watched. . . .

Walter Mondale beat Hart handily for the presidential nomination in 1984, but in the summer of 1987 Hart was the front-runner, threatened only by an uneasiness about his private life. . . . Hart was widely known to reporters as a man who fooled around.

For almost two hundred years the sex lives of politicians—especially presidents and presidential candidates—were left to the historians. However, the old rules had changed, and the new rules guaranteed scrutiny by the press if they got wind of any ongoing extracurricular sexual escapades. By 1987, the press was poking into the private lives of almost everyone, especially if they were prominent and indiscreet. And Gary Hart was both.

Many of the national reporters talked about Hart's private life among themselves . . . it seemed only a matter of time before one of those rumors erupted on somebody's front page as truth.

On May 3, 1987, the *Miami Herald* ended the suspense. Under a comparatively innocuous headline, "Miami Woman Linked to Hart," Miss Donna Rice began her fifteen minutes of fame as Hart's girlfriend, first with news of an overnight stay in Hart's Capitol Hill house, and later with reports of a two-day trip with Hart to Bimini, on the felicitously named motor yacht *Monkey Business*. A snapshot of the scantily clad Miss Rice on the would-be president's lap really sealed Hart's fate. . . .

A month earlier, I had called a special meeting . . . to discuss what we should be doing about the Hart rumors. On the one hand, if we wrote anything about them, we just added swirl to the controversy. And if we printed rumors without investigating them ourselves, we would be abandoning our principles. On the other hand, if we ignored the rumors—especially about a Democrat—weren't we courting a charge of bias? . . .

On May 3, Tom Edsall, one of the best political reporters going, was given a picture of Gary Hart leaving the house of an attractive woman—not married—whose name had been linked with his for a long time. They were together: she was pictured in the doorway of her house, and Hart leaving. The picture had been taken in December 1986, by a private detective working for a former senator who suspected his wife of having an affair with Hart. . . .

The someone was a reasonably well-known woman in Washington, a former Capitol Hill staffer turned lobbyist. I knew her casually, and volunteered to find out whether her rumored romance with Hart had ever been a fact, and whether it was then a fact. I did find out, that afternoon. The answer was yes; the romance had existed and still existed....

What did the presidential candidate already flailing away at the Donna Rice fires have to say?

To answer that question we called on Paul Taylor, who was covering Hart in New Hampshire. Taylor himself had just been in the news, after asking Hart pointblank at a press conference: "Have you ever committed adultery?" Instead of telling Taylor that it was none of his damn business, Hart had said he thought adultery was immoral....

Why was this story so important?

The leading Democratic candidate for president had repeatedly told the American public that he and his wife were a solid unit, when more and more evidence was accumulating that they were not. They had "an understanding of faithfulness, fidelity and loyalty," Hart had told *The Washington Post* only a few days earlier. He had even challenged the press to follow him around, a challenge the *Miami Herald* had accepted....

Now, it seemed to me, our reporting plus the picture plus the *Miami Herald*'s reporting all suggested that Gary Hart was lying about his private life. The changes in the rules now gave the public a right to know, and even a need to know before Election Day. There has to be some line beyond which the truth is essential, and lying is not allowed. And it had just been drawn.

Taylor told Hart's press secretary, Kevin Sweeney, about the picture, the private detective's report, and the confirmation I had received of the relationship. Sweeney paled, and asked for time.... It wasn't until early next morning that Taylor got his answer. He bumped into Joe Trippi, the deputy political director of Hart's campaign, in a parking lot. "You're looking at the end of a candidacy here," Trippi said with a sigh. "Hart's going to get out of the race tonight or tomorrow."...

The story of Hart's withdrawal was all over page one for days, of course, but we never ran a story about the private detective's report, and we never identified the other woman, even though they had specifically triggered the withdrawal. Our reasoning was simple: since Hart was no longer a presidential candidate, his private life was his own business again. And since the woman was not in public life, her private life was her own business.

Hart was furious at the press in general, and at the *Post* in particular. He just didn't get it.... We felt we had behaved responsibly, after determining a legitimate public interest in his private life. Our position was well stated by George Reedy, once President Lyndon Johnson's press secretary and then a journalism professor. "What counts with a candidate for president," he told Taylor, "is his character, and nothing shows it like his relationship with women. Here you have a man who is asking you to trust him with your bank account, your children, your life and your country for four years. If his own wife can't trust him, what does that say? The press doesn't invent stories about the peccadilloes of candidates." . . .

James MacGregor Burns, a professor at Williams College and FDR biographer, spoke eloquently for those who disagreed with Reedy. "This is a tragedy," he told Taylor, "a real loss for all of us, that a really impressive man has been brought down this way. The character of candidates and presidents is crucial. But the media aren't able to deal adequately with real and total character; their judgments are based on such old-fashioned, puritanical pieces of evidence."

Was Hart a victim of a prurient press, or a victim of his own excesses? Had the rules changed, and if so, who changed them? How come Hart was the object of such press scrutiny, when LBJ, and especially Jack Kennedy, had escaped that scrutiny?

Yes, the rules had changed, without any formal agreement within the press, and without any formal notification to the candidates. Certainly, the sexual revolution that started in the early sixties had changed American society permanently by the eighties. It was increasingly normal to be interested in our own sexual proclivities, and especially the sexual proclivities of the burgeoning world of celebrities. The supermarket tabloids, with their voracious appetite for the sensational—true or not—had been joined by tabloid television with its equally voracious appetite. And the press had been accused of covering up Kennedy's fooling around, which had become increasingly well documented since his death. They had silently decided they were never going to be accused of covering up the fooling around of any subsequent candidate. If Hart was the victim of anything, he was the victim of these new rules. . . .

DISCUSSION POINTS

1   Why, according to Bradlee, have the rules for covering the private lives of public officials changed?

2   Is Bradlee correct when he argues that the private affairs of public officials can be the public's business? What justification does he offer for this judgment?

3   Should there be a uniform set of written rules agreed upon by the media and made available to politicians with respect to what aspects of their private lives are fair game and what are not?

— 8 —

September 11th and the Bush Presidency: Rally Around the Rubble

STEPHEN FRANTZICH

> *Presidential public opinion numbers have become news. How did that happen? Should presidential approval figures be news? Does it matter that they have become news? In this article, which was published in a special publication devoted to the president, the navy, and the war on terrorism, Stephen Frantzich of the United States Naval Academy examines these questions.*

One of the most dramatic and measurable influences of 9/11 on the American psyche was the impact it had on George W. Bush's approval ratings. While no slouch when compared to the ratings of previous presidents at similar points in their terms, Bush's 35 percent increase from 51 to 86 percent in the Gallup Poll registered the largest increase in popularity since the regular measurement of presidential approval ratings began in the 1950s. The increase was almost double the previous one-week record of 18 percent, experienced by his father during Operation Desert Storm. A few weeks later, George W. Bush's approval increased to 90 percent, eclipsing his father's record of 89 percent.

The purpose of this article is to explore the causes and ramifications of the changes in presidential approval associated with 9/11 in the context of previous patterns of presidential approval. . . .

The Origin and Nature of Rallies

The general pattern of presidential approval reflects an immediate post-inauguration "honeymoon" evaluation giving him a higher rate of approval than in the election in which he was chosen. From there on, it is usually a general downward trend over time, with minor variations usually associated with highly publicized initiatives (especially those associated with foreign policy) or events (such as the assassination attempt on Ronald Reagan) that thrust the president into public awareness. As a presidency proceeds, dashed expectations and tough decisions turn off some past supporters, lowering the overall approval rate. There is an old story around Washington about a president who called in a pollster on inauguration day and asked him how he could leave office with the highest level of approval, and the pollster replied, "That is simple, resign today."

The more atypical, yet relatively common phenomenon, is the presidential rally in which the previous decline is reversed, usually temporarily, by a significant improvement. The size of George W. Bush's rally was unprecedented, making it the "mother of all rallies" to use terminology more associated with his father's term in office.

John Mueller was the first to carefully analyze the rally effect. Mueller argued that rallies were most likely to be associated with dramatic international events directly involving the United States in general and the president in particular. The events of 9/11 could hardly fit the bill more clearly. It is hard to imagine that even in his most optimistic hopes Osama bin Laden could have anticipated two direct hits with maximum damage captured live on television. The dramatic collapse of the World Trade Center and the gaping hole in the Pentagon created images seared into the psyche of the American public.

In our increasingly visually-oriented society, the images of the 9/11 destruction were particularly important in establishing a context to which the public had to react. In an era with an ever-expanding range of media sources and extensive audience fragmentation, it has become less and less likely for Americans to have shared national experiences. Economic considerations require media outlets to compete for "eyeballs" by providing unique content to serve as magnets for television remotes and mouse clicks. In the not so distant past, a limited number of national television networks with constrained and scheduled evening news programs fed similar content to largely passive audiences. In the print realm, all but the most well-endowed newspapers depended on a limited number of wire service stories for information about most national events. With limited choices and less control over content, most people developed "shared islands of understanding" about most major issues. These "islands" were based on virtually everyone receiving the same content at the same time. This was facilitated by the existence of only three major networks all covering stories in similar ways and broadcasting at the same time. It was meaningful water fountain interaction to begin a conversation by asking "What did you feel when you saw John-John Kennedy salute his father's coffin," or "Weren't the pictures of Germans chipping away at the Berlin wall dramatic?" The emergence of multiple cable television options (with news 24 hours a day, 7 days a week) and a growing reliance on the Internet for news meant that such shared islands of understanding based on the consumption of common stories and images were less likely to form. News consumers increasingly receive different content at different times.

The morning of September 11, 2001 began with media competition, audience fragmentation and content exclusivity and ended with an agreement by the major players to share all generic video. The images of the World Trade Center towers coming down became an icon on network television, cable television, newspapers, and Web sites, summarizing the horror of 9/11 and heightening its drama. In many ways, it was a throwback to a previous era, giving the public a shared national experience with a limited number of interpretations. . . .

Presidential Approval as News

Public support for presidents becomes news in and of itself. . . . Regular assessments of presidential popularity become hooks for media stories.

News by definition is something out of the ordinary. Therefore, stories tend to focus on record-breaking events or major changes. Personal highs or lows for presidents, especially resulting from significant shifts, are likely to generate more news than continuing strings of similar evaluations. Slow increases or decreases are likely to disappear under the radar screen of journalistic observers.

Is Presidential Approval News?

The Gallup Poll measures presidential approval on an almost monthly basis, and dozens of other polling companies collect and distribute their own measures. Most poll results receive only limited coverage. A LEXIS-NEXIS search of newspaper articles and television news program transcripts indicated a dramatic increase in the coverage of presidential approval figures at rally points and on historic dates (i.e., one year after September 11th). Rallies are news and it makes sense to assume that positive coverage of a rally helps keep it going.

Framing the Story

Even though poll results are hard data that seemingly leave little room for interpretation, the media have the power to frame the story in a variety of ways. In the abstract, most measurements of presidential approval do not have an absolute interpretation. A president with fifty percent approval can easily fall victim to the "is the glass half full or half empty" question. Presidential approval is gauged against an incumbent president's previous levels and against the records of previous presidents. Two aspects of framing are possible. Individual writers have the power to frame their stories as they (and their editors) see fit, while headline writers (usually not the article author) have some leeway in encapsulating a story in a few words.

It is widely accepted that many readers see nothing but the headline, others decide to read a story based on its headline, and that headlines create a mindset for readers of an article. The first wave of the Bush rally after 9/11, pushing him to 86 percent, was greeted with numerous stories quoting the Gallup Poll and a spate of positive headlines such as: "Americans Support President in Times of Crisis" (*Buffalo News*, September 23, 2001, p. H1) and "Democrats Unite Behind Bush" (*San Francisco Chronicle*, September 20, 2001, p. A10).

Interestingly, foreign newspapers expressed even more adulation in headlines like: "Bush's Approval Rating Soars: More Popular than his Father During Gulf War," (*Ottawa Citizen*, September 18, 2001) and "Support Surges as Bush Becomes the President the People Have Yearned For," (*The Daily Telegraph* [London], September 17, 2001, p. 2).

When Bush climbed to his record-breaking 90 percent approval, positive reactions to the poll results continued, although some sources began pointing out that significant decline was likely and initiated analysis of the political utility of the current, if temporary, approval level. The headlines read: "Once-in-a-Lifetime Unity Envelops D.C.," (*San Antonio Express-News*, September 19, 2001, p. 11b), "Bush Seems Invincible—For Now," (*Boston Globe*, September 27, 2001, p. A15), and "Bush Uses Support for Long Campaign Against Terrorism" (CNN, 07:00 September 24, 2001).

As the one-year anniversary approached, Bush's approval had dropped to 66 percent (September 5th) and then jumped again to 70 percent a few days after the anniversary. Much of the press coverage emphasized the decline in presidential approval over the previous year with headlines such as: "United We Stood, Until Good Will Gave Way," (*St Louis Dispatch*, September 11, 2002, p. 6) and "Bush Strives to Regain Magic; Partisanship Erodes Unity of a Year Ago" (*Houston Chronicle*, September 10, 2002, p. A1).

Using the same poll results, one paper gave its readers two very different perspectives with seemingly contradictory headlines: "A Tragedy that Redefined a President: Despite Slippage in Polls, America Still Sees a Different Bush" (*Hartford Courant*, September 9, 2002, p. A1) and "Bush's Democratic Support Eroding" (*Hartford Courant*, September 13, 2002, p. A8).

A few months later, journalists had more fodder for analysis. In January 2003, George Bush's approval dropped to 58 percent, the lowest level since the attacks of 9/11 and then returned to 61 percent the following week. Even though approval close to 60 percent is a respectable level of approval, the news was the drop. The headlines for three stories reflect their content and express very different interpretations "As 9/11 Memories Fade so Does Bush's Luster" (*Baltimore Sun*, January 16, 2003, p. 1a), 'Bush Bounces Back in Popularity Poll" (*The New York Post*, January 19, 2003, p. 6), and "Bush Ratings Tumble Amid Iraq, Economy" (*The Times Union* [Albany, NY], January 19, 2003).

Many newspapers rely on news services for their stories. Contracts with news services limit the nature of the editing subscribers can apply but allow them to write the headlines. A more precise test of the power of framing through headlines emerges from looking at differing head lines *on the same* news service article. John Hall, senior Washington correspondent for the Media General News Service, wrote an article about George W. Bush and the emerging slate of Democratic contenders. Hall's article is quite positive about the president's approval rating arguing that "President Bush was bound to begin sliding in the polls ... it was extraordinary that he kept it rolling through the November election," and "In parlous times, Americans look for a tower of strength. None of the Democratic candidates has yet shown signs of reaching very high, and an incumbent president may have slipped a notch or two. But it is way too early to tell what any of it means." Four outlets, which printed the article in *exactly the same way*, headlined it in quite different ways: "Bush's Shiny Armor Showing Wear" (*Reidsville Review*, January 15, 2003), "For Now Democrats Can Chip Away At Bush's Approval Ratings" (*The Tampa Tribune*, January 16, 2003), "Bush Dips and 2004 Comes Early" (*The News Virginian*, January 16, 2003), and "Earlier Campaigns Mean Less Time for Teamwork" (*The Richmond Times-Dispatch*, January 16, 2003). Readers would clearly expect, and perhaps take away, very different information from articles with such widely varying headlines.

What Difference Does News Media Coverage Make?

The importance of news reports of presidential approval lies in the fact that they become one more piece of data the public uses in determining their own level of approval. For most individuals, presidential approval is not an article of faith or deep commitment impervious to outside forces. Emerging conventional wisdom of a highly effective president or a floundering one is likely to push less interested and less committed citizens to follow the lead of their fellow citizens as reflected in the polls. It is instructive to note that the record breaking 35 percentage point surge of George W. Bush bringing him to 86 percent approval, was followed a week later with another increase to 90 percent approval. If Bush's approval was simply an outpouring of nascent patriotism, we should not have expected the second wave of the rally. This phenomenon adds some credence to the fact that elite opinion leadership and/or the publication of previous poll results play some role in the level and duration of approval ratings. Bush maintained his atmospheric 80 percent plus support for sixteen weeks. Individuals wavering in their support were faced with disagreeing with the vast majority of their fellow citizens.

The media and the conventional wisdom it spawns not only affect the public, but also impinge on the evaluations of other politicians as well. Politicians use approval ratings as surrogate measures of whom it is safe to criticize and whom it is wise to give a pass. In reality, the relationship is interactive. By holding back their criticism, other public officials make it more acceptable for the public to approve of a president's performance, opening the door to higher approval ratings, which in turn discourage those same public officials from taking a swipe at the president. Active support by other politicians and the media gives the wheel another spin, allowing further increases in presidential approval among the public. The process, of course, can also go the other way. Low or declining approval makes a president fair game for criticism by other politicians and the media. Negative comments by other politicians and the media can then speed the downward spiral.

What Presidential Approval Buys

Presidential approval easily gets caught up in the political jockeying associated with promoting one's party, issues and political future. . . .

It has been shown empirically that popular presidents have more influence with Congress. Along with his extraordinarily high public approval ratings, George W. Bush also secured a near record high rate of legislative victory in Congress. By stating a clear preference on a very narrow agenda and using his popularity, Bush was successful with Congress 87 percent of the time in 2001 and 88 percent in 2002. Only Lyndon Johnson in 1965 surpassed that record with a 93 percent support level. While a lot more than presidential approval goes into legislative success, Bush did much better than many previous presidents who had larger party majorities in both houses of Congress.

. . . Bush's popularity certainly did not hurt his party's fortunes in the 2002 midterm elections. . . . no president since 1934 had gained seats in both houses. . . .

Conclusion

George W. Bush's 9/11 rally was an historic event the likes of which we hope we will never see again. While it could be viewed as an historical anomaly linked to a tragic enigma, it allows us to apply our analytical tools to events and behaviors occurring at the margins of political reality.... The more impressionistic analysis of the media justifies the fact that far from simply reflecting reality like a mirror, the media refracts it like a prism. In its power of framing, the media has the potential for consistently changing the nature of perceived reality, especially under conditions where the new rules of media competition and audience fragmentation are at least temporarily rebuffed. While analysis of presidential popularity as a cause of the behavior of other political actors is less precise, it is clear that presidents do need to be concerned about their level of approval from a political perspective. Garnering public approval is clearly better than engendering disdain. Leadership and followership are closely intertwined phenomena, each influencing the other.

DISCUSSION POINTS

1 Are public opinion numbers news? Should they be news? In what ways do they matter?

2 Consider how phenomena about the media described in other selections in this book might help explain how and why presidential approval ratings have become news.

3 What do you think higher public approval ratings for presidents really measure? Is it the public's true expressions of support or does the public take its lead from elites in public life and in the media who may influence public opinion?

PART THREE

The Media and Campaigns

WINNING VOTES AND GAINING SUPPORT are perhaps the most basic of all functions performed by politicians in a democracy. Politicians compete for votes from the public during elections as well as among their fellow office-holders when it comes to passing or defeating legislation or nominations. Increasingly, effective media campaigns can make the difference between success or failure on a legislative vote or in an election itself. Thus, politicians often view the media as the means to desired ends. The politicians' role in campaigns is obvious: they seek to use their influence with the public or with fellow politicians to obtain votes and support. The media's role is a bit more complex. Unofficially, the American media is responsible for helping the public to identify and screen out the bad candidates or the bad policy positions from the good ones. There is a certain subjectiveness to this role that the media enjoys that may make many uncomfortable. Because of the stakes, politicians rarely sit back and just allow the media to perform this screening on its own without their input. Politicians have surrounded themselves with consultants who specialize in media and public relations. The media knows this and spends a great deal of energy and resources resisting being "spun" in one direction or another by political campaigns. The media's resistance to such efforts often anger or frustrate candidates who believe that the candidates not the media should control the issues that the public considers. This in turn may cause the media and politicians to be at loggerheads or it may cause campaigns to limit press access to candidates in the hope that the media will not be able to directly raise issues with candidates (in particular on film or on tape) that the candidates do not want to address. There is, therefore, a game within the campaign game—one that may have more to do with media access, tone, and coverage and less to do with informing or serving the public. The reading selections in this part examine several important aspects of this game within the game.

Electoral tactics, and the electoral landscape, frequently change. Politicians and their aides need to be aware of how to incorporate effective media strategies into their campaigns. Consequently, politicians and their aides need to be well-informed about the most up-to-date information affecting elections and running for office. It is with such politicians in mind, perhaps, that Daniel Shea and John Michael Burton published *Campaign Craft*. Intended as a kind of "how to" guide to electoral politics, *Campaign Craft* provides office-holders with valuable insight and lessons on how to run a successful modern media campaign.

Picking up on the theme of constant change in elections, Katherine Seelye examines how technological changes affected the 2004 race for the Democratic Party's nomination to run for president. Seelye finds that technological advances are revolutionizing how successful candidates campaign. She also finds that these changes have had a number of effects on the media itself.

Aides to former President Bill Clinton described a phenomenon that they called the "continuous" or "permanent" campaign. This describes a political environment in which elected officials govern as if they are still running for office. In effect, the type of events that mark campaigns such as public appearances and photo opportunities, editorial letter writing, public opinion polling, fundraising, advertising, and efforts to seize the public agenda never end. Instead, they continue long past the last counted ballot. The media has helped to fuel this strategy by covering politics as if it were a sporting event and treating its audience as interested spectators hungry for knowledge about what tactics were used to win or lose the big game. Enter into this political world judicial nominations. Starting in the 1950s, federal courts have emerged as significant policymakers. This has been true in disputes over social and legal policy as well as in conflicts over separation of powers and checks and balances. This rise in judicial policymaking has coincided with an electorate and a Senate that are arguably more divided politically, regionally, and ideologically than at any time since the American Civil War. Judicial nominations, especially for the United States Supreme Court, have become high stakes political contests with the prize being the control of America's political-legal-economic agenda. Presidents and their administrations, imbued with the "continuous" or "permanent" campaign mentality, have come to treat judicial nominations as another campaign to win. As a result, Richard Davis tells us, what was once a simple process about a nominee's professional competence has morphed into a choreographed dance involving White House press announcements and photo-opportunities, advertisements, interviews with surrogates for nominees and their opponents, political polling, focus groups, and visits to senatorial offices for personal interviews and more photo-opportunities. The question, Davis suggests in the final reading of this part, is whether we are better off for such changes.

9

Campaign Craft

DANIEL SHEA
JOHN MICHAEL BURTON

Candidates for public office need clear, coherent, easy to understand, easy to recall, and timely messages. In this article, two veteran campaign advisors, Daniel Shea and John Michael Burton, provide a kind of "how to" guide for campaigns and candidates. Pay attention to their five strategies for success and look for key terms such as earned media, paid media, and new media.

Political communication is a complex endeavor. Armchair analysts sometimes think that it is all about money and message—and it *is* about these things—but it is about much else. Communications directors must know the fine points of television (broadcast and cable), radio, print, and new media (primarily the Internet). They need to appreciate the tactical differences between paid media (advertising) and earned media (news coverage)—how to buy one and how to attract the other. They must also be able to orchestrate all these media into a coherent, strategic unit. This chapter discusses some of the general strategies that campaigns use to maximize the power of their message, the fundamentals of media strategy, the differences among the various types of paid media, . . .

Media Strategy

Coordination is crucial. The overall image of the candidate is created largely by the general strategy of campaign media. If the media do not mesh, then voters will not know where the candidate stands on the issues.... To build a coherent image, a campaign must commit itself to consistency, efficiency, proper timing, effective packaging, and a well-played expectations game.

Consistency

Media consultants seek "message discipline"—trying to stay "on message" and never getting "off message." During Campaign 2000, George W. Bush kept the focus on "leadership." Whether the specific issue was foreign policy, the domestic economy, or the need to change the education system, leadership always held center stage. Likewise, Bush's main rival in the primaries, Senator John McCain, also held a singular theme. For him it was good government....

Consistency is demanding. A campaign's theme must be communicated up and down the chain of command. Typically, only designated staffers speak for the campaign—the candidate, the campaign manager, and the press secretary or communications director.... The campaign theme must also be consistent with the candidate's past record. One function of opposition research is to locate discrepancies between a candidate's actions on the job and words on the campaign trail. A candidate who says one thing and does another courts misfortune—even if the statement fits with the campaign theme. Finally, the theme must be reasonably consistent with the views and actions of a candidate's supporters....

Efficiency

Despite complaints that consultants drive up the cost of campaigns, new-style political operatives are known for their efficient use of resources in difficult media environments. They want to... maximize the number of times that persuadable voters can be reached with a campaign pitch, either through paid advertising or through news coverage.

For electronic media, communications specialists think in terms of "reach" and "frequency." Reach is the portion of the viewership that actually receives a given message. The concept is typically bounded by some time frame. For example, a campaign might reach 30 percent of the market in a given week. Frequency, on the other hand, is the number of times that a person is reached. The principal measurement, however, is neither reach nor frequency but a combination of the two, expressed as "gross rating points" (GRPs). GRP is nothing more than reach times frequency. A message that plays three times on a show having an 11.2 percent reach adds up to 33.6 GRPs. These notions offer communications personnel a powerful means of analyzing media efficiency.

Demographics matter. *NYPD Blue* may offer the largest viewership but it is not necessarily the best audience for every candidate. The show's reach skews toward a cosmopolitan audience aged eighteen to forty-nine. Would *NYPD Blue* be the right show for a campaign that wants to reach older, more socially conservative voters? The better approach might be to place ads on reruns of *Matlock*—a much smaller audience but a much more efficient media buy. . . . MTV's audience is not large, but it is valuable to some advertisers because it skews toward a narrow, youth-based demographic. If people of all ages watched MTV, its audience would be valued less—even if it attracted more people—because fewer advertisers would be interested in a scattershot viewership.

As a rule of thumb, a political campaign thinks not in terms of simple GRPs but in terms of the cost-per-point (CPP) of persuadable voters. Everything outside the district is waste. Everything outside the targeted demographics is inefficiency. The more precisely that a campaign can aim its message at targeted voters, and the more options that it has for reaching them cost-effectively, the more efficiently the campaign can spend its money.

Note that these considerations are relevant for news coverage as well as paid advertising and for print as well as electronic media. Ads consume campaign cash whereas news coverage consumes the precious time of the candidate, staff, and consultants. A congressional candidate in Chicago has to work hard to win a profile piece in the *Chicago Tribune*, and if this widely circulated paper eventually decides to run the story, many of the candidate's new admirers will be Wisconsin voters. Additionally, the demographics may be all wrong. For some campaigns, an interview with a reporter from *Crain's Chicago Business* would be a far more efficient use of a candidate's time. More likely, however, the best investment would be a neighborhood weekly, which might reach targeted voters more efficiently. . . .

Timing

Part of the efficiency equation is the timing of the message. A standard sequence for a challenger campaign might be to establish the candidate in the public mind by doing a series of press interviews combined with "establishment" ads—those designed to let viewers know who the candidate is in the broadest terms. Once a positive impression of the candidate is created, the campaign might build credibility with a series of "issue" ads, laying out the high points of a candidate's agenda. If the incumbent starts to respond, the challenger might return fire with "attack" ads. At the end of the campaign, it is the responsibility of the campaign strategists to decide whether the challenger should go negative, go positive, or stay the course. Incumbents might follow roughly the same pattern, but they start off with better name identification, so they may not have to get into the business of establishment ads. Incumbents must, however, decide whether they want to strike back at a challenger who attacks their record.

Timing is important to message development for another reason. ... Only a fixed number of radio and television spots are available during the course of a race.... A campaign must make early determinations about how much money it will be able to raise and when it will be able to get the cash in hand. A campaign's income and outflow must match an odd quirk in the tactics of ad buying: the last days have to be purchased first. Because every campaign wants to grab the last few days before the election, a campaign that waits until a month before Election Day to buy the final slots will likely walk away empty-handed ...

Packaging and Effectiveness

Campaign ads fall into three general categories: positive, comparative, and negative. Advertising designed to establish a candidate's credentials and to lay out a policy agenda are usually positive in nature.... In a 1998 Georgia race Republican Dylan Glenn was trying to become the first black Republican congressman from the South since Reconstruction. To introduce himself, he ran a biographical sketch—"From Georgia; for Georgia." Comparative ads lay out differences between the candidates. In the 1998 Ohio race between Congressman Ted Strickland and Lieutenant Governor Nancy Hollister, one thirty-second ad was literally split in half. It began with a harsh attack on Hollister's record ("41% Income Tax Increase"), complete with black-and-white imagery and a discordant musical score, and then in midcommercial, the music lifted, the colors flowed, and the ad turned decidedly positive ("Ted Strickland is working to cut taxes"). Across the Ohio River in Kentucky, the 1998 Senate campaign of Republican congressman Jim Bunning included a fiercely negative ad against his opponent, Scotty Baesler. Baesler was shown shouting into the microphone at a campaign rally, to which was added Richard Wagner's "The Ride of the Valkyries," a score often associated with Nazism. ...

Expectations

An important element of communications strategy is something that political professionals call the "expectations game." ...

George W. Bush suffered from inflated expectations in early Campaign 2000. Through most of 1999, Bush was the presumptive winner of the next year's primaries. As such, he had nowhere to go but down. When Steve Forbes ran just eleven points behind Bush in Iowa, and John McCain won New Hampshire by 19 percent, virtually all attention shifted to Forbes and McCain. The question was whether the front-runner had hit a roadblock.... [O]peratives for Bush's nationwide campaign—ahead in virtually all of the post-New Hampshire states—were forced to call supporters with reassurances that Bush still had good prospects.

The expectations game demonstrates the relative nature of news. The question is not, Did Bush win Iowa? but rather, Did Bush win Iowa by the number of votes anticipated? Critics say that the outcome is all that counts, but it is not clear that the failure to meet expectations does not signify underlying truths.... Perception becomes reality. Campaigns must therefore do their best to control expectations.

Paid Media

The unique value of paid media is that it gives campaigns the ability to control their message. Unlike news coverage, which puts a reporter between the campaign and the public, paid media allows campaign operatives to script the message, target the audience, and, for the most part, to select the timing that best suits the needs of the campaign. The downside is that paid media costs money (by definition). Television ads can run tens of thousands of dollars. Even a small display ad in a college newspaper can cost hundreds. The costs of paid media can be staggering. According to congressional scholar Paul Herrnson, "Hopeful challengers committed an average of $410,000 to campaign communications" (2000, 230). Campaigns must be efficient in their targeting, and they must choose the right medium for their message.

... Campaigns in the new millennium have a wider variety of options, from new broadcast channels, to cable systems, to Internet media. Each has its own advantages. Cable allows for narrow targeting. Broadcast television and radio have wide reach and are required to sell ad time to candidates at bargain prices. Newspapers, while losing market share, are doing their best to remain competitive by offering deep discounts. Campaign Web sites ... are ... a critical means of voter outreach.

Television

Television is a powerful medium. Combining audio with visual imagery, it absorbs its viewers in ways that radio and print cannot. ...

Production costs are high, to be sure. Assembling a television spot requires the assistance of a producer, photographer, assorted gaffers, and a postproduction house to edit the raw footage.... The process is complicated, taking time that campaigns cannot spare. Campaigns that shoot on film, which is strongly preferred over video, need to factor in the hours, or even days, required to develop film stock. The competitive nature of politics puts a premium on speed, and television is the slowest and most expensive of the media to produce. It is cumbersome and resistant to real-time changes, but no campaign turns down the opportunity to use television ads if it has the money to do so....

The most familiar means of receiving television is via broadcast. In the mid-1970s, it was practically the only way to see a television program, but with the rise of cable in the 1980s and 1990s, broadcast lost a significant share of the video audience. Videocassette recorders, digital video players, and video game systems reduced the broadcast television audience further still. Furthermore, the increasing number of channels available to the viewer—especially those who watch network broadcast television on cable television systems—means that there is a greater tendency for people to "zap" commercials, including political spots. Nonetheless, broadcast television continues to be the mainstay of larger, new-style campaigns.

The reason is reach. A campaign can send a powerful message to wide swaths of the electorate with a single ad buy....

... Because it is regulated by the Federal Communications Commission as a public resource and because the FCC's mission is to render broadcasting friendly to political discourse, federal candidates have a legal right to buy ad time at discount rates.... Low-cost purchases provide no guarantee of placement. If a candidate buys a spot at a certain time using anything less than the higher "non-preemptable rate," another of the broadcaster's clients can pay top dollar to bump the candidate's ad from its time slot. To use low rates well, ad buyers must pay attention to day-to-day fluctuations in the broadcast marketplace.

Close monitoring is possible because candidate ad-buy records are public by law. Everyone has a right to view up-to-the-minute reports and to make copies for a reasonable fee.... Keeping a close eye on public records can let a campaign know when it should jump into the market....

Broadcast television reaches the largest audience, while cable television targets the most specific selection of voters.... [T]he ability to run ads in a single cable market fundamentally changes the tactics of video ad placement. Cable offers narrowly defined markets. Local cable companies have fixed borders—towns, cities, counties, and other municipal entities—and these boundaries are contiguous with many electoral districts. Waste is minimized. Moreover, because cable offer dozens of channels, cable channels and networks are forced to "narrowcast" their programming. That is, the History Channel, A&E, BET and MTV each seeks its own slice of the pie. Candidates have started to work their way into Spanish-language networks like Telemundo. . .

The benefits of cable are not without cost. First, the cable audience tends to be highly desirable to product marketers. . . . While it has been reported that cable customers vote more regularly than broadcast viewers (Friedenberg 1997, 184–85), campaigns that wish to target these voters are competing with powerful economic interests. Hence, to those who think cable is less expensive than broadcast, media consultant Jon Hutchens replies, "Not on a cost-per-voter-impression basis, not by a long shot" (1996, 42). Second, the cable marketplace is decentralized. Because there are more than 10,000 cable companies across the country, buying cable ads can be a tough job. . . . [T]here is some question as to whether an all-cable strategy is politically wise. Cable penetration is deep, but it is not total. Says Hutchens, "Excluding any significant-sized audience from receiving your communications only invites peril" (42). . . .

Radio

Radio obviously lacks the visual element of television, but in some ways it offers the best of broadcast combined with the best of cable. Like broadcast, it has a powerful reach, and it follows the same discount rules as broadcast television. Like cable, it can be used for precision targeting and constant repetition. For example, talk radio attracts a decidedly more conservative audience than pop stations. A radio-based strategy is therefore low-cost, allowing a campaign to buy a great deal of time. Moreover, fast production means that radio is suitable for rapid response. Campaigns can react to events in a matter of hours. In an interesting tactical twist, a radio-based strategy helps a campaign "fly under the radar," escaping the sorts of "ad watch" scrutiny that sometimes makes negative advertising difficult. As Friedenberg points out, "Generally, radio ads are not taped, nor are the transcripts of them closely analyzed by the press" (1997, 143). . . .

Newspapers

Newspapers, once the primary means for propagating partisan ideas, have lost a great deal of market share. Fewer people are reading newspapers, and less money is spent advertising in them. There are, however, a few reasons that newspaper ads remain part of new-style campaigns. First, ad space is always available. Whereas television and radio are scarce commodities, newspapers can always find space for display ads.... Second, newspapers are responding to market pressures by segmenting their markets. High-tech printing operations allow for geographic variations in advertising content, whereby each suburb in a metropolitan area might receive its own set of display ads. Finally, there is a fear factor at play. Many political operatives believe that failure to buy newspaper ad space can lose a campaign its rightful endorsement and might even creep into decisions about news reporting. It is an economic pressure that is presumed to work both ways. One former elected official recommends the following to candidates in local races: if a paper never runs with a campaign's news release, "threaten to cancel [campaign] ads and ask for your money back. The editors will hate me for telling you this, but for a small paper on a tight budget, this is an effective technique for your campaign" (Grey 1999, 182).

New Media

Newspapers are old media; campaign Web sites are new media. In the mid-1980s such resources did not exist, but now a presence on the World Wide Web is considered essential to campaigns at almost all levels. A candidate without a Web site seems to lack seriousness. A candidate with a disheveled site gives the impression of having a disorganized campaign. A visually attractive, user-friendly Web site that offers an abundance of informational content—one study showed that visitors spend the most time with "issue sections, candidate biographies and comparative sections" (Hockaday and Edlund 1999, 14)—can help deepen voters' impression of the candidate....

The difficulty with campaign Web sites is that people must make a conscious effort to travel to the site. Radio and television reach all the listeners and viewers who do not zap the ad. They are "opt-out" media. The Web, however, is an "opt-in" medium, meaning that some sort of off-site market is necessary to bring a substantial surfer-base or user-base to a Web site....

Another strategy is the political use of "banner ads." The digital version of newspaper display ads, these banners are the small advertisements that most Web surfers know from the top of major search engines and online directories such as Yahoo! and Lycos. In 1998, New York City Council speaker Peter Vallone used banner ads in his bid for the New York governorship. Banners are similar to traditional voter contact media in that they build name identification, but "[w]hen a user clicks on your banner ad (called a 'click through'), they immediately leave the site they were on and move to your site" (Hockaday and Edlund 1999, 14). Furthermore, "[c]lick-through rates on banner ads are comparable to direct mail prospecting rates, and there is strong evidence that voters who visit campaign Web sites make good use of the resources available" (14). One consultant notes the specificity with which banner ads can be placed: "Current local ad-targeting capabilities by national newspapers such as *The New York Times* and *USA Today* mean they can now be included in your media plan. Each site has different targeting abilities. Some target by market, others by state, ZIP code or phone number prefix. National TV and cable sites (such as MSNBC.com and CNN.com) can, in most cases, be bought by state or market" (Mentzer 2000, 69). By reaching out to other sites and even other media—both paid and earned—a campaign can increase traffic and broaden the reach of its strategic communications.

Finding the Media

Finding media outlets requires careful research. Take, for example, the search for print media. While just about everyone knows the major papers in a big city, a number of smaller publications might go unnoticed. With geographically large districts, such as rural congressional districts, just getting a handle on the television stations that serve the electorate can become a chore. Media advisers must inventory the outlets that serve a district—not just those that are published in the district but all those that reach the district's voters. The principal resources are Editor and Publisher's *International Year Book, The Gale Directory of Publications and Broadcast Media, SRDS TV & Cable Source, Broadcasting & Cable Yearbook*, and *SRDS Radio Advertising Source*.

The *International Year Book* lists publications from major daily papers down to shopping guides. A researcher studying the Miami Beach market will find a handful of major newspapers serving the metropolitan area, including the *Miami Herald* (in the "Dailies" volume) and the Spanish-language *el Nuevo Herald* (listed in the "Hispanic Newspapers" section). For each paper, the *Year Book* lists circulation, advertising rates, special editions, special weekly sections, and the newspaper's magazine. In addition, technical specifications—ranging from the width of a paper's columns to the types of software and printers in use—help a media consultant plan the details of an ad buy. To find smaller papers, the researcher looks to the "U.S. Shoppers" section of the *Year Book*, or to the *Gale Directory*. There one finds that Miami Beach has the *SunPost*, affiliated with the Post Newspaper Group. Contacts and ad rates are supplied. Even with all these resources, a prudent operative will actually travel the district to see what publications are sold at the newsstands and offered at the local libraries. Looking at the news boxes on the sidewalks makes clear that the *Miami New Times* and *Street*, both of which focus heavily on Miami's nightclub scene, are widely read in the South Beach area.

Also in the *Gale Directory* are broadcast media. Returning to the Miami Beach example, one finds that there is a 1,000-watt gospel radio station, WMBM. Of course, those who live in Miami Beach are likely to be listening to stations aired from the city of Miami, a few miles away. A researcher should therefore look at the whole media market. These stations can be found in the *Gale Directory, Broadcasting & Cable Yearbook,* or the *SRDS Radio Advertising Source.* SRDS divides the state of Florida into markets. Miami Beach lies in the "Miami–Fort Lauderdale–Hollywood" market. In the section devoted to this region, the researcher learns about a variety of radio stations, including WLYF, a 100,000 watt "adult contemporary" station licensed out of Miami. It has women aged thirty-five to forty-four years as its primary audience and men and women aged twenty-four to fifty-four as its secondary audience. The *SRDS TV & CABLE SOURCE* shows WAMI-TV in the Miami–Fort Lauderdale market. In fact, the station is located in the heart of Miami Beach's historic Art Deco district. Through careful investigation, political researchers can efficiently pinpoint media outlets appropriate to campaign marketing.

Television resource information is structured in much the same way. Using the *SRDS TV & Cable Source*, to look at Miami Beach once again, it appears that the Miami–Fort Lauderdale market is served by a number of broadcast stations, WFOR among them. This station is shown to be a CBS affiliate out of Miami. In addition, one finds that cable spots in Miami Beach zip codes are handled by TCI Cable Advertising of Miami. With a little investigation, the astute researcher can map out a rigorous media strategy.

Conclusion

The point of such research is purely strategic. Media buying has as its primary goal the purchasing of spots and ad space that will most likely move the candidate closer to electoral victory. The business of paid advertising—the most controllable form of voter contact—becomes unpredictable as soon as the opposition candidate enters the fray. Charges are followed by countercharges as each campaign seeks to push the other side off-message. To reinforce its own themes, a campaign must use all available means of reaching the voters, including news coverage, in the quest for an integrated series of campaign messages.

DISCUSSION POINTS

1 What are the five media strategies that Daniel Shea and John Michael Burton identify? Why is each important? Which do you think is most important? Why do you select this one? Think of examples of these strategies from elections with which you are familiar that support the authors' main points.

2 What do the following terms mean or include—earned media, paid media, and new media—and why are each important to running a successful campaign?

10

Making of the Digital Press Corps, 2004

KATHERINE Q. SEELYE

There is an old saying that "a day is like a lifetime in politics." That statement made more sense when news cycles were 24 hours long and the public was limited as far as where it could get its news. As journalist Katherine Seelye tells it, in the modern era of communication technologies, candidates are fast finding that they frequently have, at the most, hours if not minutes to respond to media reports and that they and their opponents can communicate to the voters almost instantaneously. All of this suggests a re-definition of a lifetime in politics to be more like a nano-second than a day.

Howard Dean was taking questions from a crowd of New Hampshire voters the other day when a young man asked him, "Governor Dean, can I pray for you?" Dr. Dean, the Democratic presidential candidate and former governor of Vermont, responded that he could use all the prayers he could get. Whereupon the young man immediately began a dialogue with the Almighty.

"Oh, I didn't know you meant right now!" Dr. Dean interjected, before telling him to go ahead. As bizarre campaign moments go, this one was brief and not really all that bizarre. But Mike Roselli, a producer for CNN, thought it was worth alerting his bosses in case they needed fresh tape of Dr. Dean.

So Mr. Roselli quickly punched an e-mail message into his Black-Berry. He titled it "Pray For Me," concisely recounted the incident and concluded: "The prayer includes a plea to God asking him to cure Dean's cold." It ended: "Amen. Live NBC Feed. 12:47:22."

With the time code, CNN could find the comment, which was being filmed by a pooled crew from NBC. Mr. Roselli, a campaign veteran, thought the prayer was more interesting than some of the material being beamed from CNN producers who were following other candidates ("Candidate X drinks a chocolate milkshake!"), but conceded that he had sent it partly because he could. And he worried that someone else might.

"Four years ago, I wouldn't have called that in until the event was over," he said. "But there's more competition now, 24 hours a day."

A deadline every minute, once the preserve of the wire services, is now the motto for most of the press corps, from print reporters with newspaper Web sites to still photographers, cable producers, and bloggers. The news cycle has condensed into one endless loop, and with it has come a endless stream of technology to accommodate it, or fuel it, since it is hard to say which came first.

Campaign reporters, like war correspondents, are not necessarily gadget geeks. But the rapacious 24-hour news cycle has forced them onto the cutting edge to do their jobs better—or at least faster. The equipment is even altering the shape of the correspondent's day, which now includes scrolling in the morning through *The Note*, an online political briefing from ABC News, and checking one another's Web sites at night, trying all the while to get a jump on everyone else.

The great leaps forward for print reporters in this campaign cycle are wireless laptops and digital tape recorders with software that allows them to download a candidate's speech immediately onto the laptops as an audio file. For television reporters, it is the ubiquitous hand-held minicam . . . Certain accessories are also a must. Many reporters have discarded their bricklike power adapters for a versatile, much cooler-looking and more functional one that lets them charge their laptops on an airplane or in the cigarette lighter of a car. And there is no need to carry around floppy discs or CDs, when they can use a flash memory stick the size of a finger to transfer data from one computer to another. . . .

Add these to the standard arsenal of cellphones, BlackBerries and palmtops, and reporters have few excuses for why an editor can't find them, why they can't meet a deadline, or why they have no idea what's happening on Mars.

To Web-crazed gadget geeks, these items are yesterday's news. But for many reporters, such supersonic portable gear simply isn't necessary. Only when they get into the competition of the campaign bubble do they realize what they have been missing.

The digital tape recorder that produces audio files has become essential for reporters trying to keep track of multiple speeches and bang out an article before flying off to another location. With the audio software, up comes an image of a tape recorder on the computer screen. "It's so easy to play, rewind, and play a quote over and over until you've got it," said Glen Johnson of *The Boston Globe*, who has been following Dr. Dean and Senator John Kerry of Massachusetts.

Mr. Johnson said his Sony digital recorder solved two problems. "It's got a much longer capacity than the standard reel-to-reel recorder, with up to five hours," he said. "And I can archive and organize all the speeches and permanently keep everything that's said on the trail without having to lug around a bunch of tapes and be out on the road without the tape I want."

He can also e-mail the audio files back to *The Globe*, which can put the sound bite on its Web site.

With an air card—a modem using a cellular connection—a reporter can file from the bus itself, without worrying about finding a phone line (or missing the bus).

If the reporter's news organization has not paid the $80 per month for air-card service, wireless service is often provided by Nathan Naylor, a 36-year-old entrepreneur and former press aide to Vice President Al Gore. During the Gore campaign in 2000, Mr. Naylor was responsible for making sure that phone lines and power cords were in place for the traveling press corps. . . .

After the 2000 campaign, he went to work for Senator Harry Reid, Democrat of Nevada. Both the terrorist attacks of 9/11, when cellphone lines were jammed, and the subsequent anthrax scare, which forced Mr. Reid into ancillary quarters, prompted Mr. Naylor to brainstorm about how to maintain communications during emergencies. The result is an oasis of mobile Internet access that he calls Soapbox. He advertises it as a way to "get in the bubble," although its great advantage for reporters is that it allows them to reach outside the bubble.

Mr. Naylor essentially hops from campaign event to campaign event, locating or arranging connections from which he can create portable Internet hot spots. On Jan. 19, the night of the Iowa caucuses, he set up his Soapbox and sold high-speed Internet access to more than 150 reporters sitting with their computers in the Polk County Convention Center in Des Moines . . . He also planted auxiliary boxes at the caucus-night parties held around town by four candidates—Mr. Kerry, Dr. Dean, Senator John Edwards of North Carolina and Representative Richard A. Gephardt of Missouri. A reporter could get access at all five spots for $100; installing phone lines at each site would have cost five times as much . . .

But there is a drawback. Because reporters can now file around the clock without a hard phone line, campaigns have reduced the filing time that they build into a candidate's schedule. This has also reduced the need for a filing center, an often-intense place that campaigns would set up at least once a day with phone lines and power outlets for the traveling press corps.

For reporters, filing time in the filing center was relatively sacred. It was a chance to sit still, hook up with the home office, check e-mail, focus, and usually eat. But on a bad news day for a candidate, the campaign handlers might restrict that time.

"Sometimes, campaigns would limit the time you had for filing so they could control the amount of research you did and who you talked to," said Mr. Johnson of *The Globe*. With wireless Internet access, "we're free from that shackle,' he said. "The wireless card works in 75 percent to 80 percent of the places where we are. You don't have to work within the parameters of the filing center."

Mr. Naylor agreed. "This rewrites the rule book of the little chess game that the media and the campaigns play, and it tilts the advantage more toward the reporters," he said. "A campaign operative can't use a filing center or a phone cord to limit your access to what's happening in the world."

Wireless access is also important because campaigns rely heavily on e-mail to send out schedules, schedule changes and statements, not to mention attacks on their opponents . . . Not every reporter, to be sure, is enamored of what technology has wrought. Jules Witcover, 76, a columnist for the Baltimore *Sun*, who covered his first campaign in 1960 by handing his copy to a Western Union boy, said he prefers to stick with the basics. He writes on a laptop. He confesses he carries a cellphone, but has told his editors that it doesn't accept incoming calls; in truth, he just doesn't answer it. And he uses a tape recorder because he realized some years ago that note-taking can be fairly unreliable.

But he does not like what the proliferation of gadgets has done to journalism, or to journalists. "Technology has impinged on reporting," he said. He said that candidates used to schmooze with reporters on the plane because they could pick whom they wanted to talk with and others would respect their privacy. Now, he said, if a candidate comes back, everybody gathers around. And with boom microphones and discreet recording gear and phones that can secretly take pictures and transmit them instantly, the candidate cannot relax.

"Rather than take a chance, they don't do it," Mr. Witcover said. "It has eroded the relationship that you could build up with a candidate."

Beyond that, he said, even a long bus ride at night is no fun anymore because most people are on their cellphones—and always on deadline.

DISCUSSION POINTS

1 Select and discuss how one change in communication technologies affected the 2004 presidential election. Consider how subsequent changes may affect future elections. What are some of these changes? Can you recall specific examples of news reporting shaped by these technologies that you have experienced?

2 What are the implications for a democracy when there is so much information available and at such a speed? Does such rob the electorate of the ability to give adequate time and attention to matters before they are swept aside with the newest batch of video, counter-ad, sound-bite, or posting?

3 From the perspective of the media or candidates for public office, what are some of the drawbacks associated with the changes in communication technologies that Seelye describes?

11

Electing Justice: Fixing the Supreme Court Nomination Process

RICHARD DAVIS

Richard Davis, a noted commentator on the media, describes how U.S. Supreme Court nominations have become like electoral campaigns. According to Davis, administrations leave little to chance and seek to control every aspect of a nomination beginning with the leaking to the press of possible candidates. Thus, begins a process through which nominees often become symbols for values or causes that they may or may not really share or favor. Pay attention to key concepts such as a "candidate with a story" and a "stealth candidate."

The new roles of external players have transformed the Supreme Court nomination process from an insider game dominated by the political interplay among the administration, senators, and, often, the legal community into one with a broader array of players, including interest groups (outside the legal community), the press, and the public. With this change, judicial selection has become a public process prone to the same emphases as other public selection processes such as elections and executive branch appointments—that is, image making to shape mass perceptions. As presidential campaigns seek to shape voters' images of a candidate, so Supreme Court nominations have become an attempt by the White House to secure certain perceptions of the nominee in the minds of elites and the public. . . .

White House Image Making

The primary (and typically initial) image maker is the White House. The times when the White House could offer a nominee and anticipate rapid, favorable confirmation by the Senate, sometimes within days, are over. The White House must sell the nominee to the other players, including groups, the press, and the public.

Such "selling" requires creating an image of a nominee. Because an image inevitably will form, the nominee and the White House want to be the first to shape it. As we will see later, failure to do so can result in a vacuum filled by other players, particularly groups and the press.

White House efforts in image making are not designed merely to aid the nominee. Their primary concern is the public's perception of the president. The nominee's image is a means to the end of shoring up the president's persona before voters. When confirmation is achieved, presidents seek to bask in the glory of their success, hoping it will stick to them and not just to the nominee. . . .

The White House image-making process starts even before the announcement of a nominee. The administration's release of names under consideration guarantees group, media, and Senate reaction. That reaction can be helpful in predicting confirmation chances before the president becomes committed to a certain nominee. Obviously, it becomes an opportunity for the press and groups to sabotage a nominee they oppose. . . .

Presidents know that their image-making strategies can be ruined if others can set images first, hence the importance of establishing a frame for a nominee at the outset. This frame is the story of the nominee.

The Nominee's Story

In an era of symbolism . . . it is no surprise that Supreme Court nominee image making is primarily based on a symbolic story. The story defines the nominee in a way that enhances public appeal and makes confirmation more likely, because senators are unlikely to want to oppose a nominee with an alluring personal story. When nominees offer a story of themselves, the story is designed to appeal to certain stereotypes in American life.

The classic example of symbolic story was Clarence Thomas's. The Bush administration labored from the outset to create a highly positive public image of Clarence Thomas. Thomas's upbringing, with a strong, influential grandfather and his rise out of poverty, resonated with the public because it fit the American ideal. . . .

Consequently, even though Thomas's accuser, Anita Hill, carried her own image of a sober, staid Oklahoma law school professor with no apparent motive for accusing a Supreme Court nominee [of sexual harassment], initial public opinion tilted toward Thomas. To some extent, Thomas had been inoculated by his own image.

Nor was Thomas's image making an aberration. Ruth Bader Ginsburg's story focused on the gender discrimination she experienced in her early years and portrayed a woman who was oppressed by societal limitations but overcame them. Stephen Breyer talked about his youthful experiences as a ditchdigger.

Although none of these stories or incidents, on their own, was false, the image was not a total one. Clarence Thomas had long since abandoned the poverty of his youth. . . . Ruth Bader Ginsburg had long since been accepted as part of the legal establishment . . . Stephen Breyer was primarily an academic whose real-world experiences were far more exceptions to his reality than the rule. Both Ginsburg and Breyer were wealthy individuals whose lives had been spent primarily in law schools or legal chambers.

Because the nominees' public life stories were not complete, they were not wholly accurate. Nevertheless, administrations extract from personal backgrounds those parts of the past that would be viewed as appealing to the general public. . . .

Why do nominees go through this transformation? The public nature of the process requires it. Because external players can weigh in on the fate of nominees, they want to be convinced that the individual embodies American democratic principles. Ideally, their life stories reflect the American dream—the ethnic whose ancestors came nearly penniless to American shores, the woman who overcomes gender discrimination, the African American who escapes poverty to achieve high political office. They become symbols for values and groups.

Explicit story making is a fairly new tactic and has emerged because the White House had created a vacuum that allowed others to define the nominee. Robert Bork was not made appealing to the public by the Reagan administration. In fact, Bork was almost demonized by opposition interest groups and some press articles. For example, a *Time* magazine cover story showed Bork dressed in black with the headline "Bork: How a young socialist became a conservative and one of history's most controversial Supreme Court nominees." Within the story, one photograph displayed a young Bork holding a snake with the caption "his intellectual odyssey 'departs from the conventional.'"

Bork's experience was ironic, given the Reagan White House's previous success with the president's own image. In fairness, Bork was committed to the notion that the confirmation process was primarily an intellectual exercise, and he may not have cooperated, as much as was necessary, in White House image-making efforts. Nevertheless, when opposition mounted, there was no reservoir of public goodwill, no public acceptance of Bork as a person that offered a benefit of the doubt to the nominee.

The Reagan administration and Judge Robert Bork made the mistake of allowing opposing groups and the press to define the nominee's story. Rather than the image of a thoughtful conservative academic and jurist, as the White House expected him to be portrayed naturally, Bork became a wild-eyed radical who lacked understanding of the real world and the effects of his legal views on everyday people. His public persona fed the story. His unshaped beard and frizzy hair, coupled with an academic's approach to senators' questions, confirmed the veracity of the image others assigned him.

Subsequent White House image makers learned important lessons from the Bork defeat....

The "story" nominations have included Antonin Scalia (first Italian American), Clarence Thomas (second African American and embodiment of rags to riches and specifically the success of efforts to assist African Americans out of poverty), and Ruth Bader Ginsburg (second woman and a long-time advocate for women's rights)....

Other nominees have not had a strong "story," and then image making becomes more problematic for the White House. These are "stealth" nominees who lack a story, yet they also lack definable records that would engender opposition. Recent "stealth" nominees include Anthony Kennedy and David Souter....

[N]ominees who lack the "story" and whose views on a range of issues are widely known, such as Robert Bork and William Rehnquist, typically face challenges in winning confirmation. Presidents who ignore the need for a "story" or appoint those with well-known ideological views do so at their own peril.

The story or stealth routes work best when the nominee is little known to the public in advance. Why? Image making is easier with a blank slate.

Supreme Court appointments are well designed for image making because nominations often begin with that blank slate in terms of public awareness of the nominee. Over more than 200 years, few Supreme Court nominees have been widely known to the public when they were nominated....

Well-known figures, however, particularly politicians, already have public records that make image making difficult. For example, although President Clinton wanted to appoint a politician to the Court, shaping the image of that individual would have been much more difficult than doing so for a lesser known individual. Clinton encountered some of that difficulty when he publicly considered Bruce Babbitt, former Arizona governor, 1988 Democratic presidential candidate, and then Interior secretary. Floating Babbitt's name led to immediate opposition from conservatives. . . . [I]t is no coincidence that elected officials, with their strong name recognition and public and controversial records, have been passed over for nomination since Earl Warren.

Federal appellate judges, on the other hand, are particularly advantaged in this process in that they rarely carry a public image that needs to be changed. Instead, images can be made from scratch.

Meeting Public Expectations

The White House needs the nominee to appear to correspond to public expectations of a Supreme Court justice. The public imagines justices as fair-minded individuals who act like the symbol of justice, with its blind approach to arbitrating disputes in society. Therefore, Supreme Court justices are supposed to be jurists or legal thinkers who carry no specific agendas with them as they ascend the bench. Justices are not supposed to be ideological extremists who use the bench to further their own ideology. . . .

An important aspect of image making is to minimize the appearance of political factors in the selection process. Presidents present nominees to the public with the inevitable line that this person deserves the position almost wholly because of merit and that regardless of the constituency nature of the appointment, once the credentials of the individual are known, there will be consensus on granting confirmation. . . .

Meeting Supporter Expectations

The mass public is not the only attentive audience. Perhaps an even more attuned one is the administration's supporters within the electorate. Through image making, presidents also need to signal to their supporters that their picks, particularly consensual ones, reflect the president's ideological direction and therefore serve their constituency. One example is President Reagan's announcement that the individuals he chose were "attentive to the rights specifically guaranteed in our Constitution and the proper role of the courts in our democratic system." In a specific instance, when Sandra Day O'Connor was nominated by Reagan, the White House reiterated the claim that O'Connor shared Reagan's views on social issues of the day, such as school busing, abortion, and the death penalty.

Another related, vital message from the White House that is often directed specifically at supporters is a thematic element to the appointment. Since Richard Nixon, presidents have defined their Supreme Court appointments through themes. For Nixon it was "strict constructionism." Ronald Reagan and George Bush promised to appoint justices who would not legislate from the bench.

Similarly, President Clinton communicated his desire to find a nominee who would have a "big heart." One aide said the president wanted a candidate much like Thurgood Marshall, who could bring a "moral dimension" to the law. The mention of Thurgood Marshall and "big heart" suggested that the president would appoint a liberal, thus satisfying the left wing of the Democratic Party.

Groups and Images

The White House rarely engages in image making alone. Groups also attempt to shape the public image of the nominee. And that effort almost always is undertaken to contradict the administration's image. . . .

The White House carries the advantage of surprise in image making. While the administration knows who the nominee will be and can begin to construct a public image, opposition groups are operating in the dark about exactly who will be the nominee until a formal announcement is made. The fact that the White House initiates the public image campaign with the announcement of the nominee and therefore gets to set the first public impressions aids the White House in the struggle over image. The announcement usually is the commencement of the image-making campaign. . . .

Opposing groups, then, must mobilize quickly to blunt the White House image campaign. In fact, that effort must occur during the first news cycle when the nomination is announced. Groups immediately offer their leaders for interviews and issue press releases designed to blunt the White House's image. . . .

This effort is made easier by the nomination of well-known candidates whose names have circulated widely among the legal community. For example, liberal advocacy groups long counted on Robert Bork's nomination by the Reagan administration. . . .

Hence, the opposition to Bork was prepared with extensive research to dull the White House image quickly. To blunt the effect of the White House image in press coverage and stop the usual rush to support by senators, within an hour of the White House announcement, Senator Edward Kennedy stood on the floor of the Senate and announced his opposition to Bork. . . .

Kennedy, in league with opposition groups, effectively signaled to other senators, the interest group community, the press, and the public that there should be no presumption of confirmation on the part of possible opposition forces. Because Bork was defeated in his confirmation bid, Kennedy's action became a model for creating an opposing image of a nominee quickly and effectively.

However, the Kennedy model is not universally applicable. When presidents nominate stealth candidates, they cannot so easily be labeled. A surprise nominee who is little known can catch groups off guard. In those cases, groups have scanty evidence to bolster their contrasting image, and the White House image goes unchallenged. . . .

Interestingly, it is not just opposition groups who seek to shape the nominee's image; groups generally supportive of the White House do so as well. For example, a pro-Clarence Thomas group placed an ad in the *Washington Post* featuring a photograph of poor black children. The ad reinforced the White House's Pinpoint strategy in selling Thomas to the nation. . . .

However, such image making by supportive groups can be harmful to the White House's carefully crafted efforts. These groups may seek to further a more extreme image that promotes the group's interests, but they also may signal undecided senators that the nominee is not what the White House suggests.

Why do supportive groups seek to construct their own images of the nominee, even to the detriment of the White House? Image making on the part of groups is not geared exclusively to the general public. The primary intended recipients are group supporters. Image making by groups is designed to justify group support for a nominee who otherwise may be portrayed as only tepidly supportive of group interests. The separate image also reassures group constituents that the group has been successful in obtaining a nominee to the membership's liking. It enhances the image of the group as an influential player in nomination politics. . . .

DISCUSSION POINTS

1 In what ways have U.S. Supreme Court nominations become like electoral campaigns? What role has been played in this transition by the White House? Why and how has this transformation occurred? Where does the media fit in?

2 What is meant by a "candidate with a story?" What is meant by a "stealth candidate?" Think of recent life examples of each.

3 What are the various factors that interest groups weigh when getting involved in shaping public opinion of Supreme Court nominations that they either favor or oppose? How do these groups use the media in their efforts aimed at shaping public opinion?

PART FOUR

Media Coverage of War, Foreign Affairs, and National Security

PERHAPS NO OTHER GOVERNMENTAL FUNCTIONS are as important or attract as much attention as the state's powers to make war or protect its citizenry. While there have been exceptions, the press has historically been supportive of American efforts to protect herself and promote her interests. The media has a long and rich tradition of informing and even entertaining its audience about war, foreign affairs, and matters of national security. Press coverage of such matters dates to the revolutionary period when the nation's printing presses cranked out newspapers and pamphlets that both glorified and exaggerated the performance of the continental army—often past the point of objectivity or accuracy. Printers often used their publications to enable the continental army to communicate with itself about matters such as rumored enemy troop strength and maneuvers.

Eighty years later, the national press corps covered the Civil War in a manner that contributed to the Union's ultimate triumph. The reporters who covered the Civil War often traveled with the troops and attended battles side-by-side with the troops. Their accounts of the courage of Union forces, as well as their laudatory accounting of President Abraham Lincoln's "Gettysburg Address," put a face on its participants and gave an otherwise unpopular war a kind of higher purpose that resonated with Northern Americans.

During World Wars I and II, the press, which tended to be sympathetic with the Allied Powers, helped to justify involving America in her first international wars. While there were many missteps and questionable military decisions made during these wars, the press was unabashedly pro-war and its coverage helped to rally public opinion and support at home for supporting the war effort.

The press's long honeymoon with the state in the area of war, foreign affairs, and matters of national security came to a crashing halt in the late 1960s and early 1970s during the Vietnam period. Early on, the press coverage of the Vietnam conflict tended to be positive. As the war dragged on, however, and public pronouncements by government officials, civilian and military alike, often failed to square with reality, the press began to report on the conflict in negative terms. The press's skepticism toward the government in the area of war and national security continues today. During the two main American military efforts in this period, the Gulf War of 1991 and the war with and present occupation of Iraq, and the efforts of the government under President George W. Bush to combat terrorism at home and abroad, the media has vacillated between initial coverage that tended to be laudatory and more recent press coverage that has tended to focus on perceived shortcomings in American Iraqi policy.

If there is one issue related to media coverage of war, foreign affairs, and matters of national security that has remained constant throughout the years, it is the tendency of some, especially in government, to question the propriety, tone, and wisdom of certain stories. Thus, while many Americans have welcomed the often critical and skeptical press that has been associated with the post-Vietnam War era, others have been troubled by such coverage. Some have gone so far on occasion as to question the patriotism and priorities of certain members of the media. Others have criticized the press for not being critical enough when it has come to its coverage of American policies in the Middle East. The readings in Part Four have been selected with an eye toward raising issues about press coverage of war, foreign affairs, and matters of national security that may not be familiar to some readers.

This part starts with former *Washington Post* editor Benjamin Bradlee's assertion for and defense of the need for vigorous press coverage of such matters. Bradlee, a former naval officer, has expressed frustration both with a public that assumes that journalists are by nature indifferent, or worse, to national interests, as well as with those members of the press corps who would report on matters that Bradlee believes run contrary to their duty as Americans. Bradlee's defense is aimed primarily at those who question the need for a vigorous press when it comes to covering matters of war or security. Note Bradlee's repeated assertion that the government needs oversight because certain agencies have consistently proven themselves untrustworthy.

The second selection comes from a new media source, a collection of blog postings, and it offers an untraditional look at the media and war, foreign affairs, and matters of national security with a particular focus on the latter during the post-9/11 world. Danny Schechter, a former television news producer and current media-critic blogger, criticizes the media for its coverage of the war on terrorism. According to Schechter, the United States has managed to obtain mostly positive and seldom probing press coverage of this war *via* a concerted and deliberate effort on the part of its military to influence media messages. The press, Schechter asserts, has been blind to this effort and the results have been disastrous.

This part's third selection comes from a non-mainstream source. While traditional journalism preaches objectivity, using stories to report or analyze but never to advocate, peace journalism encourages journalists to use their stories to assist the cause of world peace. In a short publication, Jake Lynch provides peace journalists and would-be-peace journalists alike with a seventeen point plan for how to use their role as a journalist to assist peace-makers.

12

A Good Life: Newspapering and Other Adventures

BENJAMIN BRADLEE

Public officials regularly criticize the media for its coverage of war, foreign affairs, and national security. Benjamin Bradlee, longtime editor of the Washington Post *and himself a former naval officer, writes in support of having a vigilant press investigate such areas of public policy. Note the role that personal relationships, both civil and less than civil, can have on the media's decision to publish matters related to this subject area.*

Editors choose.

That's what they do for a living. People first, then subjects, then words. And choosing whether to print anything is often the toughest decision of them all.

In matters of national security, the question quickly boils down to this: Is the security of the nation really at stake, just because someone in authority says it is? ...

One morning in November 1976, Bob Woodward reported to me that although he had only one source, it looked as if a Middle East head of state was on the CIA payroll.... At this point, Woodward didn't know which head of which state was on the CIA payroll for how much, although there seemed no lack of candidates. I asked him for a full court press, and it took him two weeks to come up with the name: King Hussein of Jordan; the dollar amount: about $1 million a year for twenty years; and some further details. The money was "walking-around" money, not connected either to economic or military aid, which Jordan received regularly. The operation was called "NO/BEEF" inside the CIA. The money had been used variously . . . including to procure women, when Hussein was little more than a teenager, and to pay for bodyguards for his children when they were old enough to go to boarding school in the United States.

What we needed now was a second source. Woodward called [President] Carter's press secretary, Jody Powell, told him everything he knew, and asked for White House comment. . . . Next day, someone from the White House . . . called to ask me whether "it would help you make up your mind [to print or not to print the story], if you could talk to the President?"

We were there the next morning for an interview I'll never forget. . . . Carter had been president for less than a month, but looked totally comfortable, poised, friendly and hospitable. He was dressed in a pin-striped gray suit, and smiling. First, the president said, the story was true. (There was our second source.) Next, he said he had been briefed several times by the outgoing Secretary of State (Henry Kissinger), and the outgoing director of the CIA (George Bush), but neither had mentioned that we had a king on our payroll. Third, he had ordered the payments stopped. And fourth, he said he couldn't make the case that others of his staff were making that the national security was involved.

We had our story.

But, the president added gently, Jordan was vital to the Middle East settlement he had made a priority. Secretary of State Cyrus R. Vance was actually in the Middle East, scheduled to see Hussein within the next forty-eight hours. The president said he would prefer the story not be published, but added, "I can't tell you how to run your business." If we were going to publish the story, he would like twenty-four hours' notice. On the spot, I promised that we would not run the story that night, and would give him at least a day's notice, if we decided to run it. The president talked about the importance of trust. He said he wanted Woodward and me to believe in him. He said he hoped that I would come to see him on "anything." And then he ended the interview, saying, "This is your country and mine."

Back in the office, we agonized. On the one hand, the president had been so straight, so decent, that it seemed almost impolite to print anything he did not want printed. On the other hand, newspapering isn't about being polite or grateful. It's about deciding where the public interest lies. In this case, could we involve ourselves effectively in a Middle East settlement *without* our negotiators—never mind the public—knowing we "owned" a key participant in that settlement?

We had developed a policy at the *Post* to help decision making on matters of national security. We automatically delayed publication for twenty-four hours as soon as any responsible official invoked national security. Simultaneously, we reached a tentative decision to publish (so that we could arrange for the extra space normally required on a big story), and we appointed a group of reporters expert in the field at issue to talk us *out* of publishing the story.

We finally came down on the side of publishing. Because the story was true . . . we did have a king on our payroll, unknown to the public and until very recently, unknown to the president and to the Secretary of State. Because the former CIA director and the former Secretary of State had failed to tell the new president despite hours of briefings. Because the current president would not say that national security was involved. And because effective oversight of the CIA lay somewhere between ludicrous and nonexistent. No one really knew what the spooks were up to.

The day after the story ran, I got this note from President Carter, handwritten on embossed White House stationery:

To Ben Bradlee,

I think your publication of the CIA story as the Secretary of State was on his Middle East mission and about to arrive in Jordan was irresponsible.

This is offered by way of editorial comment.

Jimmy

I could understand why the president was upset. So was I. I felt we had gone the last mile to be responsible. . . .

In 1981, *The Washington Post* and the CIA were involved in an adventure most of which could have shown up in a John le Carré book or movie—which, in fact, they did.

It all started one day when Howard Simons and I "came into possession" of a manuscript, written in tiny, cramped Russian handwriting, filled with complex mathematical computations and diagrams. . . . [B]ecause we were both conspiratorial and because the Cold War was still hot, we immediately thought this material might have great value to the American intelligence community.

Howard called Admiral Bobby Ray Inman, the deputy director of Central Intelligence, and asked for an immediate appointment. (CIA director Casey was out of town.) We told Inman what we knew, what we thought we had, and what we planned to do with it. Namely, to give it to him, pronto. We asked for two things in return, without much confidence that we would get either one.

First, we wanted first crack at whatever story might develop. If it ended the Cold War, for instance. . . . Second, if there were any spare

Brownie points to be earned in this matter, we would appreciate a few, to combat the constant charge from the morons that the press in general—and the *Post* in particular—regularly disregarded the interests of the country for a scoop. We didn't have much hope here either, even after I talked to CIA director Casey. But two subsequent CIA directors volunteered on separate occasions that they were aware of the *Post*'s cooperation. That awareness, plus a token, is worth exactly one ride on the subway.

Inman "put [the manuscript] into the system," as he described it to me thirteen years later. In fact, the manuscript contained the specifics of design and function of a particular new Soviet Intermediate-Range Ballistic Missile (IRBM). Combined with satellite intelligence—from the monitoring of individual Soviet IRBM test firings, for instance—these specifics proved to be invaluable.

In September 1994, a Soviet weapons expert at the Central Intelligence Agency reported, for the record, that the document "gave us the best insights we had on Soviet Strategic Force Sea Launched Ballistic Missiles, and ICBMs, on their engineering capabilities, on their propellant capabilities." At the same time Inman described the document as "unique material . . . judged to be valuable" to our country. . . .

If stories involving questions of national security are the toughest problems for an editor, the mother of all national security stories was the Pelton case, a classic battle in the war over national security between the government and *The Washington Post*. I guess we won it, because we printed the story finally, May 29, 1986, but our "victory" was costly: NBC beat us to the punch, even though they had almost no details, and our negotiations with President Reagan, CIA director Bill Casey, NSA director William Odom, and National Security Council chief John Poindexter were so protracted I felt more like a lawyer than an editor, as we battled to get the story in the paper.

Pelton was Ronald W. Pelton, a low-level (less than $12 an hour) employee of the National Security Agency (NSA), and a spy who gave away the family jewels to the Russians in 1980, five years before he was identified as the traitor.

Actually, we backed into the Pelton case, courtesy once more of Bob Woodward. "Backed in" because Woodward learned of the U.S. intelligence capability to intercept Soviet military signals before we learned that it had been compromised, or by whom. One day Woodward told me that the United States had developed the capability of intercepting cable communications between the Soviet High Command and its submarines. This capability was code-named "Ivy Bells," and it consisted of a bell-shaped contraption installed at the bottom of the ocean over a Soviet cable. Without penetrating that cable, messages sent via the cable were recorded inside the bell-shaped contraption.

U.S. submarines regularly retrieved tapes of the Soviet messages and installed new tapes. . . . Operation Ivy Bells had the highest security classification, we were told again and again, as we began to learn the details.

I found Woodward's story appalling. First, because I could see no useful social purpose whatever in publishing news of our new intelligence capability. It was obviously of enormous value to the country, in avoiding a war, or fighting one if worse came to worst. And second, who the hell was passing on information like that to Woodward and why? Good as he was, wasn't it reasonable to assume that if Bob Woodward, investigative reporter, knew about this supersecret U.S. capability, the Soviets might learn about it one of these days? And if so, didn't we have some responsibility to tell government leaders that their secret was out?

After talking to Don Graham, by then the *Post*'s publisher, I sought and received an appointment with General William Odom, NSA director, told him what we had—limited as it was—told him we had no intention of publishing at that time, but asked him what the hell was going on. I remember wondering whether we earned any Brownie points in the process, or simply guaranteed that all our phones would be tapped, if they weren't already.

What we couldn't know then was that the Soviets knew all about Ivy Bells, and had long since removed the U.S. listening devices from their cables. The United States eventually learned that Ivy Bells had been compromised in 1985 from Soviet defector Vitaly Yurchenko, the top Soviet KGB official who redefected to the USSR a few months later, after telling the United States that Pelton had given Ivy Bells to the Soviets. . . . Woodward found all that out soon enough, and the question of to print or not to print was back on the front burner.

If the Soviets knew all about Ivy Bells, why shouldn't the American public know about it? Before we got the answer to that question, I had some twenty conversations with all the biggest shots in the intelligence community, and the *Post* publisher's wife Katharine Graham had one conversation with President Reagan. . . .

Woodward had been joined on the story by reporter Pat Tyler . . . and the pressure from them to print never stopped. . . . Woodward and Tyler must have rewritten the story a dozen times, in an effort to meet each new objection from the intelligence establishment. Two former CIA directors—Dick Helms and Bill Colby—were consulted. One of them told us that what the Soviet leaders knew wasn't as important as what might happen when the rest of the Soviet establishment learned of the U.S. intelligence coup.

We started showing various government officials different versions of our story, something we almost never did, and that boomeranged on us. . . .

CIA director Casey was on our backs . . . on Ivy Bells . . . threatening the *Post* with prosecution if we published, under a 1950 law that provides criminal penalties for anyone who "publishes" any classified information about communications intelligence. In May, Casey wanted to talk to me again, suggesting a drink at the University Club. This time I took managing editor Len Downie with me. He'd been in on all the maneuvering, and I hunched that Casey was going to muscle us—big time. And he did. After reading the latest version of the story written by Woodward and Tyler, he sipped his Scotch and water, told us he had just come from the Justice Department, and said slowly: "There's no way you run that story without endangering the national security. I'm not threatening you, but you've got to know that if you publish this, I would recommend that you be prosecuted."

Threats are truly counterproductive with me. As we waited still another couple of days, we ran a story about being threatened with prosecution. Casey called to object, saying he thought we were having a private conversation! The next day, at Casey's suggestion President Reagan made his telephone call to [Katherine Graham].

On May 19, as jury selection in the Pelton case began, NBC's James Polk broadcast a story about "Operation Ivy Bells, believed to be a top-secret underwater eaves-dropping operation by American submarines inside Soviet harbors."

On May 21, our story finally ran, under the headline: "Eavesdropping System Betrayed, High Technology Device Disclosed by Pelton Was Lost to Soviets."

On May 22, Pelton's trial began in Annapolis.

On May 26, Casey and Odom issued a joint statement cautioning against "speculation and reporting details beyond the information actually released at trial."

On May 29, Casey called to say, "I don't want a pissing match."

On June 5, Pelton was convicted and given three life sentences, plus ten years.

What lessons did the Pelton case teach me?

First, the damage to the national security was done by Pelton, not by *The Washington Post*, nor the press generally.

Second, the government tried to prevent publication to avoid national embarrassment. Once it was certain that the Russians knew everything about Ivy Bells, there was no issue of national security.

Third, the claim that publication would threaten national security is an insidious one. The public feels entitled to believe that a president, or a CIA director, or a four-star general knows more about national security than a two-stripe editor. It is a formidable task to convince the public that patriotism is not exclusively the province of administration officials. It is a formidable task to convince the public that officials often—more often than not, in my experience—use the claim of national security as a smoke screen to cover up their own embarrassment. Those of us who heard Richard Nixon claim he could not explain Watergate because matters of national security were involved will never automatically accept claims of national security. Those of us who were taken all the way to the Supreme Court for violating national security laws by publishing the Pentagon Papers got more out of that experience than an acquittal.

DISCUSSION POINTS

1   What lessons does Benjamin Bradlee draw as a result of episodes like the Pelton case?

2   What was the *Washington Post*'s policy for deciding whether to publish stories related to national security matters? Do you agree or disagree with such media policies? Does the press have an obligation to be Americans first and journalists second as Bradlee suggests? Why or why not? What would be the legal or ethical justification for such a conclusion?

3   Why does the media consult with mainstream, retired or active, national security officials before deciding whether to publish stories? Does it appear, based on this reading, that enough weight is given to non-authority opinions held by those outside of the government? Is this important? Why or why not?

13

Information Warriors: From the News Dissector's Weblog

DANNY SCHECHTER

Danny Schechter is a former television news director and the founder of a blog that examines the western media's coverage of politics and world affairs. In this excerpt from his 2003 book, Media Wars: News at a Time of Terror, *Schechter examines the Pentagon's policy of "IO" (Information Operations). This policy is aimed at limiting news coverage of wars. According to Schechter, it is both a successful and dangerous policy for a democracy to have.*

An acronym we haven't seen too much in the flow of reporting from every media pore over the course of our "holy war" on terror is IO. But "I" and "O" are two letters that have great importance among those charged with steering and massaging media coverage to ensure that it puts the military in the best possible light.

"IO," short for Information Operations, is the Pentagon's Ministry of Truth in the best *1984* sense of the term. Now it is time for us to focus in, and "eye-o," open our eyes to how this increasingly sophisticated military science works and why it has been so effective in shaping our images and ideas about a faraway war on many fronts.

There is an excellent exposé about this by . . . Maud S. Beelman, director of the International Consortium of Investigative Journalist. . . .

"IO groups together information functions ranging from public affairs to military deception and psychological operations or PSYOP," she writes. "What this means is that people whose job traditionally has been to talk to the media and divulge truthfully what they are able to tell, now work hand-in-glove with those whose job it is to support battle-field operations with information, not all of which may be truthful."...

Fighting On Three Fronts

[L]et's be blunt: IO is a way of obscuring and sanitizing that negative-sounding term "propaganda" so that our "information warriors" can do their thing with a minimum of public attention as they seek to engineer friendly write-ups and cumulative impact. They achieve this objective by pursuing the following strategies.

1. Overloading the Media

IO operates in some conflicts by providing too much information. During the Kosovo War, briefers at NATO's headquarters in Belgium boasted that this was the key to information control. "They would gorge the media with information," Beelman writes, quoting one as saying, "When you make the media happy, the media will not look for the rest of the story."...

2. Ideological Appeals

We saw an appeal to patriotism and safeguarding the national interest in the fall when Condoleezza Rice and other Bush administration officials persuaded the networks to nix bin Laden videos and other Al-Jazeera work. This is nothing new. All administrations try to seduce and co-opt the media. Back in 1950, President Harry S. Truman appealed to top newspaper editors to back the Cold War with a "campaign for truth" in which "our great public information channels," as Secretary of State Dean Acheson referred to the media, would enlist. Nancy Berhard, author of *U.S. Television News and Cold War Propaganda, 1947–1960* (1999, Cambridge University Press), says "none of the assembled newsmen blanched" at Truman's "enlistment to propagandize."

It is this ideological conformity and worldview that makes it relatively easy for a well-oiled and sophisticated IO propaganda machine to keep the U.S. media in line. The Pentagon enjoys the avid cooperation of the corporate sector, which owns and controls most media outlets. Some of those companies, such as NBC parent General Electric, have long been a core component of that nexus of shared interests that President Eisenhower called the military–industrial complex. As Noam Chomsky and others have argued, that complex has expanded into a military, industrial, and *media* complex, in which IO is but one refinement.

3. Spinning Information

Spinning has become an art form. We see this every day at Pentagon briefings where what's really happening is, at best, secondary. For example, the weekly *Washington Post* edition of January 14-20 tells how reporters who scoured the bombed-out ruins of the town of Qalai Niazi in Afghanistan found an estimated eighty civilians dead, yet little or no evidence of Taliban or al Qaeda forces. The villagers they interviewed insisted, "there was nothing of the Taliban here." Yet most of the media minimized their own findings and instead relied on pronouncements by Pentagon officials who insisted that they were right to bomb the village to smithereens. In Washington, Secretary of Defense Rumsfeld gave the story what struck me as an IO spin: "There were multiple intelligence sources that qualified the target," he insisted. No reporter challenged him to produce evidence. Rumsfeld's words were enough, apparently because he is so personable, in an aw-shucks kind of way. In the end, newspapers like the *Post* always seem to conclude that what their reporters saw is insufficient. "There is much that is not known—and maybe never will be—about what happened on that December night," concludes Edward Cody, who filed the dispatch. Translation: No one is to blame, especially not the United States.

4. Withholding Information

"Sorry, I am not at liberty to explain. But do I really have to?" says Ted Gup, who teaches journalism at Case Western Reserve University in Cleveland and writes about the secret lives of CIA operatives: "It is easy operating behind the curtain of secrecy to conceal setbacks and pronounce progress." Underline that word "easy."

Another disclosure appears in the *New Yorker*, where Seymour Hersh reveals that Pakistan, with U.S. permission, airlifted out its own military officers from Konduz on the eve of a battle. His version of these events contradicts the impression we had that the U.S. military explicitly prohibited any negotiations or escapes by forces under attack. Clearly, an exception had been made for our Pakistani "allies" who were still advising Taliban forces. This information was suppressed at the time in line with a policy of selective disclosure.

5. Co-Option and Collusion

But why do we in the media go along with this approach time and again? We are not stupid. We are not robots. Too many of us have *died* trying to get this story (and other stories). Journalists will tell you that no one tells them what to write or what to do. Yet there is a homogenized flavor and Pentagon echo to much coverage of this war that shames our profession. Why? Is it because reporters buy into the ideology of the mission? Is it because there are few visible war critics to provide dissenting takes? Or is it because information management has been so effective as to disallow any other legitimate approach? An uncritical stance is part of the problem. Disseminating misinformation often adds up to an inaccurate picture of where we are in this war.

Stratfor.com, a global intelligence consulting website says.. "Coverage of the 'war on terrorism' has reversed the traditional role between the press and the military. Abandoning the hypercritical coverage of the past, the media have become cheerleaders—allowing the conflict in Afghanistan to become synonymous with the war at large and portraying that war as an unalloyed success. The reversal of roles between media and military creates public expectations that can affect the prosecution of the war."

Pentagon-Media Rules

After the Gulf War, the bureau chiefs of the networks sat down with the Pentagon to work out guidelines that would permit independent access and end the pool system used during Desert Storm by the military to manage the press so successfully. The negotiations took eight months of haggling within the media, and between media and Pentagon representatives. Nine general principles were agreed on. The key one was this: "Open and independent reporting will be the principal means of coverage of U.S. military operations."

Once the "war on terror" began, the Pentagon reaffirmed its commitment to these principles and then promptly forgot about them, applying an IO strategy of appearing to be open while defining the terms and framing the story themselves whenever possible. Did the media chiefs yell bloody murder? Hell no. They acquiesced and seemed to forget that independence should govern the relationship between Washington and those that write about its machinations.

I will give the last word to Stanley Cloud, who ran *Time* magazine's Vietnam reporting, and was one of the post-Gulf War media negotiators: "No government can be depended upon to tell the truth, the whole truth, and nothing but the truth—especially not when that government makes mistakes or misjudgments in war time. The natural inclination then is to cover up, to hide, and the press's role, in war even more than in peace is to act as a watchdog and truth seeker."

If the press is not playing this role, it may be because the media is no match for IO specialists who have learned all too well how to massage, manipulate, and manage news coverage.

DISCUSSION POINTS

1   What are the five strategies that the Pentagon's "IO" policy employs? How does each work?

2   Does the Pentagon's "IO" policy surprise or bother you? Why or why not?

3   Should there be limits on what the media can publish, post, or broadcast about a war? If so, why? If not, why not? What would the limits be? Who would impose them and how?

14

Tips for Covering Conflict

JAKE LYNCH

Jake Lynch practices what is called "peace journalism." Peace journalists use their stories to encourage non-violent solutions to international conflicts. In this short piece, Lynch offers seventeen bits of advice to aspiring peace journalists so that they may avoid adopting an anti-Middle Eastern bias.

Middle East Media Bias

1. Avoid portraying a conflict as consisting of only two parties contesting one goal. The logical outcome is for one to win and the other to lose. Instead, a peace journalist would disaggregate the two parties into many smaller groups who are pursuing many goals, thus opening up more creative potential for a range of outcomes.

2. Avoid accepting stark distinctions between "self" and "other." These can be used to build the sense that another party is a "threat" or "beyond the pale" of civilized behavior—both key justifications for violence. Instead, seek the "other" in the "self," and vice versa. If a party is presenting itself as "the goodies," ask questions about how different its behavior really is to that it ascribes to "the baddies"—isn't it ashamed of itself?

3. Avoid treating a conflict as if it is only going on in the place and at the time that violence is occurring. Instead, try to trace the links and consequences for people in other places now and in the future. Ask:

Who are all the people with a stake in the outcome?
Ask yourself what will happen if . . . ?
What lessons will people draw from watching these events unfold as part of a global audience?
How will they enter the calculations of parties to future conflicts near and far?

4. Avoid assessing the merits of a violent action or policy of violence in terms of its visible effects only. Instead, try to find ways of reporting on the invisible effects—for example, the long-term consequences of psychological damage and trauma, perhaps increasing the likelihood that those affected will be violent in future, either against other people or, as a group, against other groups or other countries.

5. Avoid letting parties define themselves by simply quoting their leaders' restatement of familiar demands or positions. Instead, inquire more deeply into goals:

How are people on the ground affected by the conflict in everyday life?
What do they want changed?
Is the position stated by their leaders the only way or the best way to achieve the changes they want?

6. Avoid concentrating always on what divides the parties, the differences between what they say they want. Instead, try asking questions that may reveal areas of common ground, and try leading your report with answers that suggest some goals may be shared or at least compatible, after all.

7. Avoid only reporting the violent acts and describing "the horror." If you exclude everything else, you suggest that the only explanation for violence is previous violence (revenge); the only remedy, more violence (coercion/punishment). Instead, as a way of explaining the violence, show how people have been blocked and frustrated or deprived in everyday life.

8. Avoid blaming someone for starting it. Instead, try looking at how shared problems and issues are leading to consequences that all the parties say they never intended.

9. Avoid focusing exclusively on the suffering, fears, and grievances of only one party. This divides the parties into "villains" and "victims," and it suggests that coercing or punishing the villains represents a solution. Instead, treat as equally newsworthy the suffering, fears, and grievance of all sides.

10. Avoid "victimizing" language, such as "destitute," "devastated," "defenseless," "pathetic" and "tragedy," which only tells us what has been done to and could be done for a group of people. This characterization disempowers them and limits the options for change. Instead report on what has been done and what could be done by the people. Don't just ask them how they feel; also ask them how they are coping and what do they think? Can they suggest any solutions? Remember, refugees have surnames as well. You wouldn't call President Clinton "Bill" in a news report.

11. Avoid imprecise use of emotive words to describe what has happened to people.

> "Genocide" means the wiping out of an entire people.
> "Decimated" (said of a population) means reducing it to a tenth of its former size.
> "Tragedy" is a form of drama, originally Greek, in which someone's fault or weakness proves his or her undoing.
> "Assassination" is the murder of a head of state.
> "Massacre" is the deliberate killing of people known to be unarmed and defenseless. Are we sure? Or might these people have died in battle?
> "Systematic," as in raping or forcing people from their homes. Has it really been organized in a deliberate pattern or have there been a number of unrelated, albeit extremely nasty incidents?

Instead, always be precise about what we know. Do not minimize suffering. Reserve the strongest language for the gravest situations, or you will beggar the language and help to justify disproportionate responses that escalate the violence.

12. Avoid demonizing adjectives like "vicious," "cruel," "brutal," and "barbaric." These always describe one party's view of what another party has done. To use them puts the journalist on that side and helps to justify an escalation of violence. Instead, report what you know about the wrongdoing and give as much information as you can about the reliability of other people's reports or descriptions of it.

13. Avoid demonizing labels like "terrorist," "extremist," "fanatic," and "fundamentalist." These are always given by "us" to "them." No one ever uses them to describe himself or herself, and so, for a journalist to use them is to always take sides. They mean the person is unreasonable, so it seems to make less sense to reason (negotiate) with them. Instead, try calling people by the names they give themselves. Or be more precise in your descriptions.

14. Avoid focusing exclusively on the human rights abuses, misdemeanors, and wrongdoings of only one side. Instead, try to name *all* wrongdoers and try to treat equally seriously allegations made by all sides in a conflict. Treating seriously does not mean taking at face value, but instead, it means making equal efforts to establish whether any evidence exists to back them up; it means treating the victims with equal respect; and it means presuming that the chances of finding and punishing the wrongdoers are of equal importance.

15. Avoid making an opinion or claim seem like an established fact. ("Eurico Guterres, said to be responsible for a massacre in East Timor . . .") Instead, tell your readers or your audience who said what. ("Eurico Guterres, accused by a top U.N. official of ordering a massacre in East Timor . . .") That way, you avoid signing yourself and your news service up to the allegations made by one party in the conflict against another.

16. Avoid greeting the signing of documents by leaders, which bring about military victory or cease-fire, as necessarily creating peace. Instead, try to report on the issues that remain and that may still lead people to commit further acts of violence in the future. Ask what is being done to strengthen means on the ground to handle and resolve conflict nonviolently, to address development[al] or structural needs in the society, and to create a culture of peace?

17. Avoid waiting for leaders on "our" side to suggest or offer solutions. Instead, pick up and explore peace initiatives wherever they come from. Ask questions from ministers, for example, about ideas put forward by grassroots organizations. Assess peace perspectives against what you know about the issues the parties are really trying to address. Do not simply ignore them because they do not coincide with established positions.

DISCUSSION POINTS

1 Which of these so-called lessons do you consider the strongest or most important? Why?

2 Which of these so-called lessons do you consider the weakest or least important? Why?

3 Should journalists be advocates for such causes as world peace or should they seek to remove all biases from their writings? Why?

─── PART FIVE ───

Entertainment Media and Politics

IN THE 1970S AND 1980S TWO FILMS, *Network* (1976) and *Broadcast News* (1987), appeared, and both of them, from different perspectives, made a similar statement about the news business: the entertainment media and the news media have become so intertwined that they are sometimes indistinguishable. Media typically associated with audience entertainment now often seek to educate or influence their audience about public affairs issues. The fact that non-news media have grown political and now have the potential to influence their audiences has not been lost on politicians. Nor has the audience's desire for consuming public affairs information in an entertaining fashion been lost on news and programming executives. As a result, the entertainment media, while perhaps always loosely aligned with political causes or prone to making political statements, have gotten more attention from policymakers and non-governmental organizations (NGOs) than in the past. The same can be said of politicians who run or oversee the public broadcast media. The readings selected for this section examine the entertainment media and politics as they have come to look and act in the early 2000s.

Part Five starts with an excerpt from a speech given by Irvin Sonny Fox. Fox, a television executive and an advocate for woman's rights and world population control, describes how he and his colleagues in television and in the world of interest groups have worked to convince the makers of many of the world's most popular soap operas to alter their scripts and storylines to promote justice for women and to achieve reductions in world population numbers.

In separate articles, *New York Times* reporters Emily Nussbaum and Elizabeth Jensen both examine television programming and politics. They do so from different perspectives but during similar times. Nussbaum looks back at how the Columbia Broadcasting System (CBS) used a sitcom in the early 1970s to famously and subtly criticize American foreign policy in Vietnam. Jensen examines efforts by politicians, long since wise to the power of the small screen to influence viewers, to influence, to their political advantage, the shows broadcast on public sponsored networks. The authors ask different questions: Nussbaum questions if commercial networks today would challenge a government during a war in the manner that CBS did. Jensen questions whether politicians ought to interfere with the creative act broadcast on public airwaves with public monies to achieve political balance or, as she sees it, advance their political causes.

The next two readings focus on films and politics. The first, written by Cesar Soriano, calls attention to the fact that many viewers view films as purely entertaining and miss out on political statements that the film maker is making. He then explores different points of view as to the propriety of films' containing political messages. David Robb also explores politics and films, only he looks at how the Pentagon works to change films. After documenting numerous examples in which the Pentagon succeeded in getting films changed due to their political message, Robb explores the ethical and legal correctness of such an unofficial public policy.

The final selection in this chapter comes from legendary author Ray Bradbury and it concerns literature as a force for voicing a writer's personal philosophies or beliefs. Like Robb, Bradbury examines censorship, only he details how private persons and businesses rather than any public entities have attempted to censor his works. Bradbury calls attention to just how much pressure to censors exists and how insidious a process it can be if one does address it head on. The arts, political or otherwise, have long been censored. As entertainment arts become more and more political, and as the state and non-governmental interests exercise greater influence, if not direct control, over these art forms, the chances that censorship will grow rise exponentially.

15

Using Soap Operas to Confront the World's Population Problem

IRWIN SONNY FOX

Long-time television executive Irwin Sonny Fox describes how Population Communications International (PCI), an international organization dedicated to slowing world population growth, convinced the makers of many of the world's most popular soap operas to alter their storylines to support causes such as women's rights, family planning, adoption, and efforts to reduce domestic violence. Fox, who is affiliated with PCI professionally, offers a first-hand look into how interest groups have quietly come to use nontraditional strategies to achieve their objectives.

In India, in a Doordarshan television network prime time serial, a fourteen-year-old girl is forced into an arranged marriage by her father. Angouri has a dream of becoming a barrister, and objects to being forced into consummating the marriage until she has had a chance to realize that dream. Her aspirations are destroyed by her mother-in-law who burns her books and beats her. Many months into the soap opera, the young girl dies in childbirth at the age of 15. The audience of 150 million viewers who watched this prime time series went into mourning, and a crucial point was made. Delaying the onset of childbearing is a good idea. Forcing children to start bearing children at 15 is not a good idea. For India, rapidly approaching a population of one billion, for the world, rapidly approaching six billion, and for all the Angouris of the world, this drama carried an impact no documentary or tract could possibly approach.

In Tanzania, the Philippines, St. Lucia, Brazil, and other countries where population and related health and social issues are of critical importance, other soap operas designed to change people's attitudes and behavior regarding family planning, health, women's empowerment, and other pro-social issues are being broadcast on radio and television. Behind this unique employment of the mass media is Population Communications International (PCI). Headquartered in New York, PCI has been developing this technique for 12 years.

The objective is to motivate individuals and communities to make choices in reproductive health and development that will contribute significantly to slowing world population growth. The work of PCI, based on the social learning theories of Professor Albert Bandura of Stanford University, is designed to complement the efforts of those involved in providing health services in these countries. With their emphasis on motivating audience members, these soap operas can break through the encrustation of many years of sexism and other anachronistic aspects of traditional culture that keep people from making sensible family planning decisions.

PCI works creatively with the media and other institutions to motivate individuals and communities to make choices resulting in population trends that will yield sustainable development and environmental protection. We at PCI operate in tandem with established groups who share our goals by forming relationships with government agencies as well as with nongovernmental organizations in host countries.

PCI values promotion of health and education and sensitivity to national and local cultures. Often we work with organizations that represent a variety of interests within a particular country, interacting, for example, with officials from the ministries of health, education, and population. In those nations with a national radio or television system, government cooperation is necessary to ensure that our programs are broadcast. Financial support for PCI's work comes in many forms. In general, PCI invests its money in training, research, and start-up costs associated with developing a soap opera. The production costs can come from foundations, corporate sponsors (such as in India), the United Nations (such as in Tanzania), or a combination of commercial and governmental sources (such as in China).

PCI has selected the soap opera format to communicate its messages for a number of important reasons. The longevity of a soap opera, in many cases several hundred episodes, allows characterizations and story lines to play out over a period of months or even years. The identification of the audience with characters they see regularly over a long period of time is substantially greater than it is for the less regular and less sustained presentations of other formats. Therefore, when a soap opera script models good or bad behavior, its impact can be exponentially greater than it is for other formats. The impact of the Angouri story was no doubt much more substantial than if it had played out as a two-hour movie.

Furthermore, the duration of soaps allows for the introduction of characters without immediately inserting social messages. This allows the audience to identify with the characters before they start their transition or journey through which they will deliver their message.

In all cases, the productions are country-specific. They are written, acted, and produced by talent in each country. PCI's role is in the training of the creative talent, in conducting research to help determine the issues, and in making the arrangements necessary for a program to be aired.

To create and produce a PCI serial drama, we cooperate with a wide range of groups that share a common goal to reduce family size and promote reproductive health. An example of such a collaboration is *Tinka Tinka Sukh*, a family planning radio soap opera first broadcast in India in February 1996. The program was broadcast by All Radio India, a national station, and made possible by a generous grant from the Indian government. In concert with the airing of the show, a comprehensive research project to evaluate the impact of the soap opera was conducted by Ohio University and the Centre for Media Studies of India.

In China, PCI has contracted with the China Population Information Service, a nongovernmental organization headquartered in Beijing. The goal of the program there, in keeping with China's national population policy, is to promote norms supporting small families and to reduce the strong preference for sons.

In Tanzania, where PCI has begun its third year presenting the radio soap *Twende na Wakati*, the collaboration involves Radio Tanzania, five Tanzanian ministries, representatives from PCI-Kenya and PCI-New York, and independent research teams from the University of New Mexico and the Population/Family Life Education Program in Tanzania. The Rockefeller Foundation provided financial support for the research.

Research is a critically important component of PCI's work. We facilitate the creation of independent research projects to measure the effects of its entertainment-education programs in various countries. In selected countries, these take the form of controlled field experiments that serve to isolate the effects of the programs.

Evaluative research includes nationwide surveys conducted before, during, and after a broadcast series; collection of clinic intake data; focus groups; in-depth interviews; analysis of letters from audience members; and analysis of other research findings such as those found in demographic and health surveys. In each case, the research is designed to measure changes in knowledge, attitudes, and behavior of audience members and within regions receiving the programs as opposed to those not receiving them.

In addition, similar research techniques are used to help form characters and story lines for programs in each country in order to ensure that all the elements of the programs are culturally accurate, relevant, appropriate, and acceptable.

Two recent reports on Tanzania and Kenya prepared by independent researchers have added substantial weight to the evidence that PCI's mass media entertainment-education programs are effective in changing behavior. The most recent study shows that 28% of the new adopters of family planning in Tanzania cited the PCI soap opera by name as a reason for seeking family planning services. In the areas of the broadcast, 52% of the population aged 15 through 45 indicated that they listened to the program, and 82% of the listeners said that the program had caused them to change their behavior in regard to AIDS prevention.

The Tanzanian program was designed under the guidance of Tom Kazungu, PCI's representative in East Africa, who applied his experience to produce *Ushikwapo Shikamana* (*When Assisted, Assist Yourself*) in Kenya in 1987–89. That serial was the top-rated program in the history of radio broadcasting in Kenya according to the advertising agencies of the time. A study of rural health centers by the University of Nairobi's School of Journalism pointed to the radio program as the most effective communications activity in the area of family planning in Kenya up until that time and credited it with convincing men that their wives should be allowed to seek family planning services.

The communications situation in the United States is different, so PCI's strategy here is different as well. There is a plethora of daytime dramas from which viewers can choose. Moreover, the competitive nature of the business makes it difficult for advocacy groups to promote their perspectives. Unlike many nonprofit organizations that try to encourage social consciousness through letter-writing campaigns or public relations efforts, PCI has developed a novel approach to gain the trust and cooperation of writers, producers, and executives in the soap opera industry and to foster their support.

PCI has organized three Soap Summits. The participants have included the head writers, executive producers, and network executives from the 11 daily American soap operas and the Fox shows "Beverly Hills 90210," "Melrose Place," and "Party of Five." We start each summit with a keynote address. In 1996 the keynote address was delivered by Secretary of Health and Human Services Donna Shalala. In 1998 the keynote speaker was Rob Reiner. We continue with a closed session the next day during which experts make 15-minute presentations on health and social issues that are not being adequately addressed in this country and ask the soap opera creators and network executives for help in addressing these problems. Attendees have been exposed to topics that include teen pregnancy, reproductive health, violence against women, and world population. Secretary Shalala emphasized the importance of soap operas in her opening speech: "Believe it or not you are part of the public health system in this country.... You increasingly fill the vacuums in this country once occupied by traditional institutions. From family to religion, from schools to communities, with light and with shadow, with words and with emotion, you reach over 40 million viewers a day and you reach them where they live."

Following the 1996 Soap Summit, PCI decided to conduct an evaluative research study to measure the effect of the conference. With a generous grant from the Ford Foundation we have been able to track the results of the meeting through extensive interviews with attendees. Participants reported that the summit reinforced their motivation to positively address social issues and generated awareness of the profound impact of their work. In addition, the summit fostered internal support for script and character changes by engaging a variety of decision makers—including executive producers, head writers, and breakdown writers. Said Lucy Johnson, CBS vice president for daytime programming, "The value of the summit . . . [was] to make us more aware of some of the consequences and the power of the message we put across."

Within a short period of time four of the ten programs that sent representatives to the summit made changes to specific scenes and plots to reflect some of the issues discussed at the conference. The writers of "All My Children," for example, abandoned a story line that would have given a single teen father custody of his baby. Instead, while the program cotinued to have the teen interested in his child, the baby was adopted by a married couple. At the end of episodes about domestic violence, "The Young and the Restless" broadcast information about 800-number help lines which were staffed and funded by the Department of Health and Human Services and the Kaiser Family Foundation.

Follow-up research demonstrated that the summits not only lead to changes in characterizations and story lines, but also contribute to an increased awareness of the topics presented, as well as of the important roles that writers and producers play in society.

DISCUSSION POINTS

1 Why would groups like PCI use entertainment vehicles such as television shows to achieve their objectives?

2   Can you think of additional television shows that you think have been used, or might be used, to broadcast an interest group's message?

3   Should groups such as PCI use entertainment vehicles such as television shows to achieve their objectives? Should the producers of such shows have to reveal if their plots were influenced by groups such as PCI which profess specific social, economic, religious, or political objectives?

16

When a TV Network Could Be Cynical About a War

EMILY NUSSBAUM

M*A*S*H was a ground-breaking sitcom that ran on CBS between 1972 and 1983. It first aired in an era of considerable social and political unrest. Most prominently, the era featured protest over the Vietnam War, women's rights, and civil rights for minorities. M*A*S*H was set during the Korean War (1950–53) and it chronicled the lives of certain members of a mobile army surgical hospital. The show, however, was clearly intended to be a critical commentary on the Vietnam War. Casting such a show, in particular, the episode Emily Nussbaum highlights, took guts. This reading reveals how television changed in 1973 with the airing of a single M*A*S*H episode.

"All wars are popular for the first 30 days," wrote the historian Arthur Schlesinger Jr. By the time *M*A*S*H* hit the airwaves in 1972, the year the last American ground troops left Vietnam, that deadline had long expired. An antiwar sitcom that blossomed during wartime, *M*A*S*H* ran for 11 years, and it was explicitly intended as a commentary on Vietnam. But the show's setting was the Korean War of the 1950's, a chronological remove that gave the show's creators a perverse freedom, as well as a stamp of universality. To watch it now is to gaze back at an era of angry skepticism, personified by the prankster antihero Hawkeye Pierce (Alan Alda). In the bleak universe of *M*A*S*H*, spokespeople are liars, generals are bullies and anyone who mouths patriotic slogans is a dupe or a hypocrite. "By the time we waded in, by the time we came on the air, people really wanted to get the hell out of Vietnam," recalled Larry Gelbart, one of the producers. "And even a corporation like CBS was ready to do a show like that."

Depending on your politics, the show's caustic vision of authority might now seem like adolescent cynicism, or a desperately needed corrective. Tomorrow's episode on FX, "For the Good of the Outfit" from October 1973, provides a particularly searing example of its take on power. While performing surgery on Koreans from a local village in their Mobile Army Surgical Hospital, Pierce and his colleague Trapper John McIntyre realize that the shrapnel they're plucking out comes not from the enemy but from American weaponry. When they try to report this "friendly fire" incident, their worst suspicions are quickly confirmed: the hierarchy is rotten all the way to the top. A slick investigator first sweet-talks Pierce, then stonewalls, and finally "loses" the evidence. *Stars and Stripes* prints a piece of propaganda blaming the Koreans for the shelling. When a general is called in to settle the dispute, he suggests that Pierce could be sent to the front lines as punishment for being a whistleblower. "I've got to hand it to you, General," Hawkeye deadpans. "You buried the evidence, you got rid of the guy who knew the evidence, and now if we press this, you'll take away our breathing privileges."

The script is studded with such bitter zingers. "Now we know how Dreyfus felt when he read the story in *Stars and Stripes*," Hawkeye says when he reads the newspaper's false account. Hawkeye's squirrely colleague Frank Burns describes the destruction of the Korean village as "this terrible but very human mistake made by a few of our brutal but well-meaning servicemen." But it's the final scene that truly gets across the episode's seemingly bottomless darkness: after initially having his mail blocked by the Army, Hawkeye finally gets a letter from his father back in Maine, a response to Hawkeye's request that his father help expose the incident by calling in a favor from a local senator. "Dear Son, I am afraid Senator Baxter can't be of much help to you," Hawkeye's dad writes. "It seems he was just indicted for influence peddling and faces 20 years in the pokey. Sure makes me sorry I stuffed a ballot box for him!"

According to Mr. Gelbart, CBS was generally "supportive or silent" about such portrayals of American corruption; its censors were far more concerned about sex jokes and blasphemy. The one major struggle the creators did lose was their battle against a laugh track. "Absent the laugh track, you hear the real tone of the show," Mr. Gelbart noted. "No comment, however bitter and angry, isn't trivialized by a mechanical laugh." (Mr. Gelbart is grateful for the advent of DVDs, where episodes can be seen uncut and free of canned chuckles.) In its first season, *M*A*S*H* had shaky ratings. But once it was renewed and given a plum spot following *All in the Family,* its viewership spiked; the final episode, in 1983, was watched by roughly half the country's population. It was a case of perfect synchronicity between audience and show, as the series' creators reflected back viewers' Watergate-era distrust of the government. "My rationale with the network was, if you can let Walter Cronkite criticize the country at 6:30, why can't we do it at 8:00?" Mr. Gelbart recalled.

Of course, military sitcoms with rule-breaking heroes had existed before, including *Gomer Pyle* and *McHale's Navy.* But Hawkeye Pierce was a notably difficult breed of prankster—more Lenny Bruce than Dennis the Menace. A prickly truth-teller whose integrity mingled with a Groucho Marx aggression, the character had a self-righteousness that at times slid into mild sadism. As Jim Wittebols, author of *Watching M*A*S*H, Watching America,* points out, as the years passed, the show began to soak up other 70's movements, including feminism, and the nastier undercurrents of Hawkeye's womanizing softened, leaving him a more sentimental figure. But in early episodes like "For the Good of the Outfit," the purity of Hawkeye's rage is rather awe-inspiring. Informed that the government plans to rebuild the village, complete with the "first soft-serve ice cream stand in Southeast Asia," Mr. Alda responds in a low-voiced fury: "Well, that's terrific. I'm glad. Now what about rebuilding the truth?"

Such a corrosive vision is hard to find these days: the most similar sensibility shows up not on TV but in the cult online comic strip *Get Your War On,* where the artist David Rees has used clip art characters of ordinary office workers to rage in Hawkeye-like despair since Sept. 11. "I think the trick now is to do something that's just not part of the noise," Mr. Gelbart said. "All the debate just goes by us, downstream. Nobody seems to convert anybody." He added, "There's a certain arrogance about the people in power today that makes them immune to criticism and satire. And then again, there's the argument Tom Lehrer made: that satire died when Henry Kissinger got the Nobel Peace Prize."

DISCUSSION POINTS

1   Was *M*A*S*H* a product of its times or would a network consider broadcasting a similar show concerning American forces deployed in the Middle East? Support your answer.

2   Can you think of other television sitcoms that have been politically inspired? What are they? Were they effective? Why or why not?

3   Should television networks using public airwaves be free to run entertainment shows that are critical of government policies and actions? Should there be some sort of warning before the show or equal time provided to its detractors? Should the public entity that issues television frequency licenses (the Federal Communications Commission) be empowered to review such scripts? Why or why not?

17

Public Broadcasting and Political Balance: A New Twist

ELIZABETH JENSEN

A political furor erupted in the mid-2000s over the political direction and nature of the shows aired by the Corporation for Public Broadcasting (CPB). The CPB is a private, non-profit corporation that was created by Congress in 1967. It is charged with the task of developing high quality, non-commercial broadcast shows for the public. Political conservatives have long charged that the CPB represents a certain liberal bias. (It was created by a Democratic Congress and President.) In recent years, conservatives have sought to balance the CPB's programming by broadcasting shows that represent less liberal or more conservative political views. Some associated with the CPB have sought to award film contracts to film makers on an equal basis so that a film made by a liberal about the war in Iraq would be balanced by a film on the same subject made by a conservative film maker. Elizabeth Jensen examines this new spirit of balance and raises questions about its propriety as well as the logistics associated with seeking such balance in films.

Richard Perle, the former Bush administration adviser and Iraq war advocate, would make a ripe subject for many filmmakers. But when the Corporation for Public Broadcasting awarded a preliminary grant for a film on Mr. Perle's neoconservative worldview, it gave the money to the British producer Brian Lapping, Mr. Perle's friend of four decades.

Not surprisingly, Mr. Lapping, an award-winning filmmaker, is sympathetic to Mr. Perle's outlook . . .

So the corporation took another unusual step. Seeking political balance on a charged topic, in late April it asked a half-dozen filmmakers to submit proposals for a separate film critical of White House foreign policy.

Sherry Jones . . was chosen, with an associate. They will examine "how the implementation of the so-called Bush doctrine has alienated traditional American allies, tarnished America's image abroad and possibly made the world more dangerous," the corporation said in a news release.

The grants to both Mr. Lapping and Ms. Jones, announced Monday, are part of the corporation's ambitious "America at a Crossroads" project, which will devote $20 million over three years to films examining America's role in the post-Sept. 11 world. The project, controversial from the start, comes even as the corporation, charged with overseeing public broadcasting, is embroiled in a debate over how to achieve balance and objectivity. Its chairman, Kenneth Y. Tomlinson, has pushed for more programs reflecting conservative viewpoints, to balance what he says is public television's liberal bias.

The corporation funnels most federal funds directly to local stations, but keeps $65 million a year for program grants. Along with a $20 million program to teach history and civics to teenagers, "Crossroads" was designed to impress Congressional patrons.

"I felt that we had to do something that would demonstrate to the people trying to make difficult decisions about the appropriation that it was still worth investing big bucks in public television," Robert T. Coonrod, who was the corporation's president when "Crossroads" began in March 2004, said in an interview.

Michael Pack, the corporation's senior vice president for television programming, said, "We want this initiative to make clear to both Congress and the public that we are fulfilling the mission of public television to raise the level of debate on public affairs issues." . . .

With public television facing severe funding challenges, the corporation received 440 "Crossroads" applications, which it says was a record. They were subjected to detailed screening by, among others, a bipartisan panel of policy experts.

The chosen films, Mr. Pack said, will cross party lines. It has not yet been decided how and when they will be shown. One option is to group them as a PBS series tied to the fifth anniversary of the Sept. 11 attacks, in 2006. "I believe it will spark a national debate," he said of the series. . . .

PBS has aired opinionated films, under the rubric of personal essays, in its "P.O.V." series and elsewhere. Mr. Pack said that the Perle film will make the case at length for an assertive United States foreign policy, and that "we also want to make sure the American people have the chance to hear at length that policy criticized." He emphasized that the "Crossroads" producers must adhere to PBS's journalistic standards.

Just how the concept of dueling films fits those standards is unclear. "What the new policies say now is that producers should enter into any work of journalism with an open mind and not a predetermined view about where the piece should come out," said Tom Rosenstiel, director of the Project for Excellence in Journalism, who helped PBS update its editorial guidelines. "I think the American tradition of journalism is that if something is controversial, the initial treatment of it would provide sufficient balance," he said.

PBS's Ms. Atlas said the guidelines also emphasized transparency. "Under our expanded definition of objectivity, the viewer will understand the process by which the filmmaker will come to his or her conclusions," she said.

Ms. Jones, whose film is examining the Bush doctrine, said she considered herself a broadcast journalist. "I don't come to things with a predetermined point of view," she said. "I think the record of our bazillion awards suggests that we spend a lot of time in research and reporting and then we present programs that are based on facts, often based on documents and on getting people who have been involved in decision-making to talk to us on camera."

Given the debate over Republican pressure on public television, Ms. Jones said she had reservations before agreeing to make her film, worrying that "instead of being allowed to do what I do, which is to report, there would be some other agenda." But, she said, she has not seen one.

Mr. Lapping's work has been shown on PBS and the Discovery Times Channel . . . He said his "very longstanding friendship" with Mr. Perle, an assistant secretary of defense under President Ronald Reagan, dated to the early 1960's.

The film, Mr. Lapping said, will be "mostly a journey, through his life and experiences," and will show Mr. Perle interacting with his critics, who say he was overly optimistic about American prospects in Iraq . . .

Mr. Lapping said the film originated at a dinner party in Provence, where he and Mr. Perle have neighboring homes. Among the guests was a former Clinton administration State Department official. "I could see they were distinctly suspicious of this right-wing hawk," Mr. Lapping said, but added that Mr. Perle won them over. "He's a very gentle performer, a very persuasive performer."

Of the Corporation for Public Broadcasting's decision to commission a counterfilm, Mr. Lapping said, "I can understand the pressure for an opposite point of view, but I didn't see the need for it."

DISCUSSION POINTS

1 Should the Federal Government be supporting political films of any kind? Why or why not?

2 What questions does Jensen raise about the CPB's new policy stressing political balance?

3 What are the implications of the type of balance that Jensen finds the CPB to be seeking?

18

Politics Creates a Disturbance in the Force

CÉSAR G. SORIANO

In the spring of 2005, film maker George Lucas released the final installment in his Star Wars *saga. Journalist César Soriano ventured out among film goers to survey their reaction to the film. He found many viewers were surprised, a few even put off, by the film's apparent political commentary on the United States's war with and occupation of Iraq.*

Since early screenings of *Episode III: Revenge of the Sith* began last month, film critics, commentators and Internet bloggers have been debating whether filmmaker George Lucas is comparing President Bush and the Iraq war to the Dark Side of the Force. The conservative film site Pabaah.com has called for a boycott. The topic even made NBC's *Today* show.

Lucas said Sunday at the Cannes Film Festival that the movie was written before the Iraq war. "We were just funding Saddam Hussein and giving him weapons of mass destruction," he said, adding, "The parallels between Vietnam and what we're doing in Iraq now are unbelievable."

Still, some see echoes of Bush in the film.

In one scene, Anakin Skywalker/Darth Vader tells his onetime mentor, Obi-Wan Kenobi, "If you're not with me, you're my enemy." The line is seen as a reference to Bush's post-Sept. 11 threat "Either you are with us, or you are with the terrorists."

The White House declined to comment on the controversy.

Josh Griffin, a self-described "conservative *Star Wars* fan," says he cringed when he heard the dialogue at a recent advance screening of *Sith*. "*Star Wars* is meant to be a children's movie . . . not to be a political statement about someone's liberal ideology."

Even a perception of bias could hurt a film's bottom line, some say. The crucial summer moviegoing season usually makes up 40% of a year's box office revenue; this year, ticket sales are down 7% from 2004.

"If people feel Lucas is pushing a parallel between the Galactic Empire and present-day America, I think people will be turned off," says filmmaker Jason Apuzzo, co-editor of the conservative film blog Libertas (libertyfilmfestival.com/libertas).

But others applaud Lucas for taking a stand.

"As a liberal and a Democrat, it was comforting," says *Slant* magazine film critic Ed Gonzalez. "*Star Wars* is created by real people, starring real people, so it s inevitable it will reflect real-life issues," even if it is sci-fi fantasy.

Freelance writer Craig Winneker, who accused *Sith* of bias on the webzine *Tech Central Station*, says he nonetheless loved the film. "I'm not going to hold a grudge against the movie or base my opinion on world events because of something Yoda says."

Political Spoilers

People who have seen early screenings of *Star Wars, Episode III: Revenge of the Sith* are noting parallels to the Bush administration:

Sith plot: Seeking to strengthen security during wartime, Chancellor Palpatine persuades the Senate to give up civil liberties and elect him emperor for life. "So this is how liberty dies—to thunderous applause," Senator Amidala laments.

Bush plot: Seeking to strengthen security after the terrorist attacks of Sept. 11, 2001, President Bush urged legislators to pass the PATRIOT Act, which opponents say infringes on civil liberties.

Sith's war: Palpatine starts a war to divert attention from his true political motives.

Bush's war: Bush persuades Congress to go to war with Iraq based on evidence that has now been largely dismissed.

DISCUSSION POINTS

1 Are you surprised to learn that certain film genres, such as adventure or fantasy, might be political?

2 Why would film makers use traditionally non-political film genres to make political films?

3 Can you think of films that you have seen that have been more political than you expected? Were you pleased by that or turned off? Why?

19

Operation Hollywood: How the Pentagon Shapes and Censors the Movies

DAVID ROBB

Ever wonder why the films with the best and most realistic American military equipment or with access to real American military bases seldom seem to present the American armed forces and American armed conflicts in a negative light? Think it is a coincidence? David Robb, a veteran entertainment industry reporter, thinks he knows the answer. In his book, Operation Hollywood, *Robb finds that the Pentagon uses its considerable influence with Hollywood to influence how war and the American military are portrayed in its films and television shows.*

The cantina was crowded. Waiters dashed from table to table, balancing spicy dishes and exotic drinks on wooden trays. Ivy covered the walls and flowers adorned the tables. The restaurant was beautiful, but the smell of horse shit was overwhelming.

Producer Mace Neufeld and director Phillip Noyce sat at a large table with their location manager, Stuart Neumann, taking in the local color and flavor of Medellin, Colombia—the cocaine capital of the world and the setting for their next movie, *Clear and Present Danger*. Based on the Tom Clancy novel, the film would star Harrison Ford as CIA agent Jack Ryan, who battles drug kingpins in Colombia—and dangerous men in his own government....

The filmmakers had flown into Medellin from Bogotá the night before. Their studio bosses back at Paramount Pictures were worried for their safety, and with good reason. Murders and kidnappings were common in this part of the world. And airplanes were crashing—or being bombed out of the sky—on a regular basis. Just before their plane took off from Bogotá, somebody came onboard, knocked on the cabin door, and handed the pilot a revolver. And just a few weeks earlier, cartel bandits had blown up several radar beacons along their route—instruments that were needed to navigate over the vast mountain range that separates the two cities.

But a State Department employee stationed in Medellin had been looking out for them. He showed them the sights, and steered them clear of the worst neighborhoods, and before long they were back home in Hollywood with some good stories to tell and a real sense of intrigue and danger that would permeate their movie.

But dealing with the Pentagon would prove even more difficult.

Right up until the day shooting was to start, Neufeld didn't know if he was going to get the Pentagon's approval for his movie. Phil Strub, the Pentagon's chief liaison to the film industry, was playing hardball. He wanted major changes in the script before he would give Neufeld what he wanted, which was the use of several F-14 jet fighters, three state-of-the-art Black Hawk attack helicopters, and access to Arlington National Cemetery.

In a July 20, 1993, letter to Neufeld, Strub said that the Pentagon wouldn't be providing assistance to the production because of its "very negative portrayals of the U.S. President and his national security advisor; U.S. military combat forces conducting illegal, covert operations in Colombia; very negative portrayal of Colombia."

Neufeld had read the Pentagon's guidelines for assisting film productions. They required filmmakers to accurately portray the military, but they didn't say anything about making the government of Colombia look good—or even the president of the United States, for that matter.

Neufeld was in a jam. Jet fighters would be hard to find, but he could get the special effects department to whip up something resembling an F-14 in flight; and he could rent Huey helicopters, put some machine guns in the doors, and paint them to look like army choppers. And he got the prop department busy at work in case they had to turn a park into Arlington National Cemetery.

"We had some fake tombstones standing by," location manager Neumann recalls. "A couple hundred."

But it would be a lot more expensive to do all this, so Neufeld was still pressing the Pentagon for assistance. But it wasn't going to be easy, and large parts of the script would have to be changed to satisfy Strub. Neufeld was reluctant to cave in at first, and battled Strub for weeks to keep the script intact. But in the end, Neufeld realized that unless he gave the Pentagon what it wanted, he wouldn't get what he wanted.

"Perhaps the biggest hurdle the [Department of Defense's] public affairs officers had to overcome was the filmmakers' sense of our meddling in their product and our sense that they weren't taking us seriously," said Army Maj. David Georgi, the technical advisor that the army assigned to the film, in an internal memo dated July 26, 1994—a few days after shooting was completed.

"There was a tension, almost until the day filming began, which manifested itself in our comments which went unanswered in subsequent drafts of the script," Georgi wrote. "When the filmmakers realized that unless the services were satisfied with the script, approval would not be granted, the changes were finally made."

One of the script changes that the Pentagon insisted on was a line spoken by the president of the United States at the end of the movie. Frustrated by the violence and lawlessness of the drug cartels, the president says, only half-jokingly, in a November 10, 1992, draft of the script, that he wishes he could blow up most of South America.

"Those sons-of-bitches," the president says, referring to the Colombian drug lords. "I swear, sometimes I'd like to level that whole damn country—and Peru and Ecuador while we're at it."

Strub, however, was not going to allow anything like that in a movie that the Pentagon was supporting.

"At the end of the script, the President of the United States swears that, sometimes, he'd like to level Colombia, Ecuador and Peru," wrote Air Force Col. Edward B. Ellis, chief of the Joint Chiefs of Staff's Strategic Plans and Policy Directorate, Western Hemisphere Division, in a June 9, 1993, memo to Strub. "This statement will not win friends in Latin America."

So at the request of the Pentagon, the offending dialogue was eliminated. But that's not all Strub wanted changed.

In the original script, the film begins when a Coast Guard cutter discovers the luxury yacht *Empire Builder* adrift in the warm waters of the Gulf of Mexico, its owner—a close personal friend of the president—brutally murdered. We soon learn that the president's friend and his wife were murdered by Colombian drug lords, and during a meeting at Camp David, the president tells his national security advisor and the director of the CIA that he wants revenge for his friend's death.

"I am sick and tired of those monkeys," the president says in the November 10, 1992, draft of the script. "I promised the American people I'd do something about this drug problem, and we haven't done squat. I want these goofs to get a message."

"What sort of message, Mr. President?" asks his national security advisor.

"That poison of theirs is gonna stop flooding in here like piss from a tall cow," the president angrily responds. "We're gonna shut 'em down! And while we're at it, I wouldn't mind bustin' some butt, if you know what I mean."

"I hear you, sir," says the director of the CIA.

"Let those jaboloneys know we're all fed up with their bullshit!" the president fumes.

"Sir—what you're asking for—it can't be accomplished through routine police agencies," says his national security advisor.

"What the hell you think I got CIA here for?" the president bellows.

"But, Mr. President, even we have limits in this kind of effort," the CIA director responds.

"This type of endeavor requires maximum resources," says the national security advisor.

"Interpret that for me, please," the president says.

"Sir, either our national security is threatened by these people, or it is not," the national security advisor says.

"Yeah—well, I said that, too, didn't I?" the president asks.

"Yes, sir, you did," says the national security advisor.

"Boys, let's just put it this way," the president says. "I want some payback—and y'all better see I get it."

This revenge motif was too much for Strub and the Pentagon, however. It would have to be eliminated if the producers were to get military assistance for their picture. And it was eliminated.

In the final draft of the script, the president comes off much more diplomatically in the scene where he gives the orders to strike back at the drug lords. Gone is any mention of "payback." Gone is any mention of "bustin' some butt." Gone is any cursing. Gone is any reference to the Colombian drug dealers as "monkeys" and "jaboloneys."

In the final shooting script, the president is more resolute—angry about the murder of his friend, to be sure, but his orders are based on national security, not revenge. This scene has now been boiled down to its bare essence. The president simply says: "These drug cartels represent a clear and present danger to the national security of the United States."

Numerous other changes demanded by the military were also made in the script, including the elimination of a scene in which a navy jet shoots down an unarmed civilian airplane that's transporting a shipment of cocaine. At the Pentagon's request, the script was changed so that the plane is blown up on the ground by American soldiers—without any loss of life.

"The script has been revised to reflect DOD [Department of Defense] concerns regarding military command and control, recognition of Colombian sovereignty and an improved depiction of the Presidency," wrote Major Georgi, on December 8, 1993, in his after-action report on the film's production. "In short, military depictions have become more of a 'commercial' for us, more than damage control, and the production offers good public information value."

Turning films into "commercials" for the military is what it's all about for Strub and the Pentagon. Whether they succeed or fail is largely dependent on how craven the producers are, and there is no shortage of craven producers in Hollywood.

For Major Georgi, *Clear and Present Danger* was the last of a dozen movies and twenty television shows that he worked on for the Pentagon as a technical advisor before retiring from the army in 1994. He still works occasionally as a military consultant for Hollywood movie producers.

Georgi, a candid man who loves the army, doesn't pull any punches when discussing the role he and the military play in shaping movies.

"Nothing was easy, but the process was simple," he says. "I'd get a call at my office in L.A. and they'd say they want military support, and I'd say, 'Okay, send me a treatment.' And right then, you could tell if it was going to get support. If they hesitated, it usually meant they had something to hide—something in the script that might not portray the military so well."

Once a film got approved for military assistance, Georgi would be on the set everyday to make sure that the producers stuck to the approved script and didn't try to sneak antimilitary scenes into the film that hadn't been approved.

"On *Clear and Present Danger*, if things were being changed, if they were shooting scenes in different ways, I'd say, 'Well, I'm taking my toys and I'm going home,'" he recalls with a laugh. "'I'm taking my tanks and my troops and my location, and I'm going home.' And that would draw the attention of the producer. That occurred on nearly every production that I supported at some time. On almost every production, there was a disagreement that had to be resolved during shooting. I'd say, 'Shoot it like it's in the script,' and then they would want to shoot it a different way. There were compromises on both sides.

"Always, somewhere in the mind of the producers, they'd try and turn the picture in the direction that they had originally presented to us. They always had that in the back of their minds. It would be my job as a technical advisor to make sure that the movie did not stray substantially from the original approved version."

But is that an appropriate role for the military? Making sure that scripts don't change substantially from their original "approved versions"? What does that do to the filmmaking process? Many movies undergo script changes right up until the last day of shooting. The director may not know if something is working on film until he shoots it and sees the rushes—the day's footage. In Hollywood, the guiding principle is: If something isn't working, change it. But the job of the Pentagon technical advisor is to put a brake on that process, to keep filmmakers from changing their minds and changing their scripts—which is antithetical to the filmmaking process. . . .

Many legal experts, including famed First Amendment attorney Floyd Abrams and renowned constitutional law professor Irwin Chemerinsky, believe that this form of censorship is a blatant violation of the First Amendment.

"This sort of viewpoint-based discrimination by the government in which it favors one form of speech over another is flatly inconsistent with the First Amendment," says Abrams, who has argued many cases before the Supreme Court and who was cocounsel to the *New York Times* in the Pentagon Papers case. "There are two types of limitations on speech by the government that are especially suspect. The first involves limitations based on the subject being discussed. For example, if the army said, 'We don't want any movies about the army, so we won't help anyone who is making a film about the army,' that would be a limitation on the subject and would be constitutionally suspect. But the second category of speech is even more disturbing from any First Amendment perspective; that is, a limitation on speech based upon the viewpoint expressed by the speaker. So if the army says, 'We will cooperate with some filmmakers, but only ones which please us because of the position it takes about the armed forces,' that is even more clearly unconstitutional."

Chemerinsky, a professor of constitutional law at the University of Southern California, agrees.

"The Supreme Court has said that above all, the First Amendment means that the government cannot participate in viewpoint discrimination," Chemerinsky says. "The government cannot favor some speech due to its viewpoint and disfavor others because of its viewpoint. The Court has said that when the government is giving financial benefits, it can't decide who to give to, or not give to, based on the viewpoint expressed." . . .

Asked why he thinks the Pentagon has been able to get away with this unconstitutional activity for all these years, Professor Chemerinsky says that the reason is simple: "Nobody has sued."

Abrams agrees.

"They've gotten away with it because they could get away with it," he says. "It hasn't been challenged in the courts."

DISCUSSION POINTS

1   Why do film makers and executives change or tailor their scripts to sui military objections? What leverage does the Pentagon have over Hollywood?

2   Should the Pentagon continue to seek to influence films and television shows in this manner? Why or why not? Should the Pentagon be made to support all entertainment shows or movies on an equal or all-or-none basis? Why or why not?

3   What potential legal problems could the Pentagon have with respect to this policy? Why has the policy survived so long unscathed in the legal arena?

20

Fahrenheit 451

RAY BRADBURY

> *Ray Bradbury is one of the most important American writers of all time. His 1953 classic,* Fahrenheit 451, *addressed a variety of social issues. Most prominent among them was censorship. Bradbury did more than knock censorship; he showed how censorship starts, where it starts, and how censorship is almost as much a part of human nature as the need for food or water. In 1979, Bradbury re-released* Fahrenheit 451 *with a special* coda *in which he explored public reaction to his works and the pressures on him to censor his own work on censorship to please censors. Rather than edit Bradbury's work, we re-print the entire* coda *as it first appeared.*

About two years ago, a letter arrived from a solemn young Vassar lady telling me how much she enjoyed reading my experiment in space mythology, *The Martian Chronicles*.

But, she added, wouldn't it be a good idea, this late in time, to rewrite the book inserting more women's characters and roles?

A few years before that I got a certain amount of mail concerning the same Martian book complaining that the blacks in the book were Uncle Toms and why didn't I "do them over"?

Along about then came a note from a Southern white suggesting that I was prejudiced in favor of the blacks and the entire story should be dropped.

Two weeks ago my mountain of mail delivered forth a pipsqueak mouse of a letter from a well-known publishing house that wanted to reprint my story "The Fog Horn" in a high school reader.

In my story, I had described a lighthouse as having, late at night, an illumination coming from it that was a "God-Light." Looking up at it from the viewpoint of any sea-creature one would have felt that one was in "the Presence."

The editors had deleted "God-Light" and "in the Presence."

Some five years back, the editors of yet another anthology for school readers put together a volume with some 400 (count 'em) short stories in it. How do you cram 400 short stories by Twain, Irving, Poe, Maupassant and Bierce into one book?

Simplicity itself. Skin, debone, demarrow, scarify, melt, render down and destroy. Every adjective that counted, every verb that moved, every metaphor that weighed more than a mosquito—out! Every simile that would have made a sub-moron's mouth twitch—gone! Any aside that explained the two-bit philosophy of a first-rate writer—lost!

Every story, slenderized, starved, bluepenciled, leeched and bled white, resembled every other story. Twain read like Poe read like Shakespeare read like Dostoevsky read like—in the finale—Edgar Guest. Every word of more than three syllables had been razored. Every image that demanded so much as one instant's attention—shot dead.

Do you begin to get the damned and incredible picture?

How did I react to all of the above?

By "firing" the whole lot.

By sending rejection slips to each and every one.

By ticketing the assembly of idiots to the far reaches of hell.

The point is obvious. There is more than one way to burn a book. And the world is full of people running about with lit matches. Every minority, be it Baptist/Unitarian, Irish/Italian/Octogenarian/Zen Buddhist, Zionist/Seventh-day Adventist, Women's Lib/Republican, Mattachine/Four Square Gospel feels it has the will, the right, the duty to douse the kerosene, light the fuse. Every dimwit editor who sees himself as the source of all dreary blanc-mange plain porridge unleavened literature, licks his guillotine and eyes the neck of any author who dares to speak above a whisper or write above a nursery rhyme.

Fire-Captain Beatty, in my novel *Fahrenheit 451*, described how the books were burned first by minorities, each ripping a page or a paragraph from this book, then that, until the day came when the books were empty and the minds shut and the libraries closed forever.

"Shut the door, they're coming through the window, shut the window, they're coming through the door," are the words to an old song. They fit my lifestyle with newly arriving butcher/censors every month. Only six weeks ago, I discovered that, over the years, some cubby-hole editors at Ballantine Books, fearful of contaminating the young, had, bit by bit, censored some 75 separate sections from the novel. Students, reading the novel which, after all, deals with censorship and book-burning in the future, wrote to tell me of this exquisite irony. Judy-Lynn Del Rey, one of the new Ballantine editors, is having the entire book reset and republished this summer with all the damns and hells back in place.

A final test for old Job II here: I sent a play, *Leviathan 99*, off to a university theater a month ago. My play is based on the "Moby Dick" mythology, dedicated to Melville, and concerns a rocket crew and a blind space captain who venture forth to encounter a Great White Comet and destroy the destroyer. My drama premieres as an opera in Paris this autumn. But, for now, the university wrote back that they hardly dared do my play—it had no women in it! And the ERA ladies on campus would descend with ballbats if the drama department even tried!

Grinding my bicuspids into powder, I suggested that would mean, from now on, no more productions of *Boys in the Band* (no women) or *The Women* (no men). Or, counting heads, male and female, a good lot of Shakespeare that would never be seen again, especially if you count lines and find that all the good stuff went to the males!

I wrote back maybe they should do my play one week, and *The Women* the next. They probably thought I was joking, and I'm not sure that I wasn't.

For it is a mad world and it will get madder if we allow the minorities, be they dwarf or giant, orangutan or dolphin, nuclear-head or water-conversationlist, pro-computerologist or Neo-Luddite, simpleton or sage, to interfere with aesthetics. The real world is the playing ground for each and every group, to make or unmake laws. But the tip of the nose of my book or stories or poems is where their rights end and my territorial imperatives begin, run and rule. If Mormons do not like my plays, let them write their own. If the Irish hate my Dublin stories, let them rent typewriters. If teachers and grammar school editors find my jawbreaker sentences shatter their mushmilk teeth, let them eat stale cake dunked in weak tea of their own ungodly manufacture. If the Chicano intellectuals wish to re-cut my "Wonderful Ice Cream Suit" so it shapes "Zoot," may the belt unravel and the pants fall.

For, let's face it, digression is the soul of wit. Take philosophic asides away from Dante, Milton or Hamlet's father's ghost and what stays is dry bones. Laurence Sterne said it once: Digressions, incontestably, are the sunshine, the life, the soul of reading! Take them out and one cold eternal winter would reign in every page. Restore them to the writer—he steps forth like a bridegroom, bids them all-hail, brings in variety and forbids the appetite to fail.

In sum, do not insult me with the beheadings, finger-choppings or the lung-deflations you plan for my works. I need my head to shake or nod, my hand to wave or make into a fist, my lungs to shout or whisper with. I will not go gently onto a shelf, degutted, to become a non-book.

All you umpires, back to the bleachers. Referees, hit the showers. It's my game. I pitch, I hit, I catch. I run the bases. At sunset I've won or lost. At sunrise, I'm out again, giving it the old try.

And no one can help me. Not even you.

DISCUSSION POINTS

1   What sin does Bradbury report Ballentine Books committed in publishing *Fahrenheit 451*? What is ironic about how he found out?

2   What is Bradbury's response to those who censor or request that he censor his own work?

3   Why is Bradbury so concerned about censorship, especially self-censorship, and what does he fear will be the harm to society from such acts?

───── PART SIX ─────

The "New Media"

PERHAPS THE MOST SIGNIFICANT DEVELOPMENT in the media of the last twenty to twenty-five years is the development and rise to prominence of the new media. Richard Davis, a leading scholar of the modern media, has described the new media as "mass communication forums with primarily non-political origins that have acquired political roles."* The new media can, but does not necessarily, involve new technology. In fact, it is often not the technology that is new, but rather it is how the technology is being used that is new. According to Davis, the new media has several characteristics. First, the new media forums themselves are traditionally entertainment oriented. Second, the new media forums are often bidirectional, meaning that listeners or viewers may participate in the show. Third, journalists play a reduced role in the new media. Fourth, the various forums of the new media are not traditionally political. Examples of the new media include tabloids, talk shows (radio and television alike), and the Internet.†

Why is the emergence of the new media so important? There are several reasons why the new media is so important. Perhaps the most salient of which is the fact that so many voters acquire information about politics from these media sources. Americans, as a general rule, do not pay much attention to politics. They attend few political rallies

---

* Davis, Richard. *The Press and American Politics*. 3rd Ed. New Jersey: Prentice Hall. 2001. Page 121.
† Ibid.

or speeches, they rarely, if ever, attend government meetings, and they seldom meet their public officials. The media acts as a kind of surrogate for them; it shows them their leaders or candidates for office and offers them the opportunity to see and hear, and in cases, even talk or correspond with them. In addition, the media attempts to focus public attention on what it believes are important issues. If Americans would prefer to watch political candidates interviewed by a comedian on a late night television talk show such as NBC's *Tonight Show* rather than by a professional journalist on a more traditional public affairs show or if they would prefer to read tabloids to more traditional newspapers then what they know about politics and politicians will be more likely to come from new media outlets than traditional media forums. New media forums have certain inherent biases or styles and certain limitations that will affect the lessons or the message that consumers will take away. For instance, tabloids stress sensationalism, talk radio emphasizes verbal conflict, and television talk shows typically emphasize humor and the personal lives of their guests as a means to attracting their audience. Entertaining audiences comes first to such media forums; informing them is a less important function. Internet users can access websites run by traditional news forums and many do. A growing number of Internet users gain information about politics from news blogs and public information websites such as those run by interest groups. There is nothing wrong with such sites and they can be quite beneficial and at times they are faster and more accurate than traditional news websites. Typically, however, those generating these sites do not have the same editorial oversight or professional training as those working in traditional news entities. As a result, news consumers who rely on blogs or other public websites for their news may be more susceptible to bias or avoidable mistakes.

Is the new media a good thing? The answer likely depends on whom you ask. Fans of the new media may stress the degree to which the new media has gotten more people interested in, more aware of, and more involved with public issues. They may also call attention to the fact that new media forums can raise important points about politics that more traditional forums could not and that they can do so in ways (e.g., through satire) that newspapers or public affairs programming cannot. Finally, certain new media forums may enable public officials to reach wider audiences with important messages than they would otherwise be able to do.

Critics of the new media are often of the view that comedians or talk show hosts untrained in the world of journalism and not necessarily aware of politics themselves do not make good interviewers. Television and radio entertainment shows may give unfair advantages to certain types of candidates or certain spokespeople (e.g., those who look or sound good or are funny or quick on their feet) that should have nothing to do with the resolution of public questions. New media critics also point out that the quality or level of discussions or postings or the manner in which the subjects are covered may do more harm than good. For instance, an interviewer who fawns all over a guest or fails to ask balanced questions may enable guests to mislead the audience or avoid questions. New media forums that stress entertainment or conflict may give the public the wrong impression about what we want in our policymakers or about what politics is really like. Those shows that treat politics as if it were a form of combat may make compromise, consensus and comity among public officials and interest groups harder to achieve.

Individuals involved with the new and traditional media do not always see eye-to-eye about the merits of their respective vocations. There is perhaps no better example of this fact than the exchange that occurred between Jon Stewart, host of *The Daily Show*, and Paul Begala and Tucker Carlson, co-hosts of CNN's now defunct *Crossfire*. Alessandra Stanley describes this exchange in her *New York Times* article, "No Jokes or Spin. It's time (Gasp) to talk." *Crossfire* focused on public issues and featured hosts and guests from different ends of the political spectrum. It appeared on a traditional news station and it fancied itself a traditional media show, yet on occasion, it featured viewer calls and it did stress disagreement among its hosts and their guests. Stewart was a frequent critic of *Crossfire* for its adoption of new media techniques. During his visit, which had been billed as a sort of reapproachment, Stewart and his guests soon took to squabbling over the merits of their respective shows and styles and, most importantly, their responsibilities to the public. Public reaction in the form of support for Stewart's arguments was devastating for *Crossfire*. In fact, the show was cancelled shortly thereafter. In announcing the cancellation, CNN offered an explanation that sounded similar to many of the criticisms of the show that Stewart himself had leveled.

The next four selections in this part focus on specific new media forums or behavior in practice. All four, ironically perhaps, could be found on-line. The first, penned by Sheryl Gay Stolberg, examines a spoof of television news shows known as *The Colbert Report*. The host, Stephen Colbert, offers a frequently devastating parody of the traditional media. In the course of doing so, he often ridicules real-life public officials while they appear with him as his guests. The question Stolberg explores is why are politicians willing to appear on the show. John Borland and Jim VandeHei examine the impact that blogs are having on American electoral politics. Borland, writing for an Internet news blog, tells how bloggers helped to expose a CBS story as false. VandeHei, in an article available on *The Washington Post*'s website, examines the potential for politically-biased bloggers to pull the political parties away from the political center and force them to adopt more extreme positions which, ironically, may be what new media consumers prefer.

The last article in this part appeared in the *New York Times*. Written by the founder of a well-known blog, Eugene Volokh, this piece argues that bloggers are journalists and that they should be afforded the same basic legal rights and protections that traditional news journalists enjoy.

21

No Jokes or Spin— It's Time (Gasp) to Talk

ALESSANDRA STANLEY

"New Media versus Old Media." Such could have been the tag-line to attract viewers to watch Jon Stewart, host of Comedy Central's The Daily Show, *appearing as a guest on CNN's* Crossfire. *No show epitomizes the new media's approach to politics more than* The Daily Show *and no host better exemplifies that approach than Jon Stewart. As Alessandra Stanley reports, Stewart sparred with* Crossfire *co-hosts Tucker Carlson and Paul Bagala over whether traditional public affairs shows have anything meaningful to contribute to American democracy or whether they are instead harming our political system and leaving the electorate deeply cynical and disillusioned with politics and politicians.*

There is nothing more painful than watching a comedian turn self-righteous. Unless of course, the comedian is lashing out at smug and self-serving television-news personalities. Jon Stewart could not resist a last dig at CNN's *Crossfire* during his monologue on Comedy Central on Monday night. "They said I wasn't being funny," the star of *The Daily Show With Jon Stewart* said, rolling his eyes expressively. "And I said to them: 'I know that. But tomorrow I will go back to being funny,'" Mr. Stewart said, adding that their show would still be bad, although he used a more vulgar expression.

And that is why his surprise attack on the hosts of CNN's *Crossfire* was so satisfying last Friday. Exchanging his usual goofy teasing for withering contempt, he told Paul Begala and Tucker Carlson that they were partisan hacks and that their pro-wrestling approach to political discourse was "hurting America." (He also used an epithet for the male reproductive organ to describe Mr. Carlson.)

Real anger is as rare on television as real discussion. Presidential candidates no longer address each other directly in debates. Guests on the *Tonight* show or *Oprah* are scripted monologuists who pitch their latest projects and humor the host. It has been decades since talk-show guests conversed with one another, yet there was a time when famous people held long and at times legendarily hostile discussions . . .

Nowadays, live television meltdowns seem to be pathological, not political—Janet Jackson baring a breast during the Super Bowl or Farrah Fawcett babbling incoherently to David Letterman.

The fuming partisan rants on Fox News or *Real Time With Bill Maher* are aimed at the converted . . .

The transcript of Friday's *Crossfire*, and the blog commentary about it, popped up all over the Internet this weekend. Mr. Stewart's Howard Beale (of *Network*) outburst stood out because he said what a lot of viewers feel helpless to correct: that news programs, particularly on cable, have become echo chambers for political attacks, amplifying the noise instead of parsing the misinformation. Whether the issue is Swift boat ads or Bill O'Reilly's sexual harassment suit, shows like *Crossfire* or *Hardball* provide gladiator-style infotainment as journalists clownishly seek to amuse or rile viewers, not inform them.

When Mr. Carlson took the offense, charging that Mr. Stewart had no right to complain since he had asked Senator John Kerry softball questions on *The Daily Show,* Mr. Stewart looked genuinely appalled. "I didn't realize—and maybe this explains quite a bit—that the news organizations look to Comedy Central for their cues on integrity." When Mr. Carlson continued to argue, Mr. Stewart shut him down hard. "You are on CNN," he said. "The show that leads into me is puppets making crank phone calls."

All late-night talk-show hosts make jokes about politicians. What distinguishes Mr. Stewart from Jay Leno and David Letterman is that the Comedy Central star mocks the entire political process, boring in tightly on the lockstep thinking and complacency of the parties and the media as well as the candidates. More than other television analysts and commentators, he and his writers put a spotlight on the inanities and bland hypocrisies that go mostly unnoticed in the average news cycle.

Mr. Stewart is very funny, but it is the vein of "a plague on both your houses" indignation that has made his show a cult favorite: many younger voters are turning to the *The Daily Show* for their news analysis, and are better served there than on much of what purports to be real news on cable.

And of course it was fun just to see television pundits who think they are part of the same media version of the Algonquin Round Table as Mr. Stewart lose their cool when he tore off the tablecloth and shattered the plates. "Wait," Mr. Carlson said querulously. "I thought you were going to be funny. Come on. Be funny." Mr. Stewart was funny. And it was at their expense.

DISCUSSION POINTS

1   Is Jon Stewart correct when he charges that old media forums such as public affairs shows are harming America's democracy? Why or why not?

2   Stewart bristles at the suggestion that new media shows that are entertainment oriented should be held to the same journalistic standards as traditional news shows. Is he correct or does the fact that so many viewers receive political information from shows like *The Daily Show* change the equation so that such new media shows should be held to a higher professional standard?

3   Stewart criticizes Tucker Carlson and Paul Bagala for appearing on post-presidential debate shows and "spin" the performance of their party's nominee in a way that benefits their favored candidate. This charge reflects the fact that Carlson and Bagala have maintained close and active ties to candidates for political office. Stewart's overall point, therefore, is that traditional media figures need to be more objective and not publically take sides in elections. Is he correct to level these charges? Should the same standard be applied to new media hosts like Stewart himself?

22

Laugh and the Voters Laugh with You, or at Least at You

SHERYL GAY STOLBERG

> Comedy Central's The Colbert Report, *a satire of nightly news shows, is one of television's most irreverent new media shows. Public officials, such as politicians, are regularly lampooned by the show's host Steve Colbert. Why, then, would members of Congress willingly appear as guests on* The Colbert Report? *New York Times reporter Sheryl Gay Stolberg sought to find out.*

Representative James P. Moran, Democrat of Virginia, does not have the kind of record most lawmakers would herald on national television. He has offended Jews with impolitic remarks and made news for scuffling with his wife a day before she filed for divorce. A former boxer, he threatened to slug one House colleague, and has thrown a punch at another.

So what in the world possessed him to appear on *The Colbert Report*, the late-night Comedy Central show, and allow himself to be goaded into taking a swing at the host, Stephen Colbert? "Because," Mr. Moran explained, "a little self-deprecation on the part of a politician is priceless."

Self-deprecation is often in short supply in Washington. But Mr. Colbert, playing the deadpan reporter in his "Better Know a District" segments, is injecting a new levity into politics. Tongue firmly in cheek, he is on a quest to interview—or lampoon—all [434] members of the

House. So Mr. Colbert is creating a litany of fools on the Hill. He drew Jack Kingston, a Georgia Republican and seemingly boring white guy who once lived in Ethiopia, into a discussion of his "African-American experience." He tweaked Jerrold Nadler, Democrat of New York, for proposing $300 million to stop school bullying: "Was that bill your idea, or did somebody bigger put you up to it?" He asked the Massachusetts Democrat Barney Frank, who is gay, about his wife. Mr. Frank was not amused. "Two Stooges short of a good routine," he complained.

It might sound like just another silly comedy shtick, and Mr. Colbert, whose show is a spinoff of *The Daily Show With Jon Stewart*, insists he is only trying to make himself "look like an idiot." Yet his work has a strain of anthropology. As he assembles a dupes' gallery, Mr. Colbert is showing a national audience what veteran Congress-watchers already know: the members are painfully, embarrassingly human. It is called the People's House for a reason.

At the same time, the show reveals an essential truth about Washington: being humiliated on national television can be better than not being on national television at all.

Congress has long suffered an inferiority complex, a sentiment that has only worsened under President Bush, who has flexed his executive muscles by keeping lawmakers out of the loop on matters ranging from eavesdropping to foreign control of American ports. Toss in the Jack Abramoff lobbying scandal and plunging poll ratings—61 percent of the public now has an unfavorable view of Congress, according to the latest *New York Times*/CBS News poll—and it's no wonder lawmakers are looking for laughs.

Why else would Eliot L. Engel, Democrat of New York, let Mr. Colbert comb the congressman's very thick mustache? Could there be another reason that Carolyn Cheeks Kilpatrick, Democrat of Michigan, joined Mr. Colbert in an off-key duet of "Do You Know Where You're Going To?", the saccharine theme from "Mahogany"?

Is there some other explanation for Mr. Moran's decision to let Mr. Colbert stuff his mouth with white Chiclets and then spew the gum out, like teeth, when the congressman feigned a whack at his cheek? . . .

In fact, there is a deeper reason. At a time when surveys show younger voters turning away from the mainstream media in favor of blogs and late-night television, politicians and their strategists recognize that *The Colbert Report* is a powerful way to reach a swath of Generation Y.

"We really don't have a broadcast medium anymore; we have sort of a narrowcast," said Chaka Fattah, Democrat of Pennsylvania, another Colbert guest. "So you've got to look for opportunities."

Mr. Moran said 40 percent of his Northern Virginia district was composed of highly mobile, transient voters in their 20's and 30's. "They're very difficult to develop a relationship with," he said. "Now they see me on the Colbert show, they think at least he likes the same show we like."

Rich Galen, a Republican strategist, sees the youthful hand of hip Congressional aides at work. "The younger staffs of these folks are convincing their bosses that if you really want to be president of the United States some day, you've got to get in with the crowd on Comedy Central," he said.

Thus did David All, the 26-year-old press secretary to the 50-year-old Representative Kingston, persuade his boss, who is also the vice chairman of the House Republican Conference, to be Mr. Colbert's guinea pig, his first guest. Mr. All then sent an e-mail message to other House Republican aides urging their bosses to do the same, and arranged for a showing of Mr. Kingston's Colbert clip at a recent weekend Republican retreat.

"We're all about the new media," Mr. All said, adding, "It's good that Republicans can be humorous."

But so far only one other Republican representative, John L. Mica of Florida, has appeared, only to suffer as Mr. Colbert poked fun of his less than elegant hairpiece. Some Democrats say that the dearth of Republicans proves that Republicans have no sense of humor, while others say that no Republican in his right mind would agree to appear on such a blatantly liberal outlet.

Mr. Colbert counters that he has no "particular political ax to grind." His head writer, Allison Silverman, insists geography is a factor. Mr. Colbert, she said, has done most of the more than a dozen interviews in New York and New Jersey, two heavily Democratic states, because his show is based in New York.

And it's not as if Democrats are getting off easy. Mr. Colbert knew just how to get under the skin of one of them, Bill Pascrell Jr. of New Jersey, by suggesting that Mr. Pascrell, a co-sponsor of legislation seeking an end to offensive media portrayals of Italian-Americans, was not a true Italian.

"Congressman," Mr. Colbert said, "your name doesn't end in a vowel."

"Italians don't have to end in a vowel," Mr. Pascrell parried. Mr. Colbert demanded that he name one.

Flustered, the congressman blurted out: "Sole! Tom Sole. S-O-L-E."

Mr. Colbert's victims—er, guests—report that the interviews can last as long as two hours, all boiled down to a few minutes on air. Most, with the notable exception of Mr. Frank, said they would do it again . . .

DISCUSSION POINTS

1 What are some reasons that would explain why members of Congress would appear on a show like *The Colbert Report*?

2 What does Stolberg mean when she writes that Colbert is reminding viewers that Congress "is called the People's House for a reason?"

23

Bloggers Drive Hoax Probe into Bush Memos

JOHN BORLAND

During the 2004 presidential election CBS News reported that it had obtained documents that suggested that President George W. Bush had lied about his national guard service. Within 24 hours of that report, a number of conservative bloggers had established that the documents upon which CBS based its report were false. This was a key event in the election, partially because it shifted attention away from the President's war record to CBS's reporting tactics. For bloggers, it was a watershed moment—one that earned blogs new respect and considerable attention.

Forget the political conventions.

When history books are written, bloggers' real contribution to the 2004 election may well turn out to be in providing leagues of amateur sleuths to fact-check political controversy.

For the last 24 hours, the Internet has been abuzz with bloggers' claims that the memos about President Bush's time in the National Air Guard publicized by CBS were actually a hoax. Keepers of online journals around the country have been analyzing the memos in excruciating detail, comparing the notes' typography to the technical specifications of early 1970s typewriters. The result? It's too early to say whether the bloggers calling "hoax" have won the day. But they have certainly helped drive questions about the veracity of CBS's *60 Minutes II* report on Wednesday night to the highest levels of the major media, and in so doing have helped shape what could be one of the most explosive—or simply weirdest—stories of the political season.

"Blogs have been characterized as places where people just go to mouth off, but what this brings out is the ability of blogs to actually help report a story," said Paul Grabowitz, professor of new media at the University of California at Berkeley's Graduate School of Journalism.

The incident could help legitimize the role that blogs and other nonprofessional online writers are already playing in the everyday business of news reporting.

Even traditional reporters working online have had to struggle to win credibility over the past decade. But nontraditional sources such as blogs—which run the gamut from high-school journal entries to war reporting from Iraq—have often had an even harder time being taken seriously.

The Drudge Report was one of the first to break into the consciousness of the mainstream media, largely by scooping the stories of old media publications before they hit the street. The report's publication of Monica Lewinsky's name before *Newsweek* ran its story on the Clinton affair catapulted the report and Lewinsky into national headlines.

But unlike the report's writer, Matt Drudge, bloggers rarely call themselves journalists. Many focus as heavily on community and discussion as on original reporting. From this can come startling insight and well-reasoned analysis, or on-the-spot news posted faster than most news outlets can manage.

The Bush memo story has shown the Internet's broader power of linking thousands of readers together, as much as it has demonstrated the intrinsic power of blogs themselves.

Not long after CBS aired its story on *60 Minutes II*, dealing with memos that allegedly showed President Bush's Texas National Guard superiors raising questions about his service, a pseudonymous message board posting on the conservative FreeRepublic.com Web site called the documents a hoax.

This kind of rhetoric is common on that site's message boards, but the author asserted that the typewriter font used in the CBS memos was anachronistic and would not have come into common use until after the alleged date of the memos.

Thursday morning, while most news services were still catching up to the CBS story, Minneapolis attorney Scott Johnson posted a link to the FreeRepublic claim on his conservative-leaning *Power Line* blog. The item sparked an eruption of e-mail from readers, ranging from former military officers to an IBM typewriter repairman, many doing detailed, expert-sounding analysis of the memos' typography. Johnson posted excerpts from the messages, most of which said the memos were likely to have been forgeries.

Other conservative bloggers chimed in, posting comparisons to Microsoft Word printouts that they said looked virtually identical. Liberal bloggers spoke up too, working to dismantle the skeptics' claims.

Ultimately the *Drudge Report* linked to Johnson's site. The resulting traffic took *Power Line* temporarily offline, but helped raise the typographical questions to a national level.

The national media has found other reasons to question the CBS story. But the issues raised by the bloggers have now been prominently featured in publications including *The New York Times* and the *Washington Post*.

"I feel a little bit overwhelmed," *Power Line*'s Johnson said Friday. "I still feel like we're in the eye of a hurricane."

DISCUSSION POINTS

1   What is it about blogs that may make them well suited to investigating and exposing mistakes made by more traditional media outlets?

2   An argument can be made that there are certain news stories that blogs would be better suited or more likely to cover or pursue by virtue of the fact that they are not members of the more traditional or mainstream media. Which stories might those be and why?

3   How much do you rely on blogs for news stories? Why is this case? Which blogs? What changes, if any, would you like blogs that cover news stories to make?

24

Blogs Attack From Left as Democrats Reach for Center

JIM VANDEHEI

Political bloggers have typically attacked officials of the opposing party. As blogs have matured, and the nation's politics has become even more fractured and divisive, bloggers on the left and right have begun to attack more moderate elements of their own parties. In this article, Jim VandeHei examines how liberal bloggers are attempting to turn the Democratic Party toward the left. Note how this is exacerbating, if not actually creating, a rift between the party's moderate inner circle and the party's more liberal base.

Democrats are getting an early glimpse of an intraparty rift that could complicate efforts to win back the White House [in 2008]: fiery liberals raising their voices on Web sites and in interest groups vs. elected officials trying to appeal to a much broader audience.

These activists—spearheaded by battle-ready bloggers and making their influence felt through relentless e-mail campaigns—have denounced what they regard as a flaccid Democratic response to the Supreme Court fight, President Bush's upcoming State of the Union address and the Iraq war. In every case, they have portrayed party leaders as gutless sellouts.

First, liberal Web logs went after Democrats for selecting Virginia Gov. Timothy M. Kaine to deliver the response to Bush's speech . . . Kaine's political sins: He was too willing to drape his candidacy in references to religion and too unwilling to speak out aggressively against Bush on the Iraq war. Kaine has been lauded by party officials for finding a victory formula in Bush country by running on faith, values and fiscal discipline.

Many Web commentators wanted Rep. John P. Murtha (D-Pa.), a leading critic of the Iraq war who advocates a speedy withdrawal, to be the opposition voice on the State of the Union night. Most Democratic lawmakers have distanced themselves from the Murtha position. "What the hell are they thinking?" was the title of liberal blogger Arianna Huffington's column blasting the Kaine selection.

"Blogs can take up a lot of time if you're on them," Kaine said to reporters Thursday. "You can get a lot done if you're not bitterly partisan."

The Virginia Democrat said he will not adjust his speech to placate the party's base. "I'm not anybody's mouthpiece or shill or poster boy for that matter. I'm going to say what I think needs to be said and they seem very comfortable with that."

Liberal activists seemed to have slightly more influence with their campaign to persuade Senate Democrats to filibuster the Supreme Court nomination of Samuel A. Alito Jr. Despite several polls showing that the public opposes the effort, Sen. John F. Kerry (D-Mass.) on Thursday strongly advocated the filibuster plan—and wrote about his choice on the *Daily Kos*, a Web site popular with liberals. Sen. Robert C. Byrd (D-W.Va.), a leading liberal and critic of the Iraq war, told reporters Kerry's viewpoint is not shared by most in a culturally conservative swing state such as West Virginia. Senate Minority Leader Harry M. Reid (D-Nev.) also opposes the filibuster.

Sen. Hillary Rodham Clinton (D-N.Y.) is another frequent target of the Internet attacks. Code Pink, an antiwar women's group with a flashy Web site, plans to protest one of Clinton's weekend fundraisers and is using the Web site to rally people against the New York Democrat. The critics say Clinton has not challenged Bush aggressively enough on Iraq.

"The bloggers and online donors represent an important resource for the party, but they are not representative of the majority you need to win elections," said Steve Elmendorf, a Democratic lobbyist who advised Kerry's 2004 presidential campaign. "The trick will be to harness their energy and their money without looking like you are a captive of the activist left."

The blogs-vs.-establishment fight represents the latest version of a familiar Democratic dispute. It boils down to how much national candidates should compromise on what are considered core Democratic values—such as abortion rights, gun control and opposition to conservative judges—to win national elections.

Many Democrats say the only way to win nationally is for the party to become stronger on the economy and promote a centrist image on cultural values, as Kaine did in Virginia and as Bill Clinton did in two successful presidential campaigns.

The new twist in this debate is the Web, which in recent election cycles emerged as a powerful political force, one expected to figure even more prominently as more people get high-speed connections and turn to the Internet for news and commentary. Unlike the past, the "pressure is conveyed through a faster, better organized, more insistent medium," said Jim Jordan, a Democratic strategist.

In the 2004 campaign, liberals used the Web to organize meetings and raise money to power the unexpected rise of former Vermont governor Howard Dean in the Democratic primaries. Dean, a newcomer to national politics who connected with liberals with his antiwar position and declaration to supporters that "you have the power" to change Washington, shattered fundraising records and for months was considered the front-runner in the race for the nomination.

But the Democratic establishment turned on Dean, and his grassroots operation was not as strong in reality as it appeared on the Internet. Since then, liberal activists have created scores of political blogs and used the Web as an organizing tool and a way to quickly vent frustrations to Democratic leaders in Washington.

The closest historic parallel would be the talk-radio phenomenon of the early 1980s, when conservatives—like liberals now—felt powerless and certain they did not have a way to voice their views because the mainstream media and many of their own leaders considered them out of touch. Through talk radio, often aired in rural parts of the country on the AM dial, conservatives pushed the party to the right on social issues and tax cuts.

The question Democrats will debate over the next few years is whether the prevailing views of liberal activists on the war, the role of religion in politics and budget policies will help or hinder efforts to recapture the presidency and Congress.

Even if they disagree with their positions, Democratic candidates recognize from the Dean experience the power of the activists to raise money and infuse a campaign with their energy. On the flip side, the Alito and Kaine episodes serve as a cautionary tales of what can happen to politicians when they spurn the blogs.

"John Kerry is beginning to bring the traditional Democratic leadership in Washington together with the untraditional netroots activists of the country," James Boyce wrote on the *Huffington Post*. "A man often accused of being the ultimate Washington insider looked outside of the beltway and saw the concern, in fact, the distress among literally millions of online Democrats."

Other Democrats, Boyce wrote, "triangulated, fabricated, postulated and capitulated."

DISCUSSION POINTS

1 How have liberal blogs affected the Democratic Party? Can one envision conservative blogs having a similar impact on the Republican Party?

2 VandeHei describes many bloggers as feeling powerless and unrepresented by the mainstream media. Does this observation surprise you? Why or why not?

3 Our founding fathers hoped to create a republic where policy decisions would be made after cool, sober, reflective, reasoned, dispassionate debate. Does the kind of intra-party battling between liberal bloggers and more moderate Democrats threaten the kind of democracy that James Madison and others of his day hoped to establish? If so, why and how? If not, why not?

— 25 —

You Can Blog,
But You Can't Hide

EUGENE VOLOKH

Blogs have emerged as a potent force in the world of modern journalism. Yet, typically bloggers and blogs are not accorded the same respect, thought of in the same terms, or provided the same legal protection as more traditional members of the media or more traditional media forums. In this op-ed piece published in The New York Times, *Eugene Volokh, UCLA law professor and founder of a blog known as the* Volokh Conspiracy, *argues that bloggers and blogs should be treated the same as more traditional members of the media.*

Say that an I.R.S. agent leaks a politician's income tax return to a newspaper reporter, an act that is a federal felony. The newspaper may have a First Amendment right to publish the information, especially since it bears on a matter of public interest. The government, meanwhile, is entitled to punish the agent, to protect citizens' privacy and ensure a fair and efficient tax system.

To punish the agent, prosecutors may need to get the leaker's name from the reporter; but if the reporter refuses to testify because of a "journalist's privilege" to protect confidential sources, the agent may never be caught. Such a pattern is evident in the Valerie Plame matter, where an independent prosecutor is trying to learn who leaked the name of Ms. Plame, a C.I.A. operative, to the press. Uncooperative journalists . . . may face jail.

The fate of the reporters involved in the Plame affair—and that of the reporter in Providence, R.I., who was convicted of criminal contempt . . . for refusing to disclose who . . . gave him a tape of a city official accepting a bribe—will of course turn on questions particular to their cases. But the solution to the larger problem turns on other questions: Should there be a journalist's privilege? What should its scope be? And who exactly qualifies as a journalist?

Thirty-two years ago, the Supreme Court held that the First Amendment does not create a journalist's privilege: like anyone else, journalists must testify when ordered to do so. But Justice Lewis Powell, in a cryptic three-paragraph concurrence, wrote that there should be a modest privilege protecting journalists from unnecessary harassment by law enforcement. In such cases, he wrote, journalists should be allowed to claim the privilege, and courts should try to strike "a proper balance between freedom of the press and the obligation of all citizens to give relevant testimony with respect to criminal conduct."

Lower courts are now split on whether the privilege exists. Legislatures likewise disagree; about two-thirds of the states have recognized a journalist's privilege of varying strengths, but the remaining states and the federal government have not . . .

So the situation is a mess—and it's getting messier. Because of the Internet, anyone can be a journalist. Some so-called Weblogs—Internet-based opinion columns published by ordinary people—have hundreds of thousands of readers. I run a blog with more than 10,000 daily readers. We often publish news tips from friends or readers, some of which come with a condition of confidentiality.

The First Amendment can't give special rights to the established news media and not to upstart outlets . . . Freedom of the press should apply to people equally regardless of who they are, why they write or how popular they are.

Yet when everyone is a journalist, a broad journalist's privilege becomes especially costly. The I.R.S. agent, for example, no longer needs to risk approaching many mainstream journalists, some of whom may turn him in. He can just ask a friend who has a blog and a political ax to grind. The friend can then post the leaked information and claim the journalist's privilege to prevent the agent from being identified. If the privilege is upheld, the friend and the agent will be safe—but our privacy will be lost.

What's the answer? On the one hand, tips from confidential sources often help journalists (print or electronic) uncover crime and misconduct. If journalists had to reveal such sources, many of these sources would stop talking. On the other hand, some tips are rightly made illegal.

The best solution may be to borrow a principle from other privileges, like those for confidential communications to lawyers, psychotherapists and spouses. The law has generally recognized that protecting the confidentiality of such communications is more important than forcing a person's testimony.

But it has also limited the privilege. Communications that facilitate crime or fraud, for example, are not protected. I may confess my crimes to a lawyer, but if I try to hire him to help me commit my crime, he may be obligated to testify against me.

Maybe a journalist's privilege should likewise be limited. Lawmakers could pass legislation that protects leakers who lawfully reveal information, like those who blow the whistle on governmental or corporate misconduct. But if a leaker tries to use a journalist as part of an illegal act—for example, by disclosing a tax return or the name of a C.I.A. agent so that it can be published—then the journalist may be ordered to testify.

Such a rule may well deter some sources from coming forward. But they will be the very sources that society should want to deter, to protect privacy and safety. In any event, the rules should be the same for old media and new, professional and amateur. Any journalist's privilege should extend to every journalist.

DISCUSSION POINTS

1   In what ways do bloggers and journalists differ? In what ways are they similar?

2   Should bloggers be treated the same as more traditional members of the media? Why or why not? What arguments does Volokh give in favor of this proposition?

3   Is Volokh correct when he argues that journalists and bloggers should be equally granted a qualified legal protection from most government efforts to compel them to reveal secret sources to grand juries or to public officials?

PART SEVEN

Assessing the Media

WHAT IS THE NATURE OF THE American media? Is it biased? If so, how so and in whose favor? What are its main strengths and weaknesses? What is the nature of journalists? Are they ethical? Are they too cynical? Are they cynical enough? Do they prepare stories that we really need or just those that we want? Are journalists powerful? If so, how powerful are they? These are among the important questions addressed by the selections that comprise this part. The answers may surprise, or even disturb you.

Michael Parenti and W. Lance Bennett examine media bias. They do so from different perspectives, ones that may surprise some readers. Parenti charges that the American media reflects corporate concerns rather than the political preferences of any one side. Thus, the American media reports on the stories that favor American business interests and in a way that favors such interests. These interests know no liberal or conservative bias *per se*. Bennett asserts that the real biases are more connected to the professional values that journalists are taught and to certain organizational pressures to which all media forms are subject if they are to succeed. Bennett argues that these biases, whether they are related to how to report stories or what stories to report or the need to report on news in fashion, all subconsciously affect the media.

The next two selections examine the extent to which the modern media stresses the need to entertain and keep an audience. Ted Koppel, a longtime member of the broadcast media, picks up on the bias issue as a part of a larger piece on the state of the media itself. Koppel examines the extent to which viewer preferences and biases are affecting or shaping the media coverage of public events or issues. In this way, the media has become a part of network programming that troubles Koppel. Michael Schudson sees many of the same developments as Koppel, but he is less troubled by their implications. Schudson views members of the media as fairly cynical when it comes to covering politics and politicians. Perhaps as a result of this cynicism, the news media, while concerned with entertaining its audience, manages to produce an insightful and comprehensive product for its audience to consider.

The final selections come from media icons Bob Woodward, Carl Bernstein, and David Brinkley. Woodward and Bernstein reveal their concerns over media ethics. Interestingly, the reporters whose ethics give them pause are themselves. The late David Brinkley gets the last word in this part. In this op-ed piece published posthumously, Brinkley offers insight into what it is like to be a news anchor and offers his answer to the question of how powerful is the media?

Inventing Reality: The Politics of News Media

MICHAEL PARENTI

The real bias affecting the media is a corporate one that places business interests—such as stories extolling the virtues of the free market or killing stories that might harm an advertiser—ahead of all others. This manifests itself in a system where newspaper owners and their advertisers all but dictate what gets printed or said in the news and, perhaps more importantly, what does not get printed or said. Editors who rock the corporate boat are seldom hired and the reporters who succeed are those who realize just how far they can push for stories and then typically stop short of crossing that line.

Does ownership of the media translate into control over information? Or are journalists free to write what they want? Reporters themselves offer contradictory testimony on this question. Some say they are independent agents while others complain of control and censorship.

Calling the Tune: Owners

The people who own the media conglomerates along with their directors and chief executive officers are drawn overwhelming from the ranks of the rich. Not surprisingly, nearly all of them are politico-economic conservatives. . . .

The top news executives are subject to the judgments of the ruling corporate directors and owners who exercise financial power over the organization and, if they so choose, final judgment over the news itself and over who is hired or fired at lower levels....

Owners often make a show of not interfering, but "the suggestions of powerful superiors are, in fact, thinly veiled orders, requiring circumlocutions in which commands are phrased as requests." Sometimes suggestions made by owners can be brushed aside by editors, but not too often. And if the owner insists, then the editor obeys....

Les Brown's observations about the ideological underpinnings of local TV stations hold for local radio and newspapers as well:

> Many of the stations are owned by persons of high right-wing bias who are pillars of the local power structure and who believe their public service obligations to be met by promoting love for the flag. They would have networks concentrate on spreading patriotism and ... would keep the air waves free from the voices of dissent.

Calling the Tune: Advertisers

Owners themselves must have a care not to offend other large financial interests, especially those of big corporate advertisers....

... Because they pay the bills, advertisers regard their influence over media content as something of a "right." And media executives seem to agree. As erstwhile CBS president Frank Stanton said: "Since we are advertiser-supported we must take into account the general objective and desires of advertisers as a whole."

Consider how, during the early 1970s, the *New York Times* covered the issues of auto safety and auto pollution. *Times* publisher Arthur Ochs Sulzberger openly admitted that he urged his editors to favor the automotive industry's position so as not to "affect the advertising." The industry was one of the *Time*'s biggest accounts at that time.

Advertisers are not hesitant to expert pressure, Mobil Oil urged PBS to suppress a film that would offend its oil partner, Saudi Arabia. Tobacco companies withdrew their ads from *Mother Jones* after the magazine ran articles citing cigarettes as a major cause of lung cancer and heart disease.... When NBC ran a documentary on the terrible conditions endured by migrant workers, citing the abuses perpetrated by Coca-Cola Food Company, Coca-Cola sharply denounced the show, and the network was unable to find a single corporate sponsor for the program....

Locally owned media are also vulnerable to the pressures of advertisers and other business interests.... After reviewing many county weeklies published in the United States, one writer concluded that very few "ever print anything that might cause discomfort to anyone with any economic power."

Advertisers will cancel ads when they feel the reporting reflects unfavorably on their own product or industry. But they just as frequently withdraw financial support because they dislike the "liberal biases" they think are creeping into the news. . . . Corporate support also explains the plethora of conservative commentators . . . on political talk shows and the absence of progressive ones. . . . In contrast, progressive commentators . . . —deprived of major advertisers—do not last long on public television, let alone on commercial outlets. Likewise, without big advertising support, progressive publications like the *Nation* and the *Guardian* are always facing insolvency, never able to launch the kind of massive mainstream promotional campaigns that might win the attention of larger public.

Business interests rail against the "anti-business bias" in the news. It is a way of keeping the press in line. But actually very little of the "investigative reporting" of the last two decades has targeted big business. No wonder when corporate leaders were asked to evaluate the treatment accorded them by the media, only 6 percent said it was "poor," while 66 percent said "good" or "excellent."

Almost all the discussion regarding freedom of the press focuses on government attempts to influence or limit the information flow. But most of the censorship occurs in the private sector, carried out by owners and advertisers who determine which facts and ideas will reach the public.

On the Line: Editors

Actual responsibility for daily (or weekly) news production rests with the newspaper editors and radio and television program producers. Without having to answer to reporters, they can cut, rewrite, or kill any story they choose, subject only to final review by their executive superiors. The top media executives meet regularly with editors and producers in order to keep tabs on story selection. They can recommend or veto a story whenever they like, even overriding their editors. However, since they have other duties and, within their corporation, are supposed to adhere to a division of labor, most often they refrain from imposing their power on a daily basis. As one editor put it: "It is not what [the executive boss] will do or will veto, but what we expect that he will do or veto; that's his influence." Daily censorship is made unnecessary by anticipatory self-censorship.

Many editors insist they are nobody's puppet. Infused with notions of professional integrity and personal autonomy, they will vehemently deny they are objects of corporate control. Indeed, editors are accorded a certain degree of independence—if they demonstrate their ability to produce what their superiors want: copy that generally does not challenge the interests of those of wealth and power. Editors perform without daily interference from their superiors because such interference is not necessary....

[M]any news editors and broadcast producers share the world view of their superiors...

Self-Censorship: Reporters

Like editors, reporters are granted autonomy by demonstrating that they will not use it beyond acceptable limits. They are independent agents in a conditional way, free to report what they like as long as their superiors like what they report. Journalistic competence is measured in part by one's ability to cover things from an ideologically acceptable perspective, defined as "balanced" and "objective." Like social scientists and other investigators, journalists rarely doubt their own objectivity even as they faithfully echo the established orthodoxy. Since they do not cross any forbidden lines, they are not reined in. Thus they are likely to be unaware they are on an ideological leash. This is why some reporters insist they are free agents. Only when they stray off the beaten path is the pressure from above likely to be felt. And they almost never do.

If every reporter had to be policed continually by superiors when producing the news, the system could not maintain its democratic appearance and probably could not function very smoothly. As it turns out, editors and owners do not have to exercise ubiquitous supervision; intermittent control will do. As already mentioned, the *anticipation* that superiors might disapprove of this or that story is usually enough to discourage a reporter from writing it, or an editor from assigning it. Many of the limitations placed on reporting come not from direct censorship but from self-censorship, from journalists who design their stories so as to anticipate complaints from superiors. This anticipatory avoidance makes direct intervention from above a less frequent necessity and leaves the journalist with a greater feeling of autonomy than might be justified by the actual power relationship....

Many people who learn to hold their fire eventually end up never doing battle. After a while anticipatory avoidance becomes a kind of second nature. Former FCC chairperson Nicholas Johnson describes the process of self-censorship:

> A reporter... first comes up with an investigative story idea, writes it up and submits it to the editor and is told the story is not going to run. He wonders why, but the next time he is cautious enough to check with the

editor first. He is told by the editor that it would be better not to write that story. The third time he thinks of an investigative story idea but doesn't bother the editor with it because he knows it's silly. The fourth time he doesn't even think of the idea anymore.

. . . Journalists will treat their self-censorship as a matter of being "realistic" or "pragmatic" or "playing by the rules." In their ability to live in a constant, if not always conscious, state of anticipatory response while maintaining an appearance of independence, newspeople are not much different from professionals in other hierarchical organizations.

Journalists are subjected to on-the-job ideological conditioning conducted informally through hints and casual inferences that masquerade as "professional" advice. Thus, they might be admonished not to get too "emotionally involved" and not to lose their "objectivity," when they are producing copy that is disturbing to persons of wealth and power. . . .

Veteran newspeople "have remarkably finely tuned antennae for finding out the limits" to which they can go, remarked one former reporter. Some even admit there are invisible restraints. ABC correspondent Sam Donaldson says: "There is a line when you're questioning public officials, particularly in public, beyond which you don't go. I can't define that line and I have never purposely gone over it, although once in a while I come close.

The Ruling Culture

When determining what to treat as news, media organizations often take their cues from one another, moving in a kind of rough unison, a phenomenon that has been called "pack journalism." The pack may run in one direction or it may suddenly stampede in another. But it is not entirely free to roam as it chooses, for past images influence present ones, and if a media opinion already exists about what is true and important, it usually will shape subsequent reporting on the topic.

If an opinion prevails for any great length of time without benefit of critical examination or hard evidence (for instance, the view that a conservative president is concerned about the well-being of working people in America or that the U.S. government supports democracy and human rights in the Third World), it is usually because of a durable ideological underpinning. Opinion inertia is easier to sustain if it is rolling with, rather than against, the ideological tilt in the land. By definition, opinion inertia favors the existing framework of institution, power, and persuasion and generally operates with conservative effect. Pack journalism is a conformist journalism. But where does the conformity come from?

Journalists are exposed to the same communities, schools, universities, graduate schools, popular culture—and media—that socialize other Americans into the dominant belief system. They react to much the same news that inundates their audiences. They seldom look to the radical press for a different viewpoint or for information unreported in the mainstream media. The establishment biases that predefine what is acceptable news and commentary are subjected to no critical examination by them. With cyclical effect, they find confirmation for the images they report in the images they have already created and internalized.

The image of the reporter propagated by Hollywood films of an earlier era is of a tough-talking, two-fisted, regular guy, more at home in a local bar than in a fancy country club, scornful of bluebloods and stuffed shirts. . . .

Turning from Hollywood fantasy to reality, we find that most journalists employed by major media were raised in upper-middle-class homes. . . . Almost all have college degrees and a majority have attended graduate school. Despite journalism's reputation as a low-paid profession, most newspeople have family incomes that put them in the top 10 percent bracket. . . .

Most newspeople lack contact with working-class people, have a low opinion of labor unions, and know very little about people outside their own social class. . . .

In regard to economic and class issues, most journalists are educated into a world view that supports rather than opposes the existing corporate system. Most journalism schools offer politically conventional curricula. While repeatedly lectured to about the importance of objectivity and professionalism, a journalism student can easily go through an entire program without ever raising critical questions about how and why the capitalist economic system functions and malfunctions as it does. . . .

Suppressing the News

In defense of his profession, a journalist once told me: "We simply goes out, we gets the story, and we writes it." In fact, the process is more complex than that. Reporters carry along their past conditioning, schooling, and political socialization. Before they ever leave the office they are influenced in what they will report by (1) the assignments given them by their superiors, (2) anticipatory responses to the reactions of superiors and public officials, (3) career considerations, and (4) the general political climate and dominant ideology (sustained partly by the press itself). *Then* they observe events and report to their editors who, responding to the same influences listed above, run the stories often after cutting and rewriting them.

Despite self-censorship and the various organizational influences and controls, there is always the danger that a reporter or editor might report something that does not rest well with those at the top. On such occasions, direct interposition from owners or sometimes advertisers becomes necessary. Publishers and network bosses will rein in editors and producers who in turn will curb reporters. As the famous newscaster Edward R. Murrow observed, the top managers "make the final and crucial decisions having to do with news and public affairs." . . .

. . . Each act of suppression has a chilling effect on other staff members. Needless to say, these instances of news repression do not themselves usually become news items in the mainstream press. Most often the reporters do not resign; they learn to accept the existing state of affairs in order to survive in their profession. The consequences of this kind of control are that "coverage is limited and certain questions never get asked," according to Len Ackland, a *Chicago Tribune* writer. Reporters think twice before delving into sensitive areas. "They worry about the editing. They worry about being removed from choice beats, or being fired."

James O'Shea, former business editor of the *Des Moines Register*, argues that the media's pattern of business ownership and interlocking directorates is "going to affect the reporter, I don't care who he is; or it will affect his editors. You're more cautious. . . . A lot of reporters and editors will tell you that it has no effect on them, but I don't believe it." Chris Welles, a former journalist and director of a program on business journalism at Columbia University, commented: "I daresay anyone who has been in the business for more than a few months can cite plenty of examples of editorial compromises due to pressure, real and imagined, from publishers, owners, and advertisers.

Most reporters are probably not right-wingers but they do not have to be. Their owners are. Years ago, media mogul Henry Luce demonstrated what has been repeatedly demonstrated by other owners before and since: that you can turn out conservative publications—as he did with *Time*, *Life*, and *Fortune*—while employing liberal editors and reporters. Luce never made a fortune out of the media business by crusading for the downtrodden and attacking the large moneyed interests, favoring the have-nots against the haves.

Those conservative critics who complain that the press is composed of liberals and pinkos have failed to explain why this same "liberal press" has consistently favored conservative candidates. Lee and Solomon point out that since 1932 every Republican presidential nominee except Barry Goldwater (who was running against a conservative Southern Democrat Lyndon Johnson) has been favored by the majority of daily newspapers, that is, favored by their rich conservative owners. Ronald Reagan was endorsed by 77 percent of the dailies in 1980 and 86 percent in 1984. George Bush received 70 percent backing in 1988.

There is nothing mysterious about who controls the ideological direction and political content of the news. As with any profit-making corporation, the chain of command in the media runs from the top down, with final authority in the hands of the owners or those who represent the ownership interests of the company. "News organizations are not democratic; in fact, they are described as militaristic by some journalist. . . ." The Lnks that bind reporter to editor to news executive to corporate executive to board members to bankers and corporate advertisers are not just work relationships but class power relationships.

DISCUSSION POINTS

1 Is Parenti's thesis really another way of charging that the media is conservative or is he truly focused on a topic that is altogether different than political ideology?

2 According to Parenti, reporters are often as elitist as their corporate bosses. Is he correct about this and, if so, consider the implications for American democracy of reporters having joined the corporate culture.

3 What would be the alternatives to a corporate-owned media? Would these alternatives have their own biases or agendas?

News: The Politics of Illusion

W. LANCE BENNETT

Not all biases need to be driven by some desire, conscious or not, to achieve some objective. Others can be systemic or accidents of fate. At least this is the case, according to W. Lance Bennett, when it comes to media bias. Bennett argues that media biases reflect certain organizational and/or professional preferences or values. For instance, reporters and editors are schooled to believe that news stories need to be framed in a certain way so as to interest and keep an audience. This training, and the reward system built around it, ultimately produce a system skewed toward certain types of stories.

Here is how *The Washington Post* described President Bush's dramatic landing on the aircraft carrier *Abraham Lincoln*—the news event that set the stage for his speech announcing that the military phase of the War in Iraq was over:

> When the Viking carrying Bush made its tailhook landing on the aircraft carrier *USS Abraham Lincoln* off California yesterday, the scene brought presidential imagery to a whole new level. Bush emerged from the cockpit in a full olive flight suit and combat boots, his helmet tucked jauntily under his left arm. As he exchanged salutes with the sailors, his ejection harness, hugging him tightly between the legs, gave him the bowlegged swagger of a top gun.

This image was replayed time and again on television news shows. It was proclaimed as the mother of all photo-ops, a publicity event that would establish Mr. Bush as a world leader, and a supremely confident commander in chief. Many journalists anticipated that this news image would also help secure an easy victory over any imaginable Democratic candidate who might emerge to challenge Mr. Bush in the 2004 election. Consider how MSNBC's Keith Olberman introduced the live coverage on his program *Countdown* and then discussed it with his guest Chris Matthews, the anchor of another MSNBC program *Hardball*:

> OLBERMAN: Good evening. Franklin Delano Roosevelt was the first serving president to fly in an airplane, Theodore Roosevelt was the first to take the still risky ride in an automobile, and White House historians disagree about whether it was James K. Polk or John Tyler, who in the 1840s was the first to, as his contemporaries feared, risk his immortal soul by being photographed. Today George W. Bush skipped the safer route of declaring combat over from the White House to instead become the first president to make an arrested landing on an Air Force carrier. The president's speech is live here on MSNBC in 58 minutes. . . .
>
> OLBERMANN: This was victory lap day. I mean, we're seeing the sign aboard the Lincoln right now that reads "Mission Accomplished." . . .
>
> MATTEWS: More than that, Keith, it's a statement. It's saying to the Democratic Party or anyone else who wants to challenge this man for a full eight-year presidency, Try to do this. Look at me. Do you really think you've got a guy in your casting studio, your casting director can come up with, who can match what I did today? Imagine Joe Lieberman in this costume, or even John Kerry. Nobody looks right in the role Bush has set for the presidency—commander-in-chief, medium height, medium build, looks good in a jet pilot's costume—or uniform, rather—has a certain swagger, not too literary, certainly not too verbal, but a guy who speaks plainly and wins wars. I think that job definition is hard to match for the Dems.

Whether the story is told by the venerable *Washington Post*, or in breathless cable talk show chatter, the terms are much the same. The emphasis is on how the news story plays as an entertainment drama. Does the flight suit look good? Does the swagger seem natural? Does Mr. Bush look right for the part? Can the opposition cast anyone more convincing for the role of president? But what about the relationship between such news images and more substantial leadership qualities or the progress of the war itself? These questions will be addressed more fully in the case study later in this chapter, which uses tools developed in the chapter to analyze George W. Bush's news image.

A Different Kind of Bias

The general focus of this chapter is on a deeper but less obvious sort of news bias—one that favors *dramatic* and *personalized* aspects of events over more complex—and potentially more engaging—underlying political realities. The result of focusing on individual actors and the dramas swirling around them is to make many political situations seem fragmented and confusing. Audiences are often left hanging, waiting for daily story updates about disorder and the restoration of authority, normalcy, and control, rather than installments on news narratives that reveal the politics behind the events.

Consider some of the other choices that news organizations had in framing the aircraft carrier landing story. *Framing involves choosing a broad organizing theme for selecting, emphasizing, and linking the elements of a story. Frames are thematic categories that integrate and give meaning to the scene, the characters, their actions, and supporting documentation.* For example, the carrier landing story could have been framed as a publicity stunt. The story also could have been framed around challenges to the administration link between Iraq and the War on Terror. The path of least resistance was to fill the news frame with a well-staged White House dramatic production starring the president. This near universal news framing decision left the underlying situation fragmented: obscuring the link between terrorism and Iraq and endowing a formerly weak foreign policy leader with a Hollywood swagger. The Hollywood moment also made for a nice chapter ending in the authority-disorder narrative: a promise of return to normalcy—"Mission Accomplished."

Yet the long-term news frames offered by the administration did not comfortably contain disturbing reports of U.S. battle casualties and civil chaos in Iraq. Journalists who shifted the framing of the conflict away from White House communication strategies on their own were accused of liberal bias, or being unpatriotic. . . . The Democrats failed to offer much of an opportunity to open the news gates, as they were too busy attacking each other in the presidential primaries to agree on a party position that might shift the framing to a more substantive drama involving a clash between the president and political opponents. As a result, only 34 of 414 stories told by ABC, NBC, and CBS on the buildup to and rationale for the Iraq War from September 2002 through February 2003 originated outside the White House.

What were people to think? The polls . . . show that most people tried to accept what they saw on the news and generally supported administration framing even months after the situation in Iraq deteriorated. One factor in this public response was a poor factual grasp of the situation. New events or political developments would eventually lead news organizations to reframe the story, but the risk of such sudden frame shifts is that people feel deceived and even less sure what to believe. This is how the biases in the U.S. communication system contribute to a public that is increasingly cynical and disillusioned with politics and government.

The paradox is that journalists complain about the scripted and staged events they cover, but they seem unable to find other ways to write stories or to replace the cynical tone with perspectives that might help citizens become more engaged. . . .

. . . This begs the question: Why was there so little innovative coverage that might stimulate citizen engagement with events as they are happening? . . .

. . . [M]ost debates about journalistic bias are concerned with the question of ideology. For example, does the news have a liberal or conservative, a Democratic or Republican, drift? . . . [S]ome variation in news content or political emphasis does occur, but it can seldom be explained as the result of journalists routinely injecting their partisan views into the news. The avoidance of political partisanship by journalists is reinforced, among other means, by the professional ethics codes of journalists, by the editors who monitor their work, and by the business values of the companies they work for.

Another important point to recall is that people who see a consistent ideological press bias are seeing it with the help of their own ideology. This generalization is supported by opinion research showing that people in the middle see the press as generally neutral, whereas those on the left complain that the news is too conservative, and those on the right think the news has a left-leaning bias. If neutrality or objectivity could be achieved, citizens with strong views on particular issues would not recognize it. Moreover, even if the news contained strong ideological biases, people with a point of view are most able to detect and to defend themselves against them. Indeed, many nations favor a partisan press system as the best way to conduct public debates and to explore issues, . . .

While many Americans are caught up in dead-end debates about one kind of news bias that is less dangerous than commonly assumed, few are noticing other information bias that really are worth worrying about. A more sensible approach to news bias is to look for those universal information problems that hinder the efforts of citizens, whatever their ideology, to take part in political life. . . .

Four Information Biases That Matter: An Overview

Our expectations about the quality of public information are rather high. Most of us grew up with history books full of journalistic heroism exercised in the name of truth and free speech. . . .

Like it or not, the news has become a mass-produced consumer product, bearing little resemblance to history book images. Communication technologies, beginning with the wire services and progressing to satellite feeds and digital video, interact with corporate profit motives to create generic, "lowest-common-denominator" information formats. In particular, there are four characteristics of news that stand out as reasons why public information in the United States does not always advance the cause of democracy: *personalization, dramatization, fragmentation*, and the *authority-disorder bias*.

Personalization

If there is a single most important flaw in the American news style, it is the overwhelming tendency to downplay the big social, economic, or political picture in favor of the human trials, tragedies, and triumphs that sit at the surface of events. For example, instead of focusing on power and process, the media concentrate on the people engaged in political combat over the issues. The reasons for this are numerous, from the journalist's fear that probing analysis will turn off audiences to the relative ease of telling the human-interest side of a story as opposed to explaining deeper causes and effects.

When people are invited to take the news personally, they can find a wide range of private, emotional meanings in it. However, the meanings inspired by personalized news may not add up to the shared critical understandings on which healthy citizen involvement thrives. The focus on personalities encourages a passive spectator attitude among the public. Whether the focus is on sympathetic heroes and victims or hateful scoundrels and culprits, the media preference for personalized human-interest news creates a "can't-see-the-forest-for-the-trees" information bias that makes it difficult to see the big (institutional) picture that lies beyond the many actors crowding center stage who are caught in the eye of the news camera.

The tendency to personalize the news would be less worrisome if human-interest angles were used to hook audiences into more serious analysis of issues and problems.... American news often stops at the character development stage, however, and leaves the larger lessons and social significance, if there is any, to the imagination of the audience. As a result, the main problem with personalized news is that the focus on personal concerns is seldom linked to more in-depth analysis....

Dramatization

Compounding the information bias of personalization is a second news property in which the aspects of events that are reported tend to be the ones most easily dramatized in simple "stories."... American journalism has settled overwhelmingly on the reporting form of stories or narratives, as contrasted, for example, to analytical essays, political polemics, or more scientific-style problem reports. Stories invite dramatization, particularly with sharply drawn actors at their center.

News dramas emphasize crisis over continuity, the present over the past or future, and the personalities at their center. News dramas downplay complex policy information, the workings of government institutions, and the bases of power behind the central characters. Lost in the news drama (*melodrama* is often the more appropriate term) are sustained analyses of persistent problems such as inequality, hunger, resource depletion, population pressures, environmental collapse, toxic waste, and political oppression. Serious though such human problems are, they just are not dramatic enough on a day-to-day level to make the news until they produce crises . . .

Crises are the perfect news material because they fit neatly into the dramatization bias. The "crisis cycle" portrayed in the news is classic dramatic fare, with rising action, falling action, sharply drawn characters, and of course, plot resolutions. By its very definition, a crisis is something that will reach dramatic closure through cleanup efforts or humanitarian relief operations. Unfortunately, the crisis cycles in the news only reinforce the popular impression that high levels of human difficulty are inevitable and therefore acceptable. Crises in the news are often resolved when situations return to "manageable" levels of difficulty, yet underlying problems often continuing to grow. The news is certainly not the cause of these problems, but it could become part of the solution if it substituted illumination of causes for dramatic coverage of symptoms.

As in the case of personalization, dramatization would not be a problem if it were used mainly as an attention-focusing device to introduce more background and context surrounding events. Drama can help us engage with the great forces of history, science, politics, or human relations. When drama is used to bring analysis to mind, it is a good thing. When drama is employed as a cheap emotional device to focus on human conflict and travail, or farce and frailty, the larger significance of events becomes easily lost in waves of immediate emotion. The potential advantages of drama to enlighten and explain are sacrificed to the lesser tendencies of melodrama to excite, anger, and further personalize events. Thus the news often resembles real-life soap operas, only with far more important consequences.

One of the things that makes the news dramatic—indeed, that may even drive news drama—is the use of visuals: photos, graphics, and live-action video. These elements of stories not only make the distant world seem more real, they make the news more believable. In many ways, particularly for television, the pictures may help editors and reporters decide which stories to tell and how to tell them. Again, there is nothing inherently wrong with emphasizing visuals in news production. In fact one might argue that thinking visually is the best way to engage the senses in communicating about society and politics. There is often, however, a tension between not reporting important stories that are hard to picture and reporting possibly unimportant stories simply because they offer great visual images.... The selection of news stories primarily because they offer dramatic images is one of several important reasons why the news is often so fragmented or disconnected from larger political or economic contexts that would provide other ways to tell the story.

Fragmentation

The emphasis on personal and dramatic qualities of events feeds into a third information characteristic of the news: the isolation of stories from each other and from their larger contexts so that information in the news becomes fragmented and hard to assemble into a big picture. The fragmentation of information begins by emphasizing individual actors over the political contexts in which they operate. Fragmentation is then heightened by the use of dramatic formats that turn events into self-contained, isolated happenings. The fragmentation of information is further exaggerated by the severe space limits nearly all media impose for fear of boring readers and viewers with too much information.

As a result, the news comes to us in sketchy dramatic capsules that make it difficult to see the causes of problems, their historical significance, or the connections across issues. It can even be difficult to follow the development of a particular issue over time as stories rise and fall more in response to the actions and reactions of prominent public figures than to independent reporting based on investigation of events. In addition, because it is difficult to bring historical background into the news, the impression is created of a world of chaotic events and crises that appear and disappear because the news picture offers little explanation of their origins.

The Authority-Disorder Bias

Whether the world is returned to a safe, normal place, or whether the very idea of a normal world is called into question, the news is preoccupied with order, along with related questions of whether authorities are capable of establishing or restoring it. It is easy to see why these generic plot elements are so central to news: They are versatile and tireless themes that can be combined endlessly within personalized, dramatized, and fragmented news episodes. . . .

In the past, it could be argued . . . that the news more often resolved the authority-order balance in favor of official pronouncements aimed at "normalizing" conflicted situations by creating the appearance of order and control. A classic scenario of politics, according to political scientist Murray Edelman, is for authorities to take center stage to respond to crises (sometimes after having stirred them up in the first place) with emotionally reassuring promises that they will be handled effectively. Today's authorities still play out their parts, but the news increasingly finds ways to challenge the pronouncements of officials and the presumption of order in society. In short, the biggest change in portrayals of authority and order in the news since earlier editions of this book is that the news balance has shifted away from trusted authorities providing reassuring promises to restore chaotic situations to a state of order or normalcy. Normalizing stories continue to appear, of course, but a growing news trend is to portray unsympathetic, scheming politicians who often fail to solve problems, leaving disorder in their wake. . . .

. . . In an industry competing for fickle and shrinking audiences, images of disorder can be amplified through subtle emphases in news writing. For example, is the traditional American family *threatened* by the increase in single-parent and two-working-parent households, or is the family in America simply *changing* in these ways as part of the normal course of social change?

As news organizations take greater dramatic license with news plots, the elements of authority and disorder are often mixed to achieve the greatest dramatic effect. A typical example comes from a local newscast in Orlando, Florida, where Channel 6 announced an "exclusive" and promised a report from their "live truck" at the scene. The newscast opened with the anchor describing "A shocking scene in a Lake Mary neighborhood tonight. A home surrounded by crime-scene tape. A death police are calling 'suspicious.'" As the anchor spoke, the screen flashed the words "Neighborhood Shocker." Cut to the reporter live from the scene who further dramatized the death of a 66-year-old woman by saying that police did not know what happened. . . . Although this statement could easily have supported either an order or a disorder plot for the story, the local news format clearly favored playing the murder mystery/shocker plot. . . . The next day, it turned out that the woman had died naturally of a heart attack. So much for the "Neighborhood Shocker." As one observer noted, "Journalism Shocker" would have been a more appropriate on-screen warning. . . .

Bias as Part of the Political Information System

... The tendencies toward personalization, dramatization, and fragmentation have all been remarkably enduring over time, ... While the focus on authority and order is also an enduring defining feature of the news, the shifting balance from order to mayhem and the unreflectively negative tone toward officials has left many observers puzzled and concerned. Indeed, many politicians say they have left government because of the relentlessly negative media scrutiny, while others have surrounded themselves by legions of media consultants and handlers. At the same time that many journalists criticize their own product in these terms, they confess being helpless to change it under the current system of profit- and ratings-driven business values.

News Bias and Discouraged Citizens

The general perspective developed in this book is that each aspect of the political information system described here is influenced by the others. For example, the weakness of journalism norms and cultural values for educating citizens may result in citizens who are easily discouraged from thinking seriously about serious issues. This, in turn, may encourage political actors to employ superficial and emotional public relations techniques in their presentation of partisan political issues and policy choices. Sensing little public interest in hard news and having few resources for investigative reporting, the press passes off these strategically crafted political messages as the substance of the story of the day, perhaps overlaid with cynical commentary about the political games being played by politicians. This core of daily political news is interspersed with scandals and personal dramas justified by ratings reports suggesting that, despite their protests to the contrary, many people really do follow these spectacles.

Whether people follow scandals and mayhem as guilty pleasures or with anger and disgust, the convenient claim by media executives—that this is really what people want—misses at least two important points. First, many people are tuning out political news and homing in on more personal information about health, sports, celebrities, fashion, travel, and lifestyles.... [T]hese trends are occurring despite the abundance of available news topics and the ease of becoming informed. Perhaps most distressing for the future of political participation is that younger generations are most likely to tune out hard news. Second, according to research by communication scholars Joseph Cappella and Kathleen Hall Jamieson, even the people who consume news often become discouraged about politics and public life by cynical, negative news.

So the public information cycle goes, one element of the press-politician-public news triangle affecting another in a dysfunctional manner until nearly everyone is dissatisfied. However, few citizens possess enough understanding of the overall system to recommend convincing solutions. Rather than thinking about the information system as a rational process in which objectivity is the highest and most desirable outcome, it makes more sense to think of this system as a game in which the different players are not all playing for the same goals or even by the same rules, but in which each uses the others to achieve particular ends:

> Politicians play for public support and favorable insider buzz by using news management and public relations techniques intended to put their political bias (or "spin") on news content.
>
> The press competes for ratings, sales, and "scoops" (being first to break a story), and perhaps most importantly, to avoid being "beaten" on a story by other news organizations. Business-driven news formulas dictate manufacturing the most dramatic audience-grabbing stories for the least cost and with a minimum of attention-distracting complexity. At the end of the day, stories often end up looking much the same from one news outlet to another, but the competition for audiences and the aggression toward politicians create the illusion of independence.
>
> The people occasionally enter the game as voters or as members of organized interests, searching the news for information that helps them decide what to do politically. Sometimes they find useful information, particularly when they are motivated by interest in a particular issue. Often they turn away, confused or discouraged. For the most part, however, they are the spectators. Political scientist Murray Edelman describes the focus of the daily news as political spectacle, attracting attention for its entertainment value even if it often fails to provide much information that is useful to citizens.

Reform Anyone?

These trends offer little promise that, despite tremendous gains in communication technology and the vast potential of the Internet, the news of the future will come any closer than we are today to meeting the information needs of democracy—unless, that is, people such as the readers of this book begin to understand how this information system works and think about how to fix what is wrong with it. In place of thinking seriously about the problems of information in this information age, many people have simply withdrawn from politics and joined the chorus of those who hurl easy criticisms at politicians and press alike. Public disapproval alone has not produced an improvement in the quality of information on which the health of democracy depends. While criticisms of the news are legion, relatively few of those critics offer much in the way of solid proposals for change. Press reform is the subject of the final chapter in this book, but a brief look at one model of more useful news reporting is in order now.

The most recent attempt to create an information system with more of the qualities outlined above is a now-fading movement for *public* or *civic* journalism. Although there is no single approach to this effort at news reform, it generally involves local news organizations inviting citizen participation in shaping news coverage that "encourages civic engagement—especially in elections—and supports communities in solving problems." This movement grew impressively in the late 1990s. By 1998, the Pew Center for Civic Journalism had funded sixty-two projects, each involving more than one news organization in coordinating agendas of issue and election coverage through opinion polls and citizen forums in communities.

The irony is that this movement has drawn harsh criticism from prominent journalists and news organizations. For example, editors at the *New York Times* and the *Washington Post* have condemned the loss of journalistic independence that comes from letting citizens help decide what is important to cover. Many journalists feel that keeping the focus on a set of issues that may not be the ones government is currently addressing risks crossing the line from objective reporting to issue advocacy. A 1997 survey of media executives sponsored by the Associated Press found little in the way of broad support for the civic journalism movement in the industry. For example, only 14 percent of media executives felt that reporting was improved by news organizations listening to input from "citizens' juries" or "citizens' forums." Fully 33 percent felt that establishing such direct communication links between citizens and news organizations was a bad idea. The executives were evenly divided (35 percent to 34 percent) on the question of whether crossing the line between reporting and advocacy would further undermine journalism credibility. Perhaps the most damning charge against civic journalism is that it is little more than boosterism, a marketing ploy, or a "gimmick to make publishers feel better about themselves." A plurality of 41 percent of media executives strongly agreed with these charges, while only 33 percent strongly disagreed?

DISCUSSION POINTS

1 What are the four information biases that Bennett identifies?

2 If the present news system pushes certain types of stories to the forefront, it may mean that certain other types of stories are not told or are not told in

a fashion that is particularly effective. Can you think of examples of types of stories that would not be told?

3   How do the information biases that Bennett identifies impact the public when it comes to the news and their view of public affairs?

28

And Now, a Word for our Demographic

TED KOPPEL

A veteran reporter and on-air commentator argues that the content of what is reported by the present media is affected by the interests and predilections of the viewing public. Increasing competition and the ever-rising number of choices available to consumers have left the traditional network news divisions often at the whim of what Koppel terms "the dictatorship of the demographic." The result, he writes, is that we are in an era of "boutique journalism" in which the news-providers are selling the news and, in the course of doing so, taking direction from their audience when it comes to determing what is important and what is not.

... [H]ere I sit, having recently left ABC News after 42 years, and who should call but an editor friend of mine who ... has asked me to write this column examining the state of television news today. Where to begin? Confession of the obvious seems like a reasonable starting point: I have become well known and well-off traveling the world on ABC's dime, charged only with ensuring that our viewers be well informed about important issues. For the better part of those 42 years, this arrangement worked to our mutual benefit and satisfaction. At the same time, I cannot help but see that the industry in which I have spent my entire adult life is in decline and in distress. Once, 30 or 40 years ago, the target audience for network news was made up of everyone with a television, and the most common criticism lodged against us was that we were tempted to operate on a lowest-common-denominator basis.

This, however, was in the days before deregulation, when the Federal Communications Commission was still perceived to have teeth, and its mandate that broadcasters operate in "the public interest, convenience and necessity" was enough to give each licensee pause. Network owners nurtured their news divisions, encouraged them to tackle serious issues, cultivated them as shields to be brandished before Congressional committees whenever questions were raised about the quality of entertainment programs and the vast sums earned by those programs. News divisions occasionally came under political pressures but rarely commercial ones. The expectation was that they would search out issues of importance, sift out the trivial and then tell the public what it needed to know.

With the advent of cable, satellite and broadband technology, today's marketplace has become so overcrowded that network news divisions are increasingly vulnerable to the dictatorship of the demographic. Now, every division of every network is expected to make a profit. And so we have entered the age of boutique journalism. The goal for the traditional broadcast networks now is to identify those segments of the audience considered most desirable by the advertising community and then to cater to them.

Most television news programs are therefore designed to satisfy the perceived appetites of our audiences. That may be not only acceptable but unavoidable in entertainment; in news, however, it is the journalists who should be telling their viewers what is important, not the other way around. Indeed, in television news these days, the programs are being shaped to attract, most particularly, 18-to-34-year-old viewers. They, in turn, are presumed to be partly brain-dead—though not so insensible as to be unmoved by the blandishments of sponsors.

Exceptions, it should be noted, remain. Thus it is that the evening news broadcasts of ABC, CBS and NBC are liberally studded with advertisements that clearly cater to older Americans. But this is a holdover from another era: the last gathering of more than 30 million tribal elders, as they clench their dentures while struggling to control esophageal eruptions of stomach acid to watch "The News." That number still commands respect, but even the evening news programs, you will find (after the first block of headline material), are struggling to find a new format that will somehow appeal to younger viewers.

Washington news, for example, is covered with less and less enthusiasm and aggressiveness. The networks' foreign bureaus have, for some years now, been seen as too expensive to merit survival. Judged on the frequency with which their reports get airtime, they can no longer be deemed cost-effective. Most have either been closed or reduced in size to the point of irrelevance. Simply stated, no audience is perceived to be clamoring for foreign news, the exceptions being wars in their early months that involve American troops, acts of terrorism and, for a couple of weeks or so, natural disasters of truly epic proportions.

You will still see foreign stories on the evening news broadcasts, but examine them carefully. They are either reported by one of a half-dozen or so remaining foreign correspondents who now cover the world for each network, or the anchor simply narrates a piece of videotape shot by some other news agency. For big events, an anchor might parachute in for a couple of days of high drama coverage. But the age of the foreign correspondent, who knew a country or region intimately, is long over.

No television news executive is likely to acknowledge indifference to major events overseas or in our nation's capital, but he may, on occasion, concede that the viewers don't care, and therein lies the essential malignancy.

The accusation that television news has a political agenda misses the point. Right now, the main agenda is to give people what they want. It is not partisanship but profitability that shapes what you see.

Most particularly on cable news, a calculated subjectivity has, indeed, displaced the old-fashioned goal of conveying the news dispassionately. But that, too, has less to do with partisan politics than simple capitalism. Thus, one cable network experiments with the subjectivity of tender engagement: "I care and therefore you should care." Another opts for chest-thumping certitude: "I know and therefore you should care."

Even Fox News's product has less to do with ideology and more to do with changing business models. Fox has succeeded financially because it tapped into a deep, rich vein of unfulfilled yearning among conservative American television viewers, but it created programming to satisfy the market, not the other way around. CNN, meanwhile, finds itself largely outmaneuvered, unwilling to accept the label of liberal alternative, experimenting instead with a form of journalism that stresses empathy over detachment.

Now, television news should not become a sort of intellectual broccoli to be jammed down our viewers' unwilling throats. We are obliged to make our offerings as palatable as possible. But there are too many important things happening in the world today to allow the diet to be determined to such a degree by the popular tastes of a relatively narrow and apparently uninterested demographic.

What is, ultimately, most confusing about the behavior of the big three networks is why they ever allowed themselves to be drawn onto a battlefield that so favors their cable competitors. At almost any time, the audience of a single network news program on just one broadcast network is greater than the combined audiences of CNN, Fox and MSNBC.

Reaching across the entire spectrum of American television viewers is precisely the broadcast networks' greatest strength. By focusing only on key demographics, by choosing to ignore their total viewership, they have surrendered their greatest advantage.

Oddly enough, there is a looming demographic reality that could help steer television news back toward its original purpose. There are tens of millions of baby boomers in their 40's and 50's and entering their 60's who have far more spending power than their 18-to-34-year old counterparts. Television news may be debasing itself before the wrong demographic.

If the network news divisions cannot be convinced that their future depends on attracting all demographic groups, then perhaps, at least, they can be persuaded to aim for the largest single demographic with the most disposable income—one that may actually have an appetite for serious news. That would seem like a no-brainer. It's regrettable, perhaps, that only money and the inclination to spend it will ultimately determine the face of television news, but, as a distinguished colleague of mine used to say: "That's the way it is."

DISCUSSION POINTS

1   Compare Koppel's article on media bias to Parenti's article on the same subject. How do you explain their divergence in views?

2   Assume Koppel's observations about who or what is driving the content of the network news are correct. What are the dangers or implications?

3   Is Koppel correct to criticize the network media for listening to news consumers? Why or why not?

29

The Social Origins of Press Cynicism

MICHAEL SCHUDSON

Michael Schudson surveys the modern news media and concludes that compared to the past it is more cynical, more infotainment oriented, and, oddly enough, more comprehensive and more credible than in the past. These findings seem counter-intuitive. To learn more, Schudson examines a number of trends in journalism itself that both help account for the good and bad in the modern news media.

Recent academic critiques of the press, echoed by a variety of prominent journalists themselves (David Broder, James Fallows) and turned into a set of proposals for journalistic reform by the public journalism movement, unite around two central propositions. Both of them are unassailably correct, and yet they offer a seriously incomplete portrait of the news today. The two key propositions are (a) that news reporting—especially political reporting—is increasingly organized by presumptions that stem from cynicism in the press corps and promote cynicism in the audience and (b) that news institutions increasingly blur news and entertainment, even fact and fiction. I will briefly take up each of these claims before going on to suggest what else we need to understand about the press to put these claims in focus.

Political Cynicism

In *Out of Order*, Thomas Patterson (1993) argues that the press has an "anti-politics bias." He cited *Washington Post* reporter Paul Taylor as writing: "Our habits of mind are shaped by what Lionel Trilling once described as the 'adversary culture.' . . . We are progressive reformers, deeply skeptical of all the major institutions of society except our own." Patterson finds a growing trend from 1960 to 1992 in the news weeklies to reporting bad news rather than good. In 1960, 75% of evaluative references to Kennedy and Nixon were positive; in 1992 only 40% of evaluative references praised Clinton or Bush (pp. 18-20).

So the news is increasingly negative and cynical about politicians. Journalists leave the impression that politicians will promise anything to get elected, and they neglect to remind people, as political science studies do, that politicians with rare exception work hard and often successfully to make good on campaign pledges (Patterson, 1993, p. 11). Journalists see political careers as more oriented to politics as a game than to politics as policy (Patterson, 1993, pp. 60-61). The "game schema" directs attention to conflicts and to a few individuals, not to social conditions and the larger interests individuals may represent. For instance, over time, journalists have shifted from reporting candidates' speeches to reporting the strategic moves behind them . . . (Patterson, 193, pp. 68-69). . . . "The game sets the context" in news today. "The game, once the backdrop in news of the campaign, is now so pervasive that it is almost inseparable from the rest of election content" (Patterson, 1993, p. 69). . . .

Analysis of news coverage of Congress finds that the press has held Congress in low esteem at least since World War II but that "in recent years congressional coverage has become increasingly negative." According to political scientist Mark Rozell (1996), "Healthy skepticism has now largely been replaced with a debilitating cynicism that potentially undermines the foundations of representative government" (p. 5). . . .

Jamieson's (1992) *Dirty Politics* . . . examined both the advertising during the presidential campaign of 1988 and the news coverage of it and concluded that news coverage assumed a "strategy schema" that read all candidate moves and motives as the "calculated product of strategic choice." Jamieson objected to "polls and strategy talk" that not only "distort but . . . distract as well." The strategy schema, she argued, "disengages the electorate from the election." The strategy schema "minimizes the educational value of a campaign's most informative moments, those that occur in mass exposure to general election presidential debates." It reduces the debates to the questions of who won, why, and what impact the candidates' debate performances would have on the outcome of the election. "This constricted focus on unanswerable and silly questions reduces the panorama of information gathered by all segments of the viewing public to irrelevant data" (pp. 186-187).

The movement for public journalism or civic journalism has

turned this sort of critique into a platform for media reform. The public journalism advocates see conventional journalism as complacently assuming that we already have a democracy and only need more information to inform it. Public journalism, as Jay Rosen (1996), one of its leading proponents contends, starts from the assumption that we already swim in a sea of information but need more democracy (p. 7). Journalists, then, should be more creative in making their institutions catalysts for community dialogue. They should know their communities better; they should incorporate citizens' expressed concerns into their own agendas, even into the questions they ask candidates for office.

Infotainment

The news is regularly attacked for blurring the line between information and entertainment. This complaint is at least as old as early objections to the news interview (in the 1860s) as a humbug, a concoction of an event by a politician and a journalist for the sake of both of their careers. So this is not a new erosion. . . . The modern concern probably begins with Daniel Boorstin's (1961) complaint about "pseudo-events." The discussion was reopened when John Hersey held in 1980 that "our grasp on *reality*, our relationship with the real world, is what is at stake here." For him, genres that blur truth and fiction . . . are deeply threatening to getting straight our sense of reality. Moreover, they "lead to, or at the very least help soften the way for, or confirm the reasonableness of, public lying." . . . [T]he proliferation of radio and television talk shows; magazine-format news progams that, even at their high end, are platforms for celebrities, diseases of the week, heartwarming or heartrending tales of fortune and misfortune; next to no national political stories; and absolutely no news from beyond the national borders. Respectable news institutions have taken to citing as legitimate news the reports of sexual escapades that appear in the same supermarket tabloids that report babies fathered by extraterrestrial aliens.

With all the new sources of entertainment-oriented news proliferating, especially in broadcast and cable television, it is impossible to doubt that infotainment has grown. Still, it is of some interest to note that quantitative data to suggest its increase in the mainstream, sensible media is measurable, too. A 1998 study produced by the Committee of Concerned Journalists found a deterioration in issues coverage in television, newspaper, and news magazine journalism between 1977 and 1997, with a declining attention to policy issues and an increasing attention to scandal. In 1977, in a sample of stories from leading newspapers and news magazines, 32% of stories were "traditional" in their emphasis on policy or political process, whereas 15% concerned personalities, scandal, lifestyle, and human interest. In 1997, traditional news was down to 26%, and feature news was up to 43% (Project for Excellence in Journalism, 1998, p. 2). I am not aware of any studies that contradict the general thrust of these conclusions—that political news demeans and diminishes what citizens may hope from politics and that this has become increasingly true over the past 30 years.

Political cynicism is a cynicism of the reporter's intellect; infotainment is a cynicism of corporate structures. Both conspire to promote in the public a cynical understanding of politics and an increasingly reckless disregard of the line that responsible journalists have tried to uphold between fact and fiction. In sum, the media have developed a character and style that appear to have negative consequences for our civic culture.

There is a question, however, about whether these changes are causes of the corrosion of American political culture, or reflections of corrosion in other places, or concomitants and side-effects of other changes that might be judged either benign or healthy. Do the media, as presently constituted, generate their own cynicism? Or do they reproduce, despite themselves, the broad cynical tug of the age? Or is what appears to be cynicism a salutary antiauthoritarianism?

These questions are important because it is necessary to reconcile the critics' agreement that the media are cynical and thereby dangerous with another account that I also subscribe to: that Americans have more information today than ever. More credible information. More national sources of information. Information from a wider variety of sources, thanks to the proliferation of expert lobbying groups and the changing habits of the media to seek out contrasting opinions. More information coming to the laity through the media rather than through expert intermediaries such as politicians, doctors, and lawyers. In important respects, American journalism is better today than ever before. People today have unprecedented access to careful, conscientious, analytically sound, crisply presented information about national and world affairs....

How can it be that the news has grown more cynical, more infotainment oriented, and more comprehensive and credible at the same time? I think a number of underlying trends in journalism may help account for all of these developments. Three trends in journalism in the past quarter century may be causes of both the salutary and troubling directions the news media are taking.

Growing Professional Interventionism

The ties between news institutions and parties began to weaken near the end of the 19th century. With more and more news institutions run by megacorporations and not by egomaniacal capitalist adventurers, the straightforward use of the press to advance the political interests of an individual, faction, or party has been progressively reduced. Reporters and editors have taken on greater authority relative to ownership. They have also taken on greater authority relative to their own sources. They are less likely to defer to official authority than they were a generation ago. Vietnam, Watergate, the adversary culture of the 1960s, the revulsion in the media toward Ronald Reagan's photo opportunities and George Bush's racist and flag-waving victory over Michael Dukakis all contributed to a self-consciousness in journalism about both its possibilities and its pitfalls.

One sign of the new interventionism is the now famous shrinking of the sound bite in television news. In national network coverage of elections, the average length of time a candidate spoke uninterruptedly on camera was 43 seconds in 1968; by 1988, it was 9 seconds. This has generally been understood to mean that television news has grown worse and worse, more and more trivial, but this was not the conclusion of communication scholar Daniel Hallin (1994), who did the sound-bite research in the first place. His more cautious conclusion was simply that television news had become more "mediated," that is, that journalists intervened with growing frequency in order to provide a compact and dramatic story. What this means for the overall quality of television news, however, he acknowledges to be "not simple," critical as he is of contemporary television news. True, he finds an increase in "horse race" coverage from 1968 to 1988, but he also finds an increase in the coverage of "issues." How can both increase? The intervening journalist offers a "more highly structured, thematic" story. There is less wasted motion, less silence, more rapid-fire editing (pp. 144, 145).

Thematizing

Media critic Paul Weaver (1981) has observed that television news is more inclined than newspaper news to "tell a story." Both television and newspaper news are "essentially melodramatic accounts of current events," Weaver wrote. But television news is "far more coherently organized and tightly unified" compared to the newspaper story that still has an inverted pyramid organization in which the news account ends with a whimper, not a bang. The newspaper story has no teleological drive to wrap things up; in fact, after the opening paragraph, or lead, which can be read as a complete capsule story in itself, the rest of the story may be presented in very loose and only semicoherent order. The newspaper story is designed not to be read in its entirety, whereas the television story is meant to achieve its significance only as a full and finished object that keeps the viewer attuned throughout. The newspaper story may confine itself to reporting an event, uninflected by any effort to give it meaning or analysis. The television story, in contrast, "inevitably . . . goes into, beneath or beyond the ostensive event to fix upon something else—a process, mood, trend, condition, irony, relationship, or whatever else seems a suitable theme in the circumstance." (p. 284).

The effort of the television news story to thematize is hard to satisfy in an age suspicious of the grand narrative, and an age where the Cold War is no longer available to provide a default narrative frame. Journalism may be no more lost out in postmodernity than human intellectual life in general, but lost it is, telling stories with beginnings, middles, and ends but, even so, with no point. . . .

Growing News Coherence

A century ago, competing newspapers in the same city featured front-page stories that their rivals did not even carry in the back pages. There was little urgency in journalism about coming up with "the" picture of that day's reality. Now, news institutions monitor one another all the time. The Cable News Network (CNN) is a permanent presence in the newsrooms of daily newspapers. Newsmagazines and newspapers preview their next editions on Web sites that other reporters and editors at other news institutions examine almost the moment they are available. Newspapers advertise the next day's stories on cable news stations. The result is interinstitutional news coherence. Literary or film critics have talked of intertextuality for a long time; now news intertextuality is an electronic reality, not an accidental outcome of wars that draw reporters to the same hotel or power centers that draw them to the same bars and parties in a capital city. News is a widely distributed, seamless intertext.

This follows in part from the domination of television in the news system. Because television journalism insists on thematic coherence, it "gives credence to the idea that there exists in America a single, coherent national agenda which can be perceived as such by any reasonable and well-intentioned person" (Weaver, 1981, p. 292). But this has intensified with (a) national news distribution—*The New York Times* News Service, CNN, *USA Today*, National Public Radio, and others—and (b) the growing importance of Washington news from the Kennedy administration and Vietnam on. The Vietnam War created modern television news as nothing else had before it. Since Vietnam, more news comes from Washington. Various factors contribute to this—the growing role of the federal government in everyday life, the growing celebrity of national television journalists, the improved technological capacity of satellite-borne television signals, and the growing corporatization of the press. More newspapers are owned by nonlocals and run by nonlocals with incentives to rise in the national organization rather than create ties to local power structures or sentimental attachments to local roots. All of this not only nationalizes news but enlarges the possibilities for cynicism. When news is local, it typically remains personal, friendly, upbeat, gossipy, homey—and it very rarely probes local power structures or the assumptions, religious, ethnic, or otherwise, of local cultures. Nationalizing news distances journalists from their audiences, for better and for worse.

The growing interinstitutional news coherence is matched by a significant increase in intrainstitutional news coherence. News reporting seeks in each news institution a new comprehensiveness and cultural inclusiveness. If you walked into a newsroom 50 years ago, you would most likely not have seen any Blacks or other racial minorities, and the only women you would have encountered would have been writing for the society page. There were Black journalists, but almost all of them worked for the several hundred Black newspapers. During World War II, many Blacks were indifferent to what seemed to them a White man's war. The Black press tried to bridge this gap with its Double V campaign that sought to promote allegiance to victory against the Axis along with victory against segregation at home. It is ironic that as their aims were realized in the civil rights movement, the separate sphere that made possible a thriving Black press disintegrated. From the 1960s on, Black newspapers failed one after the other as the older papers could no longer attract the readers, especially younger readers, that national advertisers sought (Pride & Wilson, 1997, p. 246; see also Finkle, 1975). The mainstream press conscientiously, if belatedly, sought to hire and promote Black Americans and to cover the news and views of minorities.

Amid a veritable deluge of public information, people—especially the young—exhibit a declining interest in it. Sixty-five percent of people older than 50, 55% of those age 30 to 49, and 40% of those age 18 to 29 think it is "very important" to keep up with the news. Not everyone lives up to their ideals, of course. Only 51% of those older than 50, 29% of those age 30 to 49, and 19% of those age 18 to 29 say they follow government and public affairs "most of the time." Women in every age group are significantly less likely than men to follow government and public affairs—only 12% of women age 18 to 29 claim that they do so (compared to 26% of men in this age group). Young people have long lagged behind older people in following the news, but there has been a decrease over time. In 1965, 67% of those age 21 to 35 read a newspaper the day before being surveyed; in 1990, it was only 30%. For the 30 to 49 age group, the percentage who read a newspaper the prior day dropped from 73% to 44%, and for those older than 50, it dropped from 74% to 55% (Radio and Television News Directors Foundation, 1996, pp. 11, 14, 23).

Publishers are alarmed. Their newspapers still turn handsome profits, but they are losing the audience to television and other media and to nonnews as much as to rival news sources. Every newspaper faces this reality. Urging the newspaper press to higher standards is not much use if the result is that even more people desert the habit of reading. So the print media become, all at once, even more thematizing, professionally interventionist, and coherent, even more cynical and open to an entertainment orientation.

There is no reason to suppose journalists are by personality or character more cynical than they were in the past. Institutional and cultural changes are more than enough in themselves to explain the cynical turn. Journalists today are unwilling to rely exclusively on official statements as they once did. Their own professional culture pushes them to be analytical and judgmental—for literary (thematizing) reasons, for cultural reasons (a society-wide growing distrust of established authority), for political reasons (the decline of the Cold War metanarrative for news), and for commercial reasons (fear of losing an audience). It is all very well to urge that news adopt a policy framework rather than a game/strategy framework for political news, but enacting this recommendation in the face of the journalism culture's best (as well as worst) instincts is another matter. As we judge and criticize the news media and the ways it represents the nation and the world to us, it is important to see the press whole, to understand what forces enable journalists to celebrate the progress of their own profession at the same time that this "progress" contains so much that cultural observers, including journalists, find appalling.

DISCUSSION POINTS

1 What are the trends that Schudson identifies that may help explain why the modern news media is more cynical, more infotainment oriented, and, arguably, more comprehensive and more credible than in the past?

2 What is it that has changed as far as news media cynicism has gone? Is it the journalists themselves or is it something about journalism as an institution or about the larger American culture that has changed?

3 Schudson reports that Americans have more information than in the past yet are less interested in this information. What are the implications for a democracy such as the United States of such a trend? In what ways might increases in press cynicism and infotainment cause or contribute to this trend?

30

All the President's Men

CARL BERNSTEIN
BOB WOODWARD

Media critics frequently harp on what they perceive to be a lack of proper ethics on the part of the media. In perhaps the best known book concerning the American media, two Washington Post *reporters, Bob Woodward and Carl Bernstein, question some of the ethical decisions that they made while covering the most famous American political scandal of all time: Watergate. The selected passages concern the* Post's *efforts to learn more about the United States Justice Department's investigation into a variety of allegations of misuse of power as well as of campaign contributions by President Richard M. Nixon. Many of these allegations proved to be true and drove Nixon to resign. Readers are invited to attempt to identify each ethical dilemma that Woodward and Bernstein faced. Note the involvement of editors, such as Harry Rosenfeld and Benjamin Bradlee, in the discussion and ultimate resolution of many of their dilemmas.*

One late November Saturday night, a *Post* editor asked for a word with Woodward in a deserted section of the newsroom. One of his neighbors had told him that his aunt was on a grand jury. His neighbor thought it was the jury on Watergate; she'd made some remark about knowing all about it. "She's a Republican, but she says she really hates Nixon now. My neighbor thinks she wants to talk."

A few days later, the editor handed Woodward a slip of paper with the woman's name and address. Bernstein and Woodward went to Rosenfeld, who seemed to like the idea of a visit but suspended final judgment until he had checked with Bradlee for a policy decision. Bradlee asked the *Post*'s lawyers.

Bernstein and Woodward consulted the *Post*'s library copy of the Federal Rules of Criminal Procedure. Grand jurors took an oath to keep secret their deliberations and the testimony before them; but the burden of secrecy, it appeared, was on the juror. There seemed to be nothing in the law that forbade anyone to ask questions. The lawyers agreed, but urged extreme caution in making any approaches. They recommended that the reporters simply ask the woman if she wanted to talk. . . .

The next morning, the reporters drove across town, knocked at the woman's door and identified themselves. She invited them inside. . . .

It took 10 minutes to figure out that the woman was indeed on a grand jury at the courthouse, but not the Watergate one. . . .

The episode had whetted their interest. They knew the outlines of the information they needed. They lacked the details a cooperative grand juror could probably supply. That afternoon, Bernstein called the chief prosecutor, Earl Silbert, and asked for a list of the 23 grand jurors. Silbert refused flatly, rejecting Bernstein's contention that the membership of the jury was a matter of public record.

Woodward asked a friend in the clerk's office if it was possible to get a roster of the Watergate grand jury. "No way whatsoever," he was told. "The records are secret."

Next morning, Woodward took a cab to the courthouse.

The clerk's office employed about 90 people. Woodward started at one end of the large complex of file rooms and after half an hour had found someone willing to direct him to a remote corner of the main file area where lists of trial and grand juries were kept. He identified himself to another clerk as a *Post* reporter and said he wanted to look through the file. The clerk looked at Woodward suspiciously. "Okay," he said, "but you aren't allowed to copy anything. You can't take names. No notes. I'll be watching."

Woodward started going through the file drawers and finally found the master list of 1972 grand juries. Two grand juries had been sworn in on June 5. He remembered that the foreman of the Watergate grand jury had an Eastern European name and worked for the government as an economist or something like that. He found the right name on Grand Jury Number One, sworn in on June 5, 1972.

Each of the grand jurors had filled out a small orange card listing name, age, occupation, address, home and work telephones. Woodward began sifting through the cards, then glanced over his shoulder. The clerk was sitting at his desk, about 15 feet away, staring at him. Woodward took the first four cards, set them face up in the bottom of the file drawer and began studying the names, ages, addresses, phone numbers and occupations. It took about 10 minutes to memorize the information. He asked the clerk where the men's room was.

Inside the washroom, Woodward went into a stall, took a notebook from his jacket pocket and wrote out what he had memorized. . . .

Woodward memorized the next five cards. Straining not to look guilty, he asked the clerk where the chief judge's chambers were.

The man frowned. "You're sure spending a lot of time with those files. I'm not so sure that you're allowed to even look in there."

Woodward said he would be back—as soon as he had checked something with the chief judge. Upstairs, in a third-floor washroom, he wrote down the five names and the other information. That left 14. . . .

On the third try, he was able to memorize six cards. . . . It took nearly 45 minutes to memorize the last eight names and accompanying details.

At the office, he typed a list of the jury members and the accompanying data. In Bradlee's office, the editors and Bernstein and Woodward . . . look[ed] for the few least likely to inform the prosecutors of a visit. The candidate would have to be bright enough to suspect that the grand-jury system had broken down in the Watergate case and be in command of the nuances of the evidence. Ideally, the juror would be capable of outrage at the White House or the prosecutors or both; a person who was accustomed to bending rules the type of person who valued practicality more than procedure. . . .

Everyone in the room had private doubts about such a seedy venture. Bradlee, desperate for a story, and reassured by the lawyers, overcame his own. Simons doubted out loud the rightness of the exercise and worried about the paper. Rosenfeld was concerned most about the mechanics of the reporters not getting caught. Sussman was afraid that one of them, probably Bernstein, would push too hard and find a way to violate the law. Woodward wondered whether there was ever justification for a reporter to entice someone across the line of legality while standing safely on the right side himself. Bernstein, who vaguely approved of selective civil disobedience, was not concerned about breaking the law in the abstract. It was a question of *which* law, and he believed that grand-jury proceedings should be inviolate. The misgivings, however, went unstated, for the most part. The reporters' procedure would be to identify themselves, tell the juror that they had learned from an anonymous mutual acquaintance that he or she knew something about Watergate and ask if he or she was willing to discuss the matter. They would leave unless the juror, without prodding, volunteered something. Nothing would be said about the grand jury unless the juror mentioned it.

Bradlee, addressing them in a final briefing before bivouac, repeated the marching orders: "No strong-arm tactics, fellas. Right?"

Working separately over the first weekend of December, Woodward and Bernstein attempted the clumsy charade with about half a dozen members of the grand jury. They returned with no information and a clear impression that the prosecutors had warned the jurors to beware of jokers bearing press cards. . . .

On Monday, Bradlee called the reporters into his office for an urgent meeting. . . . At least one of the grand jurors had told the prosecutors he'd been visited by a *Washington Post* reporter. One of the prosecutors had called Edward Bennett Williams, the *Post*'s principal attorney. The prosecutors had gone to Judge Sirica with the juror's complaint and Williams had advised Bradlee to have his reporters sit tight. . . .

Judge Sirica wanted Bernstein and Woodward in his courtroom at 10:00 A.M. on December 19. A hearing before the Judge on another matter involving the press—a defense motion to force the *Los Angeles Times* to turn over tapes and notes of its interview with Alfred C. Baldwin—was already scheduled for that hour. . . .

Sirica, they learned at precisely 10 o'clock, was capable of expressing his displeasure with a frown so deep as to leave no doubt about his reputation for toughness. He had decided to make the reporters the first order of business. The grand jurors had entered the courtroom. The audience obeyed the command of "All rise." The Judge's frown deepened. "Oh boy," Woodward whispered to Bernstein, bouncing on his toes and sucking in his breath so the words sounded as if he were ordering a horse to stop. Bernstein was contemplating which fate he preferred—the ignominy of being stripped naked in front of his colleagues for his half-assed conduct, or the mitigating honor of being dispatched by "Maximum John."

"It has recently come to my attention . . ." Sirica began recounting the unfortunate facts . . .

The Judge peered out into the audience. "Now I want it understood by the person who approached members of this grand jury that the court regards the matter as extremely serious." . . .

Sirica was scowling. He noted thoughtfully that the person who had attempted to subvert the sanctity of the grand-jury proceedings was neither defendant nor counsel but . . . "a news media representative." A buzz in the assembled press corps. Who among them? Bernstein and Woodward waited for the Judge to unmask them and, maybe, to ask if they wished to throw themselves on the mercy of the court.

First, however, Sirica desired to point out the legal ramifications and to remind the assembly that attempting to gain information from a grand juror is, "at least potentially," a contemptuous offense. Then he excused the grand jury and strode from the court. The clerk declared a recess.

It took the reporters several moments to understand what had happened, that that was the end of it. They had gone free.

Bernstein and Woodward tried to look nonchalant as their colleagues asked who they thought was guilty. They declined to speculate. Dan Schorr of CBS, who knew a sham when he spotted one, was the first to suggest, privately, that Bernstein and Woodward were the offenders. Hearsay, innuendo and character assassination, protested Bernstein. . . .

. . . Accused again, Woodward said the first thing that came into his head: the grand-jury contact had taken place over the first weekend in December. That was six weeks after he and Bernstein had written a major story. Somehow, the compelling illogic of the syllogism got by. Bernstein, feeling grubby, listened raptly to another newsman explain why the offender was probably a radio or television reporter, not someone from a newspaper. "Sirica specifically used the phrase 'news media representative.' That's the term he always uses when he's talking about radio and television reporters. When he means newspaper reporters, he says 'the press.'" Yeah, said Bernstein, he thought he had noticed that, too.

Woodward and Bernstein were trying to avoid a colleague who was interviewing reporters in the hallway about the session in Sirica's courtroom. He caught up with Woodward near the elevator and asked point-blank if the Judge had been referring to him or Bernstein. . . .

Listen, Woodward snapped. Do you want a quote? Are we talking for the record? I mean, are you serious? Because if you are, I'll give you something, all right.

The reporter seemed stunned. "Sorry, Bob, I didn't think you'd take me seriously," he told Woodward. . . .

. . . They felt lousy. They had not broken the law when they visited the grand jurors, that much seemed certain. But they had sailed around it and exposed others to danger. They had chosen expediency over principle and, caught in the act, their role had been covered up. They had dodged, evaded, misrepresented, suggested and intimidated, even if they had not lied outright.

That afternoon, Woodward returned to Judge Sirica's courtroom for the hearing on the *Los Angeles Times'* Baldwin material. The notes, tapes and related documents of reporters Jack Nelson and Ronald Ostrow had been subpoenaed by lawyers for the Watergate defendants.

The *Times'* interview with Baldwin had been the most vivid piece of journalism in the whole Watergate saga, definitively portraying the difference between a "third-rate burglary attempt" and the brand of political gang warfare practiced by the President's men. Woodward, remembering his own dealings with Alfred Baldwin's lawyers, doubted there would have been any interview without assurances that the tapes and notes would remain in the *Times*' possession. Certainly, the stories Bernstein and he had done could not have been written without such guarantees.

The Judge ordered John F. Lawrence, the *Los Angeles Times*' bureau chief in Washington, to turn over the tapes, which the paper had placed in his custody.

"I must respectfully decline," Lawrence, a thin man in his late thirties, said mildly.

Sirica held him in contempt and ordered him jailed. . . .

Bernstein had rarely seen Woodward so shaken. They were both painfully aware of the contrast. Lawrence, whose only offense had been to act professionally and to follow his conscience, was in jail. They had gotten off with a lecture and with their secret intact.

The grand-jury adventure was not the reporters' last encounter with Judge Sirica or the prosecutors.

Several days after their court appearance, Woodward phoned a former secretary in the office of Morton B. Jackson, a Los Angeles lawyer with whom Hunt had stayed during the week following the Watergate break-in. Woodward identified himself and explained that he knew she had been interviewed by the FBI.

"Leave me alone," she said. "I have my life to live. I can't stand it. Why do you want to bother me?" . . .

The next day, Bradlee called Woodward and Bernstein to his office. "Williams got another call from the prosecutors. . . . Some woman from California complained that one of you phoned her and said you were an FBI agent."

Bernstein broke up laughing at the thought of Woodward as an FBI agent. But Bradlee was serious. During the hearing on the Baldwin tapes, Sirica had directed all potential witnesses in the case not to talk to reporters until after the trial.

"Now we're back with Sirica," Bradlee said "The prosecutors had to go to the Judge. They don't think you posed as an FBI agent. But they think you might have violated the witness rule."

Bradlee said that Ed Williams would visit Sirica again. Bernstein complained that it would be impossible to continue the investigation if he and Woodward couldn't talk to witnesses. Bradlee agreed. "Until we get it settled," he said "you're going to have to stay away from witnesses completely."

The reporters asked how they were supposed to know whether someone was a witness.

No way, Bradlee said, so you'll have to stop your reporting—that is, stop digging new ground—until this is settled. . . .

Two days later, Bradlee put new ground rules in writing. Copies went to Rosenfeld, Sussman, Woodward and Bernstein: "Williams talked to Sirica this morning. It is OK for us to talk to witnesses... PROVIDED that the minute a witness tells us he or she has been forbidden by the court to talk to us, we call off the dogs. And that means *the minute* they tell us that. In other words, we can *not* try to talk a witness into talking if that witness has expressed an understanding that he or she is not supposed to talk. We *must* live up to the spirit and the letter of this ground rule."

Later that week, they stopped by the office of [prosecutor] Earl Silbert to discuss the guidelines....

... Woodward noticed a letter on Silbert's desk, and recognized the letterhead—The Watkins-Johnson Company of Rockville, Maryland. Woodward knew it was the company where McCord had bought some of the equipment used to bug the Watergate.

He mentioned it to Bernstein as they took a cab back to the *Post*. So what? Bernstein said. Woodward didn't know, but he got on the phone to the company the next morning, and learned that McCord had left his CRP calling card when he bought the equipment, and had paid with $100 bills—35 of them.

Woodward wrote a brief story about the transaction which ran December 23 on the inside of the paper.

The next Monday, Bernstein got a call from Silbert saying that he wanted to see the two of them in his office at once. Bernstein had no idea what Silbert wanted. Woodward figured that Silbert had put together the information on the $3500 radio and their having seen the letter on his desk. Bernstein thought it was inconceivable that Silbert would be calling them down for such a trivial matter, especially since they already had some documents on McCord's purchase.

When they arrived, Silbert and his associate, Seymour Glanzer, were wearing very stern expressions. Silbert demanded to know the source of the radio story. The letter was in the same position on his desk, at the far lefthand corner, clearly in sight from where Woodward sat. Woodward said he had seen the letter and decided to call Watkins-Johnson to learn if anything new had come up about the equipment since the reporters had last checked.

"For me to believe that," Silbert said, "you're going to have to tell me your original source of information."

They refused.

Silbert was persuaded that their information had come from the letter, and only the letter. He threatened to circulate a memorandum in the U.S. Attorney's office, telling everyone about the incident and recommending that no one there ever again talk with Woodward or Bernstein. He was considering taking legal action. If he let something slip in conversation, Silbert added, it was perfectly proper for the reporters to use it. But to get information off someone's desk was "sneaky and outrageous." Glanzer said it was dishonest.

Bernstein had learned years before that the ability to read upside down could be a useful reportorial skill, but he did not disagree strongly with the prosecutors, and he apologized profusely. Woodward also apologized, but he thought Silbert and Glanzer were being irrational, and said so.

Silbert said he didn't know if he could ever trust the two reporters again.

If the prosecutors took any action on the matter, Woodward and Bernstein did not hear of it.

DISCUSSION POINTS

1   What ethical dilemmas did Woodward and Bernstein face? Do you agree with how they resolved these matters? Why or why not?

2   Are you surprised by how much contact Woodward and Bernstein had with their colleagues from other media sources as well as with officials of the Justice Department? Why or why not? What does this contact tell you about the nature of the media?

3   Woodward professes to have some unusual skills that assist him in his reporting. What are these skills and does their use raise any ethical concerns?

— 31 —

On Being an Anchorman

DAVID BRINKLEY

It may be difficult for news consumers born in the post-cable era to appreciate the role that network news anchors played in prior generations' lives. When television news began in the 1950s, viewers did not have the plethora of viewing choices that they have today. Nor were there Internet news sites. Television viewers chose among the three networks which typically offered one national news show. These anchors tended to stay in the anchor seat for significant periods of time, and as a result, many became central figures in the lives of the viewing audience. It was the anchor who told listeners what was happening, why what had happened was important, what might happen, and on occasion, what should happen. Many viewers reported that they knew or had even grown up with their favorite anchors. The late NBC anchor, David Brinkley, one of the 20th century's most prominent and influential television news personalities, looks back on a career spent in front of the television camera discussing public affairs. He discusses the special relationship of the anchor and audience as well as issues related to just what happens when journalists, especially anchors, take themselves and their powers too seriously.

... The anchor's role is difficult to assess, because there is nothing to compare to it. Newspaper reporters and editors do some of the same work, but they are not more or less personally in the living room every night and are not instantly recognizable in airports, poolrooms and saloons. But the great difference, I think, is that in a night-to-night or day-to-day relationship with tens of millions of people, the anchor gives the news a kind of dimension and character it never had before, mediated through his own voice and appearance and personality. The news then becomes not just what happened but what a familiar face and voice says happened, and the meaning of it is to some extent determined by how he says it.

It is a strange relationship, and only a few people have experienced it in the half century or so since television news became a significant force in American life. Between the anchor and the audience, there is a kind of intimate remoteness. They know his clothes and his haircuts and to some extent his likes and dislikes. They watch him get older. They feel they know him, and in a way they do. But he does not know them.

By now, it has become accepted as journalism. But it bears only a scant relationship to the journalism we knew in the past—and anc still know in news media other than broadcasting. Television news is not merely the same news delivered in a different way. It is different because the means of its delivery changes its meaning to its audience and because it reaches more, and different, people—many of them barely, if at all, reached by other news . . .

In my view, television news tends more to reinforce the existing social and political values than to change them, and the recurring cry that it and other news media excessively influence public opinion in one political direction or another seems to me an empty claim. It must be if, after a half century of news reporting that has been regularly charged with being too liberal, we have recently elected some of our most conservative presidents.

TV anchors and reporters serve the useful public function of delivering the goods, attractively wrapped in the hope of attracting some millions of people to tune in. In recent decades, I fear, the wrapping has sometimes become too attractive and much television news, in response to economic pressures, competition and perhaps a basic lack of commitment to the integrity and value of the enterprise, has become so trivial and devoid of content as to be little different from entertainment programming. But even at its best, television news is driven less by the ideology of those who deliver it than by the pressures of the medium itself. And as a result, individual journalists, from the anchors to the local news beat reporters, are all constrained in their power by the skepticism of a public that from the beginning saw in television something closer to the tradition of entertainment (movies, theater and the like) than to the tradition of the press.

The television journalist does have the power to steer the public's attention in one direction or another. He can make an obscure person famous for a day or two, but not much longer than that, unless the person is then able to hold the public's attention with his own resources. Television can keep a story alive but it cannot ensure that the public will continue to believe in it. The year or more during which the news media was obsessed with the Monica Lewinsky scandal, for example, saw a significant rise in President Clinton's public approval ratings and a significant decline in the media's.

There is no question that television anchors have become enormously famous. Most of my adult life has been shaped by that reality. But I do not believe that I, or my fellow anchors, have become famous for our power to influence uncritical masses of people, or for our ability to change the social or political order, or to elect a candidate or defeat one. So what are we famous for? Mainly, we are famous for being famous.

To survive, an anchor must convince millions of people that he is at least modestly competent, that he has some idea of what he is talking about, and that he is playing it straight, and that is about all. He might also wear a tie and keep his suits pressed and comb his hair if he has any (and virtually all anchors have quite a lot).

I believe that all of the network anchors of my time have done that pretty well, and I tried to do the same. But is there any real power? I believe not. Over the years, several television newsmen, not understanding that they were famous only for being famous, have run for political office. Most of them lost.

DISCUSSION POINTS

1   Why does Brinkley suggest that the news media's supposed power to affect the views of its viewing public are exaggerated?

2   Why does Brinkley describe the relationship between the anchor and the audience as "strange"?

3   Brinkley appears to suggest that broadcast journalism is somehow less pure a breed of journalism than other forms such as print. Why do you think he would write such? How does broadcast journalism differ from other forms of journalism?

─── PART EIGHT ───

The Media and the Law: Private Efforts to Restrict the Free Press

THE FRENCH STUDENT OF AMERICAN DEMOCRACY, Alexis de Tocqueville, has written quite famously that "there is hardly a political question in the United States that does not sooner or later turn into a judicial one." This quotation from Tocqueville's *Democracy in America* is a favorite of scholars and students alike, so much so that it has almost become obligatory to cite it. Its ubiquity traces perhaps from the fact that in American history it has been our courts that have often had the final word on important questions of legal, social, or economic policy. This has been particularly true of disputes over the right of the press in America.

This part focuses on private efforts to use the courts to curb press freedoms. Each of these episodes resulted in landmark Supreme Court cases. The opinions from these cases have been excerpted here.

Three of the conflicts involving private attempts to restrict the press are defamation suits. These defamation suits, *New York Times v. Sullivan* (1964), *Time Inc. v. Hill* (1967), and *Gertz v. Welch, Inc.* (1974), have run the gambit when it comes to the variety of parties involved: Plaintiffs include an elected local official, the reluctant subject of a play, and a private attorney, while defendants include a major newspaper, a major magazine, and a smaller publication affiliated with a right-wing political association. All three cases have involved major doctrinal decisions on the Court's part. Readers should note the promulgation of the actual malice test and pay special attention to when and to whom this test is applied.

The remaining cases do not involve the application or creation of any press doctrine. Yet, they offer important legal precedent for our system of free expression. The first, *Hustler Magazine v. Falwell* (1988), is memorable both for the parties involved (publisher Larry Flynt versus Reverend Jerry Falwell) and for the Court's refusal to allow punishing political speech because it is in bad taste. The second, *Cohen v. Cowles Media Co.* (1991), affirmed the idea that the press, which frequently promises to keep sources confidential, can be sued for breaking its word to secret sources whose identities it later reveals. This ruling opens the door to the possibility that the press might one day be squeezed between government subpoenas to reveal the identity of secret sources and the threat of being sued by the sources whom the press would name.

A Small Glossary of Legal Terms

In the pages that follow, we will encounter some legal terms that we best define here.

certiorari — From the *Latin* for "be informed of." It is a judicial order instructing a lower court to send the records of a case to a higher court for review.

petitioner — The party that brings an appeal. It is the party that lost the most recent round of a legal dispute and petitions the court for relief. Synonymous with plaintiff or appellant.

respondent — The party that responds to the petitioner's appeal. It is the party that won the most recent round of a legal dispute and petitions the court for relief. Synonymous with defendant or appellee.

injunction — A court order instructing a party not to take a certain action.

remand — To return a case back to a lower court for the purpose of instructing that court to carry out a certain action.

vacate — When a court sets aside the ruling or action of a lower court.

estoppel law — A law protecting individuals from being injured by the actions of others. A promissory estoppel protects one party in a contract from injury. In the case of *Cohen v. Cowels Media Co.* (1991) Cohen was protected against his name being revealed by the reporters (see page 234).

— 32 —

New York Times Co. v. Sullivan
376 U.S. 254 (1964)

Set during the 1960s civil rights movement, this is one of the most important, if not the most important, Supreme Court interpretation of the First Amendment's free press clause. The dispute that gave rise to the case concerned defamation.* The real issue in the case, however, was whether opponents of racial integration could run one of the nation's leading pro-racial integration newspapers, and presumably any pro-integration newspaper, out of business.

The prevalent view of defamation in the 18th and 19th centuries was that society needed to protect its "best men" from attacks on their reputation lest these "best men" shrink from public service.† Thus, courts and the law dealt with defamatory expressions quite severely. This was especially true of published defamations that typically concerned elites. Traditionally, defamation was a state issue. The U.S. Supreme Court said as much in U.S. v. Hudson & Goodwin *(1812). The Court reiterated that position in* Chaplinsky v. New Hampshire *(1942). In that case, the Court held that there are certain forms of speech that are of such slight social value that they are not entitled to full First Amendment protection. Among speech of such inferior value was defamation. Twenty years later, the Court, in* Sullivan, *revisited the principles established in* Hudson & Goodwin *and* Chaplinsky. Sullivan *stands as a sharp turn-away from* Hudson & Goodwin, *however, the Court's development of the Actual Malice Test*

---

* To defame someone is to publish or speak words that damage or injure that person's character or reputation. Published defamations are called libels. Spoken defamations are called slander.
† See article #3, Norman Rosenberg's *Protecting the Best Men: An Interpretive History of the Law of Libel*. Chapel Hill: University of North Carolina Press, 1986.

in Sullivan *allowed it to leave the central holding of* Chaplinsky *in tack while creating an exception for defamation made without actual malice.*

In 1960, the New York Times *had published an advertisement "Heed Their Rising Voices" in which the authors criticized police brutality in Alabama against civil rights protestors. The ad did not name any names, but it contained several pieces of information that were inaccurate. L.B. Sullivan, a Montgomery City Commissioner, sued the* Times *for libel. Although Sullivan was not listed by name in the ad, an Alabama jury awarded him $500,000 for damages. The* Times *appealed to the Supreme Court. Before the case was decided, eleven other local officials, all unnamed by the* Times *article, filed suit against the newspaper seeking $5 million dollars in damages. If such suits succeeded, it was likely that more would follow, and newspapers could be run out of business by excessive defamation awards stemming from publications that were critical of the government and its policies or its leaders.*

Justice BRENNAN delivered the opinion of the Court.

We are required in this case to determine for the first time the extent to which the constitutional protections for speech and press limit a State's power to award damages in a libel action brought by a public official against critics of his official conduct.

Under Alabama law as applied in this case, a publication is "libelous per se" if the words "tend to injure a person . . . in his reputation" or to "bring [him] into public contempt"; the trial court stated that the standard was met if the words are such as to "injure him in his public office, or impute misconduct to him in his office, or want of official integrity, or want of fidelity to a public trust . . . ." The jury must find that the words were published "of and concerning" the plaintiff, but where the plaintiff is a public official his place in the governmental hierarchy is sufficient evidence to support a finding that his reputation has been affected by statements that reflect upon the agency of which he is in charge. Once "libel per se" has been established, the defendant has no defense as to stated facts unless he can persuade the jury that they were true in all their particulars . . . The question before us is whether this rule of liability, as applied to an action brought by a public official against critics of his official conduct, abridges the freedom of speech and of the press that is guaranteed by the first and Fourteenth Amendments.

Respondent relies heavily, as did the Alabama courts, on statements of this Court to the effect that the Constitution does not protect libelous publications. These statements do not foreclose our inquiry here. None of the cases sustained the use of libel laws to impose sanctions upon expression critical of the official conduct of public officials . . . Like insurrection, contempt, advocacy of unlawful acts, breach of the peace, obscenity, solicitation of legal business, and the various other formulae for the repression of expression that have been challenged in this court, libel can claim no talismanic immunity from constitutional limitations. It must be measured by standards that satisfy the First Amendment.

The general proposition that freedom of expression upon public questions is secured by the First Amendment has long been settled by our decisions ... Thus we consider this case against the background of a profound national commitment to the principle that debate on public issues should be uninhibited, robust, and wide-open, and that it may well include vehement, caustic, and sometimes unpleasantly sharp attacks on government and public officials. The present advertisement, as an expression of grievance and protest on one of the major public issues of our time, would seem clearly to qualify for the constitutional protection. The question is whether it forfeits that protection by the falsity of some of its factual statements and by its alleged defamation of respondent.

Authoritative interpretations of the First Amendment guarantees have consistently refused to recognize an exception for any test of truth—whether administered by judges, juries, or administrative officials—and especially one that puts the burden of proving truth on the speaker. The constitutional protection does not turn upon "the truth, popularity, or social utility of the ideas and beliefs which are offered." *N. A. A. C. P. v. Button* (1963). As Madison said, "Some degree of abuse is inseparable from the proper use of every thing; and in no instance is this more true than in that of the press." *4 Elliot's Debates on the Federal Constitution* (1876), p. 571 ... That erroneous statement is inevitable in free debate, and that it must be protected if the freedoms of expression are to have the "breathing space" that they "need ... to survive," *N. A. A. C. P. v. Button* (1963).

Injury to official reputation affords no more warrant for repressing speech that would otherwise be free than does factual error. Where judicial officers are involved, this Court has held that concern for the dignity and reputation of the courts does not justify the punishment as criminal contempt of criticism of the judge or his decision. *Bridges v. California*. This is true even though the utterance contains "half-truths" and "misinformation." Such repression can be justified, if at all, only by a clear and present danger of the obstruction of justice ... If judges are to be treated as "men of fortitude, able to thrive in a hardy climate," surely the same must be true of other government officials, such as elected city commissioners. Criticism of their official conduct does not lose its constitutional protection merely because it is effective criticism and hence diminishes their official reputations.

If neither factual error nor defamatory content suffices to remove the constitutional shield from criticism of official conduct, the combination of the two elements is no less inadequate. This is the lesson to be drawn from the great controversy over the Sedition Act of 1798 . . . which first crystallized a national awareness of the central meaning of the First Amendment. See Levy, *Legacy of Suppression* (1960), at 258; Smith, *Freedom's Fetters* (1956), at 426, 431 . . .

Madison prepared the *Report [of the Virginia Legislature against the Alien and Sedition Acts of 1798]* in support of the protest. His premise was that the Constitution created a form of government under which "The people, not the government, possess the absolute sovereignty." . . . Earlier, in a debate in the House of Representatives, Madison had said: "If we advert to the nature of Republican Government, we shall find that the censorial power is in the people over the Government, and not in the Government over the people." *4 Annals of Congress,* p. 934 (1794) The right of free public discussion of the stewardship of public officials was thus, in Madison's view, a fundamental principle of the American form of government.

The state rule of law is not saved by its allowance of the defense of truth . . . Allowance of the defense of truth, with the burden of proving it on the defendant, does not mean that only false speech will be deterred.* Under such a rule, would-be critics of official conduct may be deterred from voicing their criticism, even though it is believed to be true and even though it is in fact true, because of doubt whether it can be proved in court or fear of the expense of having to do so . . . The rule thus dampens the vigor and limits the variety of public debate. It is inconsistent with the First and Fourteenth Amendments.

The constitutional guarantees require, we think, a federal rule that prohibits a public official from recovering damages for a defamatory falsehood relating to his official conduct unless he proves that the statement was made with "actual malice"—that is, with knowledge that it was false or with reckless disregard of whether it was false or not.

Such a privilege for criticism of official conduct is appropriately analogous to the protection accorded a public official when he is sued for libel by a private citizen . . . The reason for the official privilege is said to be that the threat of damage suits would otherwise "inhibit the fearless, vigorous, and effective administration of policies of government" and "dampen the ardor of all but the most resolute, or the most irresponsible, in the unflinching discharge of their duties." Analogous considerations support the privilege for the citizen-critic of government. It is as much his duty to criticize as it is the official's duty to

---

* The Court included at this point FOOTNOTE 19 which read: "Even a false statement may be deemed to make a valuable contribution to public debate, since it brings about "the clearer perception and livelier impression of truth, produced by its collision with error." Mill, *On Liberty* (Oxford: Blackwell, 1947), at 15; see also Milton, *Areopagitica*, in *Prose Works* (Yale, 1959), Vol. II, at 561."

administer. It would give public servants an unjustified preference over the public they serve, if critics of official conduct did not have a fair equivalent of the immunity granted to the officials themselves. We conclude that such a privilege is required by the First and Fourteenth Amendments . . .

[W]e consider that the proof presented to show actual malice lacks the convincing clarity which the constitutional standard demands, and hence that it would not constitutionally sustain the judgment for respondent under the proper rule of law . . . We also think the evidence was constitutionally defective in another respect: it was incapable of supporting the jury's finding that the allegedly libelous statements were made "of and concerning" respondent . . . There was no reference to respondent in the advertisement, either by name or official position.

The judgment of the Supreme Court of Alabama is reversed and the case is remanded to that court for further proceedings not inconsistent with this opinion.

Reversed and remanded.

Justice BLACK, with whom Justice DOUGLAS joins, concurring.

I concur . . . I base my vote to reverse on the belief that the First and Fourteenth Amendments not merely "delimit" a State's power to award damages to "public officials against critics of their official conduct" but completely prohibit a State from exercising such a power. The Court goes on to hold that a State can subject such critics to damages if "actual malice" can be proved against them. "Malice," even as defined by the Court, is an elusive, abstract concept, hard to prove and hard to disprove. The requirement that malice be proved provides at best an evanescent protection for the right critically to discuss public affairs and certainly does not measure up to the sturdy safeguard embodied in the First Amendment.

In my opinion the Federal Constitution has dealt with this deadly danger to the press in the only way possible without leaving the free press open to destruction—by granting the press an absolute immunity for criticism of the way public officials do their public duty.

To punish the exercise of this right to discuss public affairs or to penalize it through libel judgments is to abridge or shut off discussion of the very kind most needed. This Nation, I suspect, can live in peace without libel suits based on public discussions of public affairs and public officials. But I doubt that a country can live in freedom where its people can be made to suffer physically or financially for criticizing their government, its actions, or its officials. "For a representative democracy ceases to exist the moment that the public functionaries are by any means absolved from their responsibility to their constituents; and this happens whenever the constituent can be restrained in any manner from speaking, writing, or publishing his opinions upon any public measure, or upon the conduct of those who may advise or execute it."* An unconditional right to say what one pleases about public affairs is what I consider to be the minimum guarantee of the First Amendment.

I regret that the Court has stopped short of this holding indispensable to preserve our free press from destruction.

Justice GOLDBERG with whom Justice DOUGLAS joins, concurring in the result.

The Court today announces a constitutional standard which prohibits "a public official from recovering damages for a defamatory falsehood relating to his official conduct unless he proves that the statement was made with 'actual malice'—that is, with knowledge that it was false or with reckless disregard of whether it was false or not." *Ante*, at 279–280. The Court thus rules that the Constitution gives citizens and newspapers a "conditional privilege" immunizing nonmalicious misstatements of fact regarding the official conduct of a government officer. The impressive array of history and precedent marshaled by the Court, however, confirms my belief that the Constitution affords greater protection than that provided by the Court's standard to citizen and press in exercising the right of public criticism.

In my view, the First and Fourteenth Amendments to the Constitution afford to the citizen and to the press an absolute, unconditional privilege to criticize official conduct despite the harm which may flow from excesses and abuses... The right should not depend upon a probing by the jury of the motivation of the citizen or press. The theory of our Constitution is that every citizen may speak his mind and every newspaper express its view on matters of public concern and may not be barred from speaking or publishing because those in control of government think that what is said or written is unwise, unfair, false, or malicious. In a democratic society, one who assumes to act for the citizens in an executive, legislative, or judicial capacity must expect that his official acts will be commented upon and criticized. Such criticism cannot, in my opinion, be muzzled or deterred by the courts at the instance of public officials under the label of libel...

This is not to say that the Constitution protects defamatory statements directed against the private conduct of a public official or private citizen. Freedom of press and of speech insures that government will respond to the will of the people and that changes may be obtained by

---

* Justice Black inserted at this point FOOTNOTE 5 which read: "1 Tucker, *Blackstone's Commentaries* (1803), 297 (editor's appendix); cf. Brant, *Seditious Libel: Myth and Reality*, 39 N. Y. U. L. Rev. 1."

peaceful means. Purely private defamation has little to do with the political ends of a self-governing society.

The conclusion that the Constitution affords the citizen and the press an absolute privilege for criticism of official conduct does not leave the public official without defenses against unsubstantiated opinions or deliberate misstatements. "Under our system of government, counterargument and education are the weapons available to expose these matters, not abridgment . . . of free speech . . . ." *Wood v. Georgia.* The public official certainly has equal if not greater access than most private citizens to media of communication.

For these reasons, I strongly believe that the Constitution accords citizens and press an unconditional freedom to criticize official conduct. It necessarily follows that in a case such as this, where all agree that the allegedly defamatory statements related to official conduct, the judgments for libel cannot constitutionally be sustained.

DISCUSSION POINTS

1   Do you agree with the majority opinion in this case?

2   What are the likely implications of this decision? Why is this case so important? What would have been the likely effect on the press had the *New York Times* lost?

3   Note that this decision applied the Actual Malice Test, as per the facts, to defamation suits brought by public officials such as elected or appointed public officials. This means that future courts would use this test in cases brought by public officials. It did not yet apply this test to those brought by public figures such as celebrities.

4   How would you rank the three opinions by Justices Brennan, Black, and Goldberg in terms of: which is most pro-free press? which is the least pro-free press? and which would be in the middle of these two extremes? Which of these three opinions do you find most convincing and why?

5   Note that by "joining in the judgment" ("the vote on the merits" rather than "joining in the opinion") Justices Black, Douglas, and Goldberg were indicating their support for the Court's verdict rather than the rationale that the majority provided for its decision.

Time, Inc. v. Hill

385 U.S. 374 (1967)

In 1952, James Hill and his family were held hostage in their Pennsylvania home for 19 hours by three escaped convicts. They were released unharmed. The Hills later moved from their home in an effort to avoid subsequent publicity about the experience. Joseph Hayes, an author, published a novel that was loosely based on the incident. Hayes, who later turned the novel into a play, took considerable liberties with the facts. In his account, the Hills were abused both physically and verbally. In 1955, LIFE *magazine published an article about the play which seemed to suggest that the play was accurate. The story even included photographs of scenes that were staged in the Hill's former home.*

James Hill sued Time, Inc., the owner of LIFE, *both for falsely implying that the play was accurate and for invasion of privacy. He sought to invoke a New York statute enacted in 1903 that forbid the unauthorized commercial use of a person's name or picture. The statute in question limited the ability of advertisers to use a person's photographic image without obtaining that individual's permission. The law made no mention of limiting newspapers to discuss private lives. Hill, however, asked the courts to interpret New York's privacy statute in a novel way so as to look past the legislature's immediate intention (limiting the use of photos in ads) to its purpose (establishing a general right of privacy). In response to the suit,* LIFE *argued that the Hill's story was one of public interest and that it had not intended to injure the Hills. A jury found for the Hills and* Time, Inc. *appealed to the Supreme Court.*

Justice BRENNAN delivered the opinion of the Court.
 The question in this case is whether appellant, publisher of *LIFE*

magazine, was denied constitutional protections of speech and press by the application [of New York privacy laws] to award appellee damages on allegations that *LIFE* falsely reported that a new play portrayed an experience suffered by appellee and his family.

[New York courts have] made crystal clear in [its past decisions] that truth is a complete defense in actions under the statute based upon reports of newsworthy people or events . . .

If this [truth standard] is meant to imply that proof of knowing or reckless falsity is not essential to a constitutional application of the statute in these cases, we disagree with the Court of Appeals. We hold that the constitutional protections for speech and press preclude the application of the New York statute to redress false reports of matters of public interest in the absence of proof that the defendant published the report with knowledge of its falsity or in reckless disregard of the truth.

The guarantees for speech and press are not the preserve of political expression or comment upon public affairs, essential as those are to healthy government. . . . We have no doubt that the subject of the *LIFE* article, the opening of a new play linked to an actual incident, is a matter of public interest. "The line between the informing and the entertaining is too elusive for the protection of . . . [freedom of the press]." *Winters v. New York.* Erroneous statement is no less inevitable in such a case than in the case of comment upon public affairs, and in both, if innocent or merely negligent, ". . . it must be protected if the freedoms of expression are to have the 'breathing space' that they 'need . . . to survive'. . . . " *New York Times Co. v. Sullivan.*

In this context, sanctions against either innocent or negligent misstatement would present a grave hazard of discouraging the press from exercising the constitutional guarantees. Those guarantees are not for the benefit of the press so much as for the benefit of all of us. A broadly defined freedom of the press assures the maintenance of our political system and an open society. Fear of large verdicts in damage suits for innocent or merely negligent misstatement, even fear of the expense involved in their defense, must inevitably cause publishers to "steer . . . wider of the unlawful zone," *New York Times Co. v. Sullivan.*

We find applicable here the standard of knowing or reckless falsehood, not through blind application of *New York Times Co. v. Sullivan*, relating solely to libel actions by public officials, but only upon consideration of the factors which arise in the particular context of the application of the New York statute in cases involving private individuals. This is neither a libel action by a private individual nor a statutory action by a public official [But rather one involving a public figure]. Therefore, although the First Amendment principles pronounced in *New York Times* guide our conclusion, we reach that conclusion only by applying these principles in this discrete context. It therefore serves no purpose to distinguish the facts here from those in *New York Times*. Were this a libel action, the distinction which has been suggested between the relative opportunities of the public official and the private individual to rebut defamatory charges might be germane. And the additional state interest in the protection of the individual against damage to his reputation would be involved. *Cf. Rosenblatt v. Baer*, (STEWART, J., concurring). Moreover, a different test might be required in a statutory action by a public official, as opposed to a libel action by a public official or a statutory action by a private individual. Different considerations might arise concerning the degree of "waiver" of the protection the State might afford. But the question whether the same standard should be applicable both to persons voluntarily and involuntarily thrust into the public limelight is not here before us.

DISCUSSION POINTS

1   What is your opinion of the Court's decision in this case? Was it correct to side with *LIFE* magazine? Are you persuaded by the Court's rationale?

2   In this case, the court recognizes a category of defamation subjects known as public figures. Public figures are either celebrities who seek the public spotlight or otherwise private citizens who, intentionally or not, have become the subject of legitimate news stories.

3   Note that this is not a defamation case *per se*. Justice Brennan, however, who was renowned for his adroitness when it came to writing judicial opinions, all but treats Hill's case as a defamation suit filed by what has come to be called a public figure. Public figures are granted less expectation of privacy from the media either by virtue of seeking public attention (such as releasing a film) or by being the subject of matters of genuine public concern (in this case a hostage taking). By holding that the Actual Malice Test ought to be used in tort cases such as Hill's, the Court, while not formally, in essence established that the Actual Malice Test will be the test that is used in defamation cases brought by public figures. It is possible that Brennan lacked a majority to formally announce that the Actual Malice Test would be the test used in defamation cases brought by public figures. This tactic of calling the case one thing, while treating it as another, may have been Brennan's clever way of applying the Actual Malice to defamation suits involving public figures by going through the proverbial judicial backdoor.

4   How does the Court's holding affect relations between public figures and the media?

34

Gertz v. Robert Welch, Inc.
418 U.S. 323 (1974)

As far as technical matters of the law go, Gertz v. Robert Welch *(1974) is significant because it clarified the judicial standard that would be used in defamation suits brought by private citizens. Prior cases such as* New York Times v. Sullivan *(1964) and* Time, Inc. v. Hill *(1967) had only spoken to what happens when public officials or public figures are defamed. The law provides the media with pretty good protection when it defames public officials or public figures. The law was unclear about what to do when private citizens find their reputations or character attacked. What was clear was that if the states applied the Actual Malice Test to lawsuits brought by private citizens against the media, private citizens would be unlikely to be able to recover damages for defamation. Unlike public officials or public figures, private citizens would be unlikely to have much recourse outside of the courts to defend their reputations.*

Elmer Gertz was a Chicago attorney known both for his role in several high-profile criminal defenses* and for his strong advocacy of civil rights and liberties.† Under the terms of the law, Gertz was also a private citizen who was attacked in the press for doing his job. Most of us are private persons and if private

---

* Among Gertz's clients were Jack Ruby (murderer of President John F. Kennedy's assassin Lee Harvey Oswald), Henry Miller (author of *Tropic of Cancer*), and Nathan Leopold (convicted along with Richard Loeb in a 1920s kidnapping and murder trial that was dubbed "The Crime of the Century"). Gertz successfully defended Ruby against the death penalty and Miller against charges of obscenity. In 1958, after Leopold had served more than thirty years of a life sentence, Gertz convinced Illinois to parole his client.

† Gertz had played a leading role in writing and winning the adoption of an Illinois Bill of Rights.

persons can be defamed by the press for doing our jobs the effect might be to dissuade many of us from practicing our vocations in a vigilant manner.

In 1968, a Chicago policeman shot and killed a teenager. The officer was convicted of second-degree murder. The victim's family retained Gertz to represent them in civil litigation against the officer. It is Gertz's decision to represent the family that led to this case.

American Opinion, a newspaper published by a conservative organization known as the John Birch Society, alleged that the lawsuit that Gertz filed was part of a wider Communist conspiracy to discredit the nation's local police with the ultimate goal being to replace local police with a national police force which would then take over the country. The article falsely alleged that Gertz had framed the officer. It further implied that Gertz had a criminal record, and it labeled him a "Communist-fronter." Gertz sued the American Opinion's *publisher, Robert Welch, for libel. Libel refers to printed assertions that damage someone's reputation. A federal jury found for Gertz; but a federal trial court and a federal appeals court set the judgment aside because Gertz had failed to satisfy the Actual Malice Test. Gertz appealed to the Supreme Court.*

Justice POWELL delivered the opinion of the Court.

This Court has struggled for nearly a decade to define the proper accommodation between the law of defamation and the freedoms of speech and press protected by the First Amendment. With this decision we return to that effort. We granted *certiorari* to reconsider the extent of a publisher's constitutional privilege against liability for defamation of a private citizen.

In his capacity as counsel for the Nelson family in the civil litigation, petitioner attended the coroner's inquest into the boy's death and initiated actions for damages, but he neither discussed Officer Nuccio with the press nor played any part in the criminal proceeding. Notwithstanding petitioner's remote connection with the prosecution of Nuccio, respondent's magazine portrayed him as an architect of the "frame-up."

[The article] contained serious inaccuracies . . .

The managing editor of *American Opinion* made no effort to verify or substantiate the charges against petitioner. [Welch asserted that Gertz was a public figure and had the paper's editor testify that the article's author had a reputation for accuracy and that the paper did not know that the charges were false.]

The principal issue in this case is whether a newspaper or broadcaster that publishes defamatory falsehoods about an individual who is neither a public official nor a public figure may claim a constitutional privilege against liability for the injury inflicted by those statements. The Court considered this question . . . in *Rosenbloom v. Metromedia*, (1971). The eight Justices who participated in *Rosenbloom* announced their views in five separate opinions, none of which commanded more than three votes . . .

In affirming the trial court's judgment in the instant case, the Court of Appeals relied on Mr. Justice BRENNAN's conclusion for the *Rosenbloom* plurality that "all discussion and communication involving matters of public or general concern," warrant the protection from liability for defamation accorded by the rule originally enunciated in *New York Times Co. v. Sullivan* (1964) . . . [Such included] defamatory falsehoods relating to private persons if the statements concerned matters of general or public interest . . . Thus, under the plurality opinion, a private citizen involuntarily associated with a matter of general interest has no recourse for injury to his reputation unless he can satisfy the demanding requirements of the *New York Times* test.

We begin with the common ground. Under the First Amendment there is no such thing as a false idea. However pernicious an opinion may seem, we depend for its correction not on the conscience of judges and juries but on the competition of other ideas. But there is no constitutional value in false statements of fact . . .

Although the erroneous statement of fact is not worthy of constitutional protection, it is nevertheless inevitable in free debate. As James Madison pointed out in the *Report on the Virginia Resolutions of 1798*: "Some degree of abuse is inseparable from the proper use of every thing; and in no instance is this more true than in that of the press." 4 J. Elliot, *Debates on the Federal Constitution of 1787*, p. 571 (1876). And punishment of error runs the risk of inducing a cautious and restrictive exercise of the constitutionally guaranteed freedoms of speech and press. Our decisions recognize that a rule of strict liability that compels a publisher or broadcaster to guarantee the accuracy of his factual assertions may lead to intolerable self-censorship . . .

The need to avoid self-censorship by the news media is, however, not the only societal value at issue. If it were, this Court would have embraced long ago the view that publishers and broadcasters enjoy an unconditional and indefeasible immunity from liability for defamation . . .

The legitimate state interest underlying the law of libel is the compensation of individuals for the harm inflicted on them by defamatory falsehood. We would not lightly require the State to abandon this purpose . . .

The *New York Times* standard defines the level of constitutional protection appropriate to the context of defamation of a public person. Those who, by reason of the notoriety of their achievements or the vigor and success with which they seek the public's attention, are properly classed as public figures and those who hold governmental office may recover for injury to reputation only on clear and convincing proof that the defamatory falsehood was made with knowledge of its falsity or with reckless disregard for the truth. . . . For the reasons stated below, we conclude that the state interest in compensating injury to the reputation of private individuals requires that a different rule should obtain with respect to them.

The first remedy of any victim of defamation is self-help—using available opportunities to contradict the lie or correct the error and thereby to minimize its adverse impact on reputation. Public officials and public figures usually enjoy significantly greater access to the channels of effective communication and hence have a more realistic opportunity to counteract false statements than private individuals normally enjoy. Private individuals are therefore more vulnerable to injury, and the state interest in protecting them is correspondingly greater.

More important than the likelihood that private individuals will lack effective opportunities for rebuttal, there is a compelling normative consideration underlying the distinction between public and private defamation plaintiffs. An individual who decides to seek governmental office must accept certain necessary consequences of that involvement in public affairs. He runs the risk of closer public scrutiny than might otherwise be the case.

Those classed as public figures stand in a similar position . . . [Typically] those classed as public figures have thrust themselves to the forefront of particular public controversies in order to influence the resolution of the issues involved. In either event, they invite attention and comment.

[T]he communications media are entitled to act on the assumption that public officials and public figures have voluntarily exposed themselves to increased risk of injury from defamatory falsehood concerning them. No such assumption is justified with respect to a private individual . . . [In fact] private individuals are not only more vulnerable to injury than public officials and public figures; they are also more deserving of recovery.

For these reasons we conclude that the States should retain substantial latitude in their efforts to enforce a legal remedy for defamatory falsehood injurious to the reputation of a private individual. The extension of the *New York Times* test proposed by the *Rosenbloom* plurality would abridge this legitimate state interest to a degree that we find unacceptable. And it would occasion the additional difficulty of forcing state and federal judges to decide on an *ad hoc* basis which publications address issues of "general or public interest" and which do not—to determine, in the words of Mr. Justice MARSHALL, "what information is relevant to self-government." *Rosenbloom v. Metromedia, Inc.* We doubt the wisdom of committing this task to the conscience of judges. Nor does the Constitution require us to draw so thin a line between the drastic alternatives of the *New York Times* privilege and the common law of strict liability for defamatory error.

We hold that, so long as they do not impose liability without fault, the States may define for themselves the appropriate standard of liability for a publisher or broadcaster of defamatory falsehood injurious to a private individual.

Notwithstanding our refusal to extend the *New York Times* privilege to defamation of private individuals, respondent contends that we should affirm the judgment below on the ground that petitioner is either a public official or a public figure. There is little basis for the former assertion.

Petitioner has long been active in community and professional affairs. He has served as an officer of local civic groups and of various professional organizations, and he has published several books and articles on legal subjects. Although petitioner was consequently well known in some circles, he had achieved no general fame or notoriety in the community. None of the prospective jurors called at the trial had ever heard of petitioner prior to this litigation, and respondent offered no proof that this response was atypical of the local population. We would not lightly assume that a citizen's participation in community and professional affairs rendered him a public figure for all purposes. Absent clear evidence of general fame or notoriety in the community, and pervasive involvement in the affairs of society, an individual should not be deemed a public personality for all aspects of his life. It is preferable to reduce the public-figure question to a more meaningful context by looking to the nature and extent of an individual's participation in the particular controversy giving rise to the defamation.

In this context it is plain that petitioner was not a public figure. He played a minimal role at the coroner's inquest, [Welch had argued that Gertz's appearance at that inquest on behalf of the victim's family made him a public official or at least a public figure] and his participation related solely to his representation of a private client. He took no part in the criminal prosecution of Officer Nuccio. Moreover, he never discussed either the criminal or civil litigation with the press and was never quoted as having done so. He plainly did not thrust himself into the vortex of this public issue, nor did he engage the public's attention in an attempt to influence its outcome. We are persuaded that the trial court did not err in refusing to characterize petitioner as a public figure for the purpose of this litigation.

We ... conclude that the *New York Times* standard is inapplicable to this case and that the trial court erred in entering judgment for respondent. Because the jury was allowed to impose liability without fault and was permitted to presume damages without proof of injury, a new trial is necessary. We reverse and remand for further proceedings in accord with this opinion.

Justice BLACKMUN, concurring.

I joined Justice BRENNAN's opinion for the plurality in *Rosen-*

bloom v. Metromedia, Inc. (1971). I did so because I concluded that . . extending the *New York Times* doctrine to an event of public or general interest, was logical and inevitable. A majority of the Court evidently thought otherwise.

The Court today refuses to apply *New York Times* to the private individual, as contrasted with the public official and the public figure. It thus withdraws to the factual limits of the pre-*Rosenbloom* cases. It thereby fixes the outer boundary of the *New York Times* doctrine and says that beyond that boundary, a State is free to define for itself the appropriate standard of media liability so long as it does not impose liability without fault. As my joinder in *Rosenbloom*'s plurality opinion would intimate, I sense some illogic in this.

The Court, however, seeks today to strike a balance between competing values where necessarily uncertain assumptions about human behavior color the result. Although the Court's opinion in the present case departs from the rationale of the *Rosenbloom* plurality, in that the Court now conditions a libel action by a private person upon a showing of negligence, as contrasted with a showing of willful or reckless disregard, I am willing to join, and do join, the Court's opinion and its judgment for two reasons:

1. By removing the specters of presumed and punitive damages in the absence of *New York Times* malice, the Court eliminates significant and powerful motives for self-censorship that otherwise are present in the traditional libel action. By so doing, the Court leaves what should prove to be sufficient and adequate breathing space for a vigorous press. What the Court has done, I believe, will have little, if any, practical effect on the functioning of responsible journalism.

2. The Court was sadly fractionated in *Rosenbloom*. A result of that kind inevitably leads to uncertainty. I feel that it is of profound importance for the Court to come to rest in the defamation area and to have a clearly defined majority position that eliminates the unsureness engendered by *Rosenbloom*'s diversity. If my vote were not needed to create a majority, I would adhere to my prior view. A definitive ruling, however, is paramount.

For these reasons, I join the opinion and the judgment of the Court.

Justice DOUGLAS, dissenting.

The Court describes this case as a return to the struggle of "defin[ing] the proper accommodation between the law of defamation and the freedoms of speech and press protected by the First Amendment." It is indeed a struggle, once described by Mr. Justice BLACK as "the same quagmire" in which the Court "is now helplessly struggling in the field of obscenity." *Curtis Publishing Co. v. Butts* (1967). I would suggest that the struggle is a quite hopeless one, for, in light of the command of the First Amendment, no "accommodation" of its freedoms can be "proper" except those made by the Framers themselves.

Justice BRENNAN, dissenting.

I agree with the conclusion, expressed in [part] of the Court's opinion, that, at the time of publication of respondent's article, petitioner could not properly have been viewed as either a "public official" or "public figure"; instead, respondent's article, dealing with an alleged conspiracy to discredit local police forces, concerned petitioner's purported involvement in "an event of public or general interest." *Roosenbloom v. Metromedia, Inc.* (1971). I cannot agree, however, that free and robust debate—so essential to the proper functioning of our system of government—is permitted adequate "breathing space," *NAACP v. Button* (1963), when, as the Court holds, the States may impose all but strict liability for defamation if the defamed party is a private person and "the substance of the defamatory statement 'makes substantial danger to reputation apparent.'" I adhere to my view expressed in *Rosenbloom v. Metromedia, Inc.*, that we strike the proper accommodation between avoidance of media self-censorship and protection of individual reputations only when we require States to apply the *New York Times Co. v. Sullivan* (1964), knowing-or-reckless-falsity standard in civil libel actions concerning media reports of the involvement of private individuals in events of public or general interest.

Justice WHITE, dissenting.

For some 200 years—from the very founding of the Nation—the law of defamation and right of the ordinary citizen to recover for false publication injurious to his reputation have been almost exclusively the business of state courts and legislatures. Under typical state defamation law, the defamed private citizen had to prove only a false publication that would subject him to hatred, contempt, or ridicule. Given such publication, general damage to reputation was presumed, while punitive damages required proof of additional facts.

The States must now discern the meaning of such ill-defined concepts as "liability without fault" and to fashion novel rules for the recovery of damages. These matters have not been briefed or argued by the parties and their workability has not been seriously explored. Nevertheless, yielding to the apparently irresistible impulse to announce a new and different interpretation of the First Amendment, the Court discards history and precedent in its rush to refashion defamation law in accordance with the inclinations of a perhaps evanescent majority of the Justices.

DISCUSSION POINTS

1 This case produced a concurrence and several dissenting opinions. With whose opinion do you agree? Why?

2 Justice Powell wrote that "[w]e doubt the wisdom of committing this task [judging if an issue makes someone a public figure] to the conscience of judges." Why would the majority doubt such?

3 How workable do you find the various standards and definitions developed by the Court in cases such as *Sullivan, Hill,* and *Gertz?*

4 What are the likely implications of this decision for private parties? The media? The states?

35

Hustler Magazine v. Falwell
485 U.S. 46 (1988)

Hustler *magazine published a parody of a well-known liquor ad campaign that featured famous people discussing "their first time." The ad referred to the first time they drank that particular liquor, but the double-entendre made it appear as if the ad referred to their first act of sexual intercourse.* Hustler's *ad parody featured the minister Jerry Falwell, who was well known for his involvement in public affairs as well as for his opposition to adult publications such as* Hustler. *The parody of Falwell had him admitting to being drunk while preaching and to having had sex with his mother in an outhouse while both were drunk. Falwell successfully sued* Hustler's *publisher, Larry Flynt, for libel and intentional infliction of emotional distress. Libel refers to printed assertions that damage someone's reputation. The jury denied the libel charges because the ad copy contained a disclaimer at the bottom that read: "Ad parody. Not to be taken seriously." In addition, the table of contents included an entry for the ad parody. On the charge that Flynt intended to cause Falwell "emotional distress" the jury found for the minister and ordered that Flynt pay damages. Flynt appealed to the Supreme Court.*

Chief Justice REHNQUIST delivered the opinion of the Court.
    This case presents us with a novel question involving First Amendment limitations upon a State's authority to protect its citizens from the intentional infliction of emotional distress. We must decide whether a public figure may recover damages for emotional harm caused by the publication of an ad parody offensive to him, and doubtless gross and

repugnant in the eyes of most. Respondent would have us find that a State's interest in protecting public figures from emotional distress is sufficient to deny First Amendment protection to speech that is patently offensive and is intended to inflict emotional injury, even when that speech could not reasonably have been interpreted as stating actual facts about the public figure involved. This we decline to do.

At the heart of the First Amendment is the recognition of the fundamental importance of the free flow of ideas and opinions on matters of public interest and concern. "[T]he [485 U.S. 46, 51] freedom to speak one's mind is not only an aspect of individual liberty—and thus a good unto itself—but also is essential to the common quest for truth and the vitality of society as a whole." *Bose Corp. v. Consumer Union of United States Inc.* (1984). We have therefore been particularly vigilant to ensure that individual expressions of ideas remain free from governmentally imposed sanctions. The First Amendment recognizes no such thing as a "false" idea. *Gertz v. Robert Welch, Inc.* (1974).

The sort of robust political debate encouraged by the First Amendment is bound to produce speech that is critical of those who hold public office or those public figures who are "intimately involved in the resolution of important public questions or, by reason of their fame, shape events in areas of concern to society at large." *Associated Press v. Walker*, decided with *Curtis Publishing Co. v. Butts*, (1967) (WARREN, C. J., concurring in result). Justice FRANKFURTER put it succinctly in *Baumgartner v. United States*, (1944), when he said that "[o]ne of the prerogatives of American citizenship is the right to criticize public men and measures." Such criticism, inevitably, will not always be reasoned or moderate; public figures as well as public officials will be subject to "vehement, caustic, and sometimes unpleasantly sharp attacks," *New York Times* [1964].

Of course, this does not mean that any speech about a public figure is immune from sanction in the form of damages. Since *New York Times Co. v. Sullivan*, (1964), we have consistently ruled that a public figure may hold a speaker liable for the damage to reputation caused by publication of a defamatory falsehood, but only if the statement was made "with knowledge that it was false or with reckless disregard of whether it was false or not."

Respondent argues, however, that a different standard should apply in this case because here the State seeks to prevent not reputational damage, but the severe emotional distress suffered by the person who is the subject of an offensive publication. *Zacchini v. Scripps-Howard Broadcasting Co.*, (1977) . . . In respondent's view . . . so long as the utterance was intended to inflict emotional distress, was outrageous, and did in fact inflict serious emotional distress, it is of no constitutional import whether the statement was a fact or an opinion, or whether it was true or false. It is the intent to cause injury that is the gravamen of the tort, and the State's interest in preventing emotional harm simply outweighs whatever interest a speaker may have in speech of this type.

Generally speaking the law does not regard the intent to inflict emotional distress as one which should receive much solicitude, and it is quite understandable that most if not all jurisdictions have chosen to make it civilly culpable where the conduct in question is sufficiently "outrageous." But in the world of debate about public affairs, many things done with motives that are less than admirable are protected by the First Amendment. In *Garrison v. Louisiana*, (1964), we held that even when a speaker or writer is motivated by hatred or ill will his expression was protected by the First Amendment:

> Debate on public issues will not be uninhibited if the speaker must run the risk that it will be proved in court that he spoke out of hatred; even if he did speak out of hatred, utterances honestly believed contribute to the free interchange of ideas and the ascertainment of truth.

Thus while such a bad motive may be deemed controlling for purposes of tort liability in other areas of the law, we think the First Amendment prohibits such a result in the area of public debate about public figures.

Were we to hold otherwise, there can be little doubt that political cartoonists and satirists would be subjected to damages awards without any showing that their work falsely defamed its subject . . . The appeal of the political cartoon or caricature is often based on exploitation of unfortunate physical traits or politically embarrassing events—an exploitation often calculated to injure the feelings of the subject of the portrayal. The art of the cartoonist is often not reasoned or evenhanded, but slashing and one-sided . . . Several famous examples of this type of intentionally injurious speech were drawn by Thomas Nast, probably the greatest American cartoonist to date, who was associated for many years during the post-Civil War era with *Harper's Weekly* . . . Despite their sometimes caustic nature, from the early cartoon portraying George Washington as an ass down to the present day, graphic depictions and satirical cartoons have played a prominent role in public and political debate. Nast's castigation of the Tweed Ring, Walt Mc-Dougall's characterization of Presidential candidate James G. Blaine's banquet with the millionaires at Delmonico's as "The Royal Feast of Belshazzar," and numerous other efforts have undoubtedly had an effect on the course and outcome of contemporaneous debate. Lincoln's tall, gangling posture, Teddy Roosevelt's glasses and teeth, and Franklin D. Roosevelt's jutting jaw and cigarette holder have been memorialized by political cartoons with an effect that could not have been obtained by the photographer or the portrait artist. From the viewpoint of history it is clear that our political discourse would have been considerably poorer without them.

[Falwell] contends ... that the caricature in question here was so "outrageous" as to distinguish it from more traditional political cartoons. There is no doubt that the caricature of respondent and his mother published in *Hustler* is at best a distant cousin of the political cartoons described above, and a rather poor relation at that ... "Outrageousness" in the area of political and social discourse has an inherent subjectiveness about it which would allow a jury to impose liability on the basis of the jurors' tastes or views, or perhaps on the basis of their dislike of a particular expression. An "outrageousness" standard thus runs afoul of our longstanding refusal to allow damages to be awarded because the speech in question may have an adverse emotional impact on the audience.

We conclude that public figures and public officials may not recover for the tort of intentional infliction of emotional distress by reason of publications such as the one here at issue without showing in addition that the publication contains a false statement of fact which was made with "actual malice," i.e., with knowledge that the statement was false or with reckless disregard as to whether or not it was true. This is not merely a "blind application" of the *New York Times* standard, see *Time, Inc. v. Hill*, (1967), it reflects our considered judgment that such a standard is necessary to give adequate "breathing space" to the freedoms protected by the First Amendment.

Falwell is a "public figure" for purposes of First Amendment law. [Therefore] ... for reasons heretofore stated [Falwell's case must be dismissed and his jury award set aside].

DISCUSS POINTS

1 What do you think of the outcome of this case? What is your view of the Chief Justice's rationale for finding in favor of Larry Flynt. Do you agree with the Court's ruling and/or its reasoning in this case? Why or why not?

2 In what way is the Court's ruling in *Hustler Magazine v. Falwell* a victory for untraditional or non-mainstream political commentators such as late night comedians, satirists, cartoonists, bloggers, and radio talk show hosts?

3 What would have been the likely impact on the media had Falwell won this case? Why do you think the Court accepted the more vague likely harm arguments in this case but has rejected them in several others included in this text?

4 Is some speech just too vile for protection? Is this such speech? If so, should the Court decide matters of taste for society?

5   What impact, if any, does this ruling have on the "social value" theory discussed in the background to the case of *New York Times v. Sullivan*?

6   Jerry Falwell was a famous conservative and was a close ally to many conservatives including President Ronald Reagan. There is a tendency on the part of many to assume the Justices appointed by Republican Presidents will vote one way and that Justices appointed by Democrats will vote another way. Yet, all of the Justices, including those appointed by Republican Presidents, voted against Falwell. What does this tell you about the value of political party labels or political ideology when it comes to predicting Supreme Court behavior?

— 36 —

Cohen v. Cowles Media Co.
501 U.S. 663 (1991)

This case should be considered in light of Branzburg v. Hayes *(1972) in Part Nine. It should also be considered in light of the number of investigative reporters who make it a regular practice of promising to guard a source's identity from public efforts to force their disclosure.*

In 1982, Dan Cohen, an official with Wheelock Whitney's campaign for governor of the State of Minnesota, offered information to reporters from the Pioneer Press *and the* Star Tribune *pertaining to the arrest records of a leading opposition candidate for Lieutenant Governor, Marlene Johnson. Before making the leak, Cohen obtained a promise of confidentiality from the newspapers. The information that Cohen provided concerned minor offenses that Johnson had committed a decade earlier. One arrest was for unlawful assembly at a civil rights rally and the other was for petty theft of six dollars worth of sewing materials. Cohen had not told the papers of the nature of the offenses. The newspapers, which had learned of their nature when confirming the story, believed that Cohen had misled them in an effort to smear Johnson. The papers concluded that the public had an interest in the tactics being used against Johnson. Independent of each other, the* Press *and* Tribune *published stories about the leak in which they identified their source and reported on his role in the Whitney campaign. The day the stories appeared, Cohen was fired by his employer and the campaign denied any knowledge of or role in the leak. Cohen claimed that by identifying him the newspapers had committed fraud misrepresentation and breach of contract. A state trial court ruled for Cohen and awarded him damages. The Minnesota Supreme Court threw out the award on the basis that it was "inappropriate" to apply a breach on contract clause to a newspaper that is engaged in the process of gathering and disseminating information of interest to the public. Cohen appealed to the Supreme Court.*

Justice WHITE delivered the opinion of the Court.

The question before us is whether the First Amendment prohibits a plaintiff from recovering damages, under state promissory estoppel law, for a newspaper's breach of a promise of confidentiality given to the plaintiff in exchange for information. [A promissory estoppel law forbids a party to act in a way that is not equitable.] We hold that it does not.

Respondents rely on the proposition that, "if a newspaper lawfully obtains truthful information about a matter of public significance, then state officials may not constitutionally punish publication of the information, absent a need to further a state interest of the highest order." That proposition is unexceptionable, and it has been applied in various cases that have found insufficient the asserted state interests in preventing publication of truthful, lawfully obtained information.

This case however, is not controlled by this line of cases but rather by the equally well-established line of decisions holding that generally applicable laws do not offend the First Amendment simply because their enforcement against the press has incidental effects on its ability to gather and report the news. As the cases relied on by respondents recognize, the truthful information sought to be published must have been lawfully acquired. The press may not with impunity break and enter an office or dwelling to gather news. Neither does the First Amendment relieve a newspaper reporter of the obligation shared by all citizens to respond to a grand jury subpoena and answer questions relevant to a criminal investigation, even though the reporter might be required to reveal a confidential source. *Branzburg v. Hayes* (1972). The press, like others interested in publishing, may not publish copyrighted material without obeying the copyright laws ...

There can be little doubt that the Minnesota doctrine of promissory estoppel is a law of general applicability. It does not target or single out the press. Rather, insofar as we are advised, the doctrine is generally applicable to the daily transactions of all the citizens of Minnesota. The First Amendment does not forbid its application to the press.

[I]t is not at all clear that Respondents obtained Cohen's name "lawfully" in this case, at least for purposes of publishing it. Unlike the situation in *The Florida Star*, where the rape victim's name was obtained through lawful access to a police report, respondents obtained Cohen's name only by making a promise which they did not honor. The dissenting opinions suggest that the press should not be subject to any law, including copyright law for example, which in any fashion or to any degree limits or restricts the press' right to report truthful information. The First Amendment does not grant the press such limitless protection.

Nor is Cohen attempting to use a promissory estoppel cause of action to avoid the strict requirements for establishing a libel or defamation claim. As the Minnesota Supreme Court observed here, "Cohen could not sue for defamation, because the information disclosed [his name] was true." Cohen is not seeking damages for injury to his reputation or his state of mind. He sought damages in excess of $50,000 for a breach of a promise that caused him to lose his job and lowered his earning capacity. Thus, this is not a case like *Hustler Magazine, Inc. v. Falwell*, 485 U.S. 46 (1988), where we held that the constitutional libel standards apply to a claim alleging that the publication of a parody was a state law tort of intentional infliction of emotional distress.

Respondents and *amici* argue that permitting Cohen to maintain a cause of action for promissory estoppel will inhibit truthful reporting because news organizations will have legal incentives not to disclose a confidential source's identity even when that person's identity is itself newsworthy. Justice SOUTER makes a similar argument. But if this is the case, it is no more than the incidental, and constitutionally insignificant, consequence of applying to the press a generally applicable law that requires those who make certain kinds of promises to keep them. Although we conclude that the First Amendment does not confer on the press a constitutional right to disregard promises that would otherwise be enforced under state law, we reject Cohen's request that, in reversing the Minnesota Supreme Court's judgment, we reinstate the jury verdict awarding him $200,000 in compensatory damages . . . The Minnesota Supreme Court's incorrect conclusion that the First Amendment barred Cohen's claim may well have truncated its consideration of whether a promissory estoppel claim had otherwise been established under Minnesota law, and whether Cohen's jury verdict could be upheld on a promissory estoppel basis . . . Accordingly, the judgment of the Minnesota Supreme Court is reversed, and the case is remanded for further proceedings not inconsistent with this opinion.

Justice BLACKMUN dissenting.

I do not read the decision of the Supreme Court of Minnesota to create any exception to or immunity from the laws of that State for members of the press. In my view, the court's decision is premised not on the identity of the speaker, but on the speech itself. Thus, the court found it to be of "critical significance," that "the promise of anonymity arises in the classic First Amendment context of the quintessential public debate in our democratic society, namely, a political source involved in a political campaign." . . . [Because] the First Amendment protection afforded respondents would be equally available to non-media defendants . . . [t]he majority's admonition that "[t]he publisher of a newspaper has no special immunity from the application of general laws," and its reliance on the cases that support that principle, are . . . misplaced.

Contrary to the majority, I regard our decision in *Hustler Magazine, Inc. v. Falwell* (1988), to be precisely on point. There, we found that the use of a claim of intentional infliction of emotional distress to impose liability for the publication of a satirical critique violated the First Amendment. There was no doubt that Virginia's tort of intentional infliction of emotional distress was "a law of general applicability" unrelated to the suppression of speech. Nonetheless, a unanimous Court found that, when used to penalize the expression of opinion, the law was subject to the strictures of the First Amendment . . .

As in *Hustler*, the operation of Minnesota's doctrine of promissory estoppel in this case cannot be said to have a merely "incidental" burden on speech; the publication of important political speech is the claimed violation. Thus, as in *Hustler*, the law may not be enforced to punish the expression if truthful information or opinion. In the instant case, it is undisputed that the publication at issue was true.

To the extent that truthful speech may ever be sanctioned consistent with the First Amendment, it must be in furtherance of a state interest "of the highest order."

Justice SOUTER dissenting.

I agree with Justice BLACKMUN that this case does not fall within the line of authority holding the press to laws of general applicability where commercial activities and relationships, not the content of publication, are at issue. Even such general laws as do entail effects on the content of speech, like the one in question, may of course be found constitutional, but only, as Justice HARLAN observed, "when [such effects] have been justified by subordinating valid governmental interests, a prerequisite to constitutionality which has necessarily involved a weighing of the governmental interest involved." *Konigsberg v. State Bar of California*, 366 U.S. 36, 51 (1961).

Because I do not believe the fact of general applicability to be dispositive, I find it necessary to articulate, measure, and compare the competing interests involved in any given case to determine the legitimacy of burdening constitutional interests, and such has been the Court's recent practice in publication cases.

The importance of this public interest is integral to the balance that should be struck in this case. There can be no doubt that the fact of Cohen's identity expanded the universe of information relevant to the choice faced by Minnesota voters in that State's 1982 gubernatorial election, the publication of which was thus of the sort quintessentially subject to strict First Amendment protection. The propriety of his leak to respondents could be taken to reflect on his character, which in turn could be taken to reflect on the character of the candidate who had retained him as an adviser. An election could turn on just such a factor; if it should, I am ready to assume that it would be to the greater public good, at least over the long run.

This is not to say that the breach of such a promise of confidentiality could never give rise to liability. One can conceive of situations in which the injured party is a private individual, whose identity is of less public concern than that of the petitioner; liability there might not be constitutionally prohibited.

Because I believe the State's interest in enforcing a newspaper's promise of confidentiality insufficient to outweigh the interest in unfettered publication of the information revealed in this case, I respectfully dissent.

DISCUSSION POINTS

1 Do you agree with the Court's ruling and/or its reasoning in this case? Why or why not?

2 In light of a decision such as *Branzburg v. Hayes* (1972) in Part Nine, what are the implications of this decision for the media? For the public? Could the press have simply revealed that the materials had been leaked by a staffer of the Whitney campaign, that the charges appear to have been spurious, and that the staffer was trying to use the press to unfairly harm Ms. Johnson without revealing names? Or, would not revealing Cohen's name, given the original story, have damaged the press' credibility, or make it appear as if Ms. Johnson had "gotten to the press?"

3 Does the public have a right to know that should have trumped Cohen's rights?

4 Justice Souter argued that Cohen's identity and his attachment to the Whitney campaign were possible public issues that publishers not judges should determine. Was he correct? What is the majority's response to such an assertion?

PART NINE

The Media and the Law: Public Efforts to Restrict or Regulate the Free Press

AMERICANS BELIEVE THAT they have created the freest state in the history of mankind and they pride themselves on having created a system of free expression that allows for freedom of speech and of the press. We had rebelled against a monarch who, either by direct action or by act of his surrogates, the royal colonial governors, had limited or even forbidden privately-owned printing presses in the Colonies. In New York, for instance, King James II had decreed in 1685 that there could be no press without his royal governor's permission. While in Virginia, the birthplace of such intellectual bulwarks for a free press as Thomas Jefferson and James Madison, there was a royal ban on privately-owned printing presses that lasted until 1730. Yet, for all of our resentment at royal efforts to curtail press liberties, and for all of this pride and talk of freedom, public efforts in America to curtail the press date to 1798 when the Congress adopted the Alien and Sedition Acts.* Most

---

* The Alien and Sedition Acts essentially made it a crime, punishable by jail and/or fine, to criticize the government or most of its leaders (criticism of the Vice-President was allowed). The law was adopted by the Federalist controlled Congress and White House and intended to be a tool against their political opponents the followers of Vice-President Thomas Jefferson (the Democrat-Republicans as their party was known). The president was authorized to deport any alien who he deemed a security risk; this could include aliens who had published articles, pamphlets, or letters, or made speeches, critical of the United States, its government, its policies, or its leaders. The law also extended the time it took for aliens to become citizens. This was significant since most aliens of the time joined the Democrat-Republican Party. President John Adams did not deport any aliens

public efforts to curtail the press, aside perhaps from those aimed at Communists during World War I and in the 1950s, have not been nearly as extreme.*

This part includes excerpts from six landmark Supreme Court free press cases pitting the state against the press. These conflicts include public efforts to: tax the press out of business, dictate conditions for the use of public radio airwaves, ban publications critical of the government, compel the press to reveal the identity of secret sources, protect candidates for public office from unfair press, and bar the press from judicial proceedings. Most result in victories for the press, however, the facts that these cases arose is testament to the fact that restrictions of free expression can occur anywhere even in America.

(though his supporters lobbied for him to do so), however, many aliens fled the country and the Government arrested twenty-five persons under the Act (including one member of Congress). Most of those arrested were newspaper editors. Nearly half were convicted under the terms of the law. After Jefferson was elected president, the law was allowed to expire and the individuals who had been punished under its terms were later cleared of the charges and, in some cases, compensated by Congress for the Government's transgressions.
* During both periods, the United States enacted laws which echoed 1798's Alien and Sedition Act and used these laws to jail opponents of World War I and Communists living in America.

37

Grosjean v. American Press Co.
297 U.S. 233 (1936)

Imagine you are a politician who constantly faces criticisms in the press. These criticisms anger you so that you seek to extract some kind of revenge upon the press. The method you select is financial retribution in the form of a tax on selected media outlets. In the 1930s, Huey Long, a Louisiana Governor (1928–1932) and United States Senator (1932–1935) attempted to use such a tax as a weapon against his critics in the media. His actions, and the court battle that ensued, are among the most interesting in American history.

Huey Long, who nicknamed himself "Kingfish," was among the most powerful and successful American politicians of the 1920s and 1930s. Long was brash and flamboyant and not above engaging in hardball politics. In his speeches, and policies, Long, to the delight of his many poor and working class followers, often advocated "sharing the wealth" and "soak the rich." Long's dominance of Louisiana politics was so complete and his advocacy of populist causes so effusive (if not extreme) that many of his critics labeled him a dangerous demagogue. Others charged that Long was a corrupt tyrant who had gotten rich at the taxpayer's expense. Many of the State's largest newspapers took to publishing scathing criticisms of Long.

While no longer governor, Long's response to allegations of demagoguery and corruption was to convince the Louisiana legislature to levy a license tax of 2% of the gross receipts for every business that sold advertising in publications that had a circulation of more than 20,000 per week. Failure to comply was a misdemeanor punishable by fine and possible jail time. While Louisiana had nearly 150 publications that sold advertisements, only thirteen had circulations in excess of 20,000 a week. Among these thirteen were the papers that had been most critical of Long.

Long famously termed the newspaper tax a "tax on lying, at two-cents a lie." The Governor put his former personal secretary, and alleged mistress, Louisiana Secretary of State Alice Grosjean, in charge of collecting the new tax. Nine of the thirteen newspapers that the State sought to tax refused Grosjean's efforts and filed suit against the tax on the grounds that it unfairly targeted them for discrimination and that it violated the First Amendment's command that the state pass no law that restricted the free press. The newspapers won. The State appealed to the Supreme Court.

Justice SUTHERLAND delivered the opinion of the Court.

This suit was brought by appellees, nine publishers of newspapers in the state of Louisiana, to enjoin the enforcement against them of the provisions of section 1 of the act of the Legislature of Louisiana known as Act No. 23, passed and approved July 12, 1934, as follows:

> That every person, firm, association or corporation, domestic or foreign, engaged in the business of selling, or making any charge for, advertising or for advertisements, whether printed or published, or to be printed or published, in any newspaper, magazine, periodical or publication whatever having a circulation of more than 20,000 copies per week, or displayed and exhibited, or to be displayed and exhibited, by means of moving pictures, in the State of Louisiana, shall, in addition to all other taxes and licenses levied and assessed in this State, pay a license tax for the privilege of engaging in such business in this State of two per cent. (2%) of the gross receipts of such business.

The validity of the act is assailed as violating the Federal Constitution in . . . [t]hat it abridges the freedom of the press in contravention of the due process clause contained in section 1 of the Fourteenth Amendment.

[This case] presents a question of the utmost gravity and importance; for, if well made, it goes to the heart of the natural right of the members of an organized society, united for their common good, to impart and acquire information about their common interests. The First Amendment to the Federal Constitution provides that 'Congress shall make no law . . . abridging the freedom of speech, or of the press.' While this provision is not a restraint upon the powers of the states, the states are precluded from abridging the freedom of speech or of the press by force of the due process clause of the Fourteenth Amendment.

The tax imposed is designated a 'license tax for the privilege of engaging in such business,' that is to say, the business of selling, or making any charge for, advertising. As applied to appellees, it is a tax of 2 per cent on the gross receipts derived from advertisements carried in their newspapers when, and only when, the newspapers of each enjoy a circulation of more than 20,000 copies per week. It thus operates as a restraint in a double sense. First, its effect is to curtail the amount of revenue realized from advertising; and, second, its direct tendency is to restrict circulation. This is plain enough when we consider that, if it were increased to a high degree, as it could be if valid . . . it well might result in destroying both advertising and circulation.

A determination of the question whether the tax is valid in respect of the point now under review requires an examination of the history and circumstances which antedated and attended the adoption of the abridgement clause of the First Amendment . . . The history is a long one; but for present purposes it may be greatly abbreviated.

For more than a century prior to the adoption of the amendment—and, indeed, for many years thereafter—history discloses a persistent effort on the part of the British government to prevent or abridge the free expression of any opinion which seemed to criticize or exhibit in an unfavorable light, however truly, the agencies and operations of the government . . .

In 1712, in response to a message from Queen Anne (Hansard's *Parliamentary History of England*, vol. 6, p. 1063), Parliament imposed a tax upon all newspapers and upon advertisements . . . These duties were quite commonly characterized as 'taxes on knowledge,' a phrase used for the purpose of describing the effect of the exactions and at the same time condemning them. That the taxes had, and were intended to have, the effect of curtailing the circulation of newspapers, and particularly the cheaper ones whose readers were generally found among the masses of the people, went almost without question, even on the part of those who defended the act.

It is idle to suppose that so many of the best men of England would for a century of time have waged, as they did, stubborn and often precarious warfare against these taxes if a mere matter of taxation had been involved. The aim of the struggle was not to relieve taxpayers from a burden, but to establish and preserve the right of the English people to full information in respect of the doings or misdoings of their government.

In 1785, only four years before Congress had proposed the First Amendment, the Massachusetts Legislature, following the English example, imposed a stamp tax on all newspapers and magazines. The following year an advertisement tax was imposed. Both taxes met with such violent opposition that the former was repealed in 1786, and the latter in 1788.

The framers of the First Amendment were familiar with the English struggle, which then had continued for nearly eighty years and was destined to go on for another sixty-five years, at the end of which time it culminated in a lasting abandonment of the obnoxious taxes. The framers were likewise familiar with the then recent Massachusetts episode; and while that occurrence did much to bring about the adoption of the amendment . . . the predominant influence must have come from the English experience. It is impossible to concede that by the words 'freedom of the press' the framers of the amendment intended to adopt merely the narrow view then reflected by the law of England that such freedom consisted only in immunity from previous censorship; for this abuse had then permanently disappeared from English practice. It is equally impossible to believe that it was not intended to bring within the reach of these words such modes of restraint as were embodied in the two forms of taxation already described.

In the light of all that has now been said, it is evident that the restricted rules of the English law in respect of the freedom of the press in force when the Constitution was adopted were never accepted by the American colonists, and that by the First Amendment it was meant to preclude the national government, and by the Fourteenth Amendment to preclude the states, from adopting any form of previous restraint upon printed publications, or their circulation, including that which had theretofore been effected by these two well-known and odious methods.

Judge Cooley has laid down the test to be applied: 'The evils to be prevented were not the censorship of the press merely, but any action of the government by means of which it might prevent such free and general discussion of public matters as seems absolutely essential to prepare the people for an intelligent exercise of their rights as citizens.' Cooley's *Constitutional Limitations* (8th Ed.).

It is not intended by anything we have said to suggest that the owners of newspapers are immune from any of the ordinary forms of taxation for support of the government. But this is not an ordinary form of tax, but one single in kind, with a long history of hostile misuse against the freedom of the press.

The predominant purpose of the grant of immunity here invoked was to preserve an untrammeled press as a vital source of public information . . . The tax here involved is bad not because it takes money from the pockets of the appellees. If that were all, a wholly different question would be presented. It is bad because, in the light of its history and of its present setting, it is seen to be a deliberate and calculated device in the guise of a tax to limit the circulation of information to which the public is entitled in virtue of the constitutional guaranties. A free press stands as one of the great interpreters between the government and the people. To allow it to be fettered is to fetter ourselves.

In view of the persistent search for new subjects of taxation, it is not without significance that, with the single exception of the Louisiana statute, so far as we can discover, no state during the one hundred fifty years of our national existence has undertaken to impose a tax like that now in question.

The form in which the tax is imposed is in itself suspicious. It is not measured or limited by the volume of advertisements. It is measured alone by the extent of the circulation of the publication in which the advertisements are carried, with the plain purpose of penalizing the publishers and curtailing the circulation of a selected group of newspapers.

DISCUSSION POINTS

1   Do you agree with the Court's ruling and/or its reasoning in this case? Why or why not?

2   What would be the potential harm to the free press had Louisiana triumphed?

3   Exceptions to *Grosjean's* ban on a "tax on knowledge" exist. Can you think of some of these exceptions and the rationale that might distinguish them from the facts of this case?

— 38 —

Red Lion Broadcasting Co. v. FCC
395 U.S. 367 (1969)

The Federal Communications Commission (FCC) long imposed on broadcasters a "fairness doctrine" requiring that public issues be presented by broadcasters and that each side of these issues be given fair coverage. The Red Lion Broadcasting Company had an FCC license to operate a Pennsylvania radio station, WGCB. WGCB was a Christian ration station that had a preference for conservative politicians. Among its favorites was the Republican Party's nominee for president in 1964 Arizona Senator Barry Goldwater. Fred Cook published a book entitled Barry Goldwater: Extremist on the Right (Grove City Press: 1964) that was quite critical of Senator Goldwater. On November 27, 1964, WGCB carried a 15-minute broadcast that attacked Cook for his book. In the course of doing so, WGCB implied that Cook was a Communist or, at least, a Communist-sympathizer. To be called a "Communist" was no small matter in the 1960s. Communism was viewed as a threat to the United States and the United States was engaged in a global struggle against Communists. Being labeled a Communist could ruin an individual's career and livelihood. In the modern context, being labeled a Communist in the 1960s was the equivalent of being called a terrorist in the post-September 11, 2001, United States.

Upset about WGCB's attack on him, Cook requested, under the Fairness Doctrine, equal reply time. The station refused and Cook complained to the FCC. The FCC declared that Red Lion Broadcasting Co. had failed to meet its obligation under the fairness doctrine when it carried a program which constituted a personal attack on Cook, and ordered it to provide him with free air time to reply. The Red Lion Broadcasting Co. refused on the grounds that being forced by the FCC to provide free reply to Cook constituted an infringement of its editorial control and that as such it violated the First Amendment.

Justice WHITE delivered the opinion of the Court.

The broadcasters challenge the fairness doctrine and its specific manifestations in the personal attack and political editorial rules on conventional First Amendment grounds, alleging that the rules abridge their freedom of speech and press. Their contention is that the First Amendment protects their desire to use their allotted frequencies continuously to broadcast whatever they choose, and to exclude whomever they choose from ever using that frequency. No man may be prevented from saying or publishing what he thinks, or from refusing in his speech or other utterances to give equal weight to the views of his opponents. This right, they say, applies equally to broadcasters.

Although broadcasting is clearly a medium affected by a First Amendment interest, *United States v. Paramount Pictures, Inc.* (1948), differences in the characteristics of new media justify differences in the First Amendment standards applied to them . . .

The lack of know-how and equipment may keep many from the air, but only a tiny fraction of those with resources and intelligence can hope to communicate by radio at the same time if intelligible communication is to be had, even if the entire radio spectrum is utilized in the present state of commercially acceptable technology . . .

Where there are substantially more individuals who want to broadcast than there are frequencies to allocate, it is idle to posit an unabridgeable First Amendment right to broadcast comparable to the right of every individual to speak, write, or publish. If 100 persons want broadcast licenses but there are only 10 frequencies to allocate, all of them may have the same "right" to a license; but if there is to be any effective communication by radio, only a few can be licensed and the rest must be barred from the airwaves. It would be strange if the First Amendment, aimed at protecting and furthering communications, prevented the Government from making radio communication possible by requiring licenses to broadcast and by limiting the number of licenses so as not to overcrowd the spectrum . . .

By the same token, as far as the First Amendment is concerned those who are licensed stand no better than those to whom licenses are refused. A license permits broadcasting, but the licensee has no constitutional right to be the one who holds the license or to monopolize a radio frequency to the exclusion of his fellow citizens. There is nothing in the First Amendment which prevents the Government from requiring a licensee to share his frequency with others and to conduct himself as a proxy or fiduciary with obligations to present those views and voices which are representative of his community and which would otherwise, by necessity, be barred from the airwaves.

Rather than confer frequency monopolies on a relatively small number of licensees, in a Nation of 200,000,000, the Government could surely have decreed that, each frequency should be shared among all or some of those who wish to use it, each being assigned a portion of the broadcast day or the broadcast week. The ruling and regulations at issue here do not go quite so far. They assert that under specified circumstances, a licensee must offer to make available a reasonable amount of broadcast time to those who have a view different from that which has already been expressed on his station. The expression of a political endorsement, or of a personal attack while dealing with a controversial public issue, simply triggers this time sharing. As we have said, the First Amendment confers no right on licensees to prevent others from broadcasting on "their" frequencies and no right to an unconditional monopoly of a scarce resource which the Government has denied others the right to use . . .

Nor can we say that it is inconsistent with the First Amendment goal of producing an informed public capable of conducting its own affairs to require a broadcaster to permit answers to personal attacks occurring in the course of discussing controversial issues, or to require that the political opponents of those endorsed by the station be given a chance to communicate with the public. Otherwise, station owners and a few networks would have unfettered power to make time available only to the highest bidders, to communicate only their own views on public issues, people and candidates, and to permit on the air only those with whom they agreed. There is no sanctuary in the First Amendment for unlimited private censorship operating in a medium not open to all. "Freedom of the press from governmental interference under the First Amendment does not sanction repression of that freedom by private interests." *Associated Press v. United States* (1945).

It is strenuously argued . . . that if political editorials or personal attacks will trigger an obligation in broadcasters to afford the opportunity for expression, to speakers who need not pay for time and whose views are unpalatable to the licensees, then broadcasters will be irresistibly forced to self-censorship and their coverage of controversial public issues will be eliminated or at least rendered wholly ineffective. Such a result would indeed be a serious matter, for should licensees actually eliminate their coverage of controversial issues, the purposes of the doctrine would be stifled.

At this point, however, as the Federal Communications Commission has indicated, that possibility is at best speculative. The communications industry, and in particular the networks, have taken pains to present controversial issues in the past, and even now they do not assert that they intend to abandon their efforts in this regard. It would be better if the FCC's encouragement were never necessary to induce the broadcasters to meet their responsibility. And if experience with the administration of these doctrines indicates that they have the net effect of reducing rather than enhancing the volume and quality of coverage, there will be time enough to reconsider the constitutional implications. The fairness doctrine in the past has had no such overall effect.

That this will occur now seems unlikely, however, since if present licensees should suddenly prove timorous, the Commission is not powerless to insist that they give adequate and fair attention to public issues. It does not violate the First Amendment to treat licensees given the privilege of using scarce radio frequencies as proxies for the entire community, obligated to give suitable time and attention to matters of great public concern. To condition the granting or renewal of licenses on a willingness to present representative community views on controversial issues is consistent with the ends and purposes of those constitutional provisions forbidding the abridgment of freedom of speech and freedom of the press. Congress need not stand idly by and permit those with licenses to ignore the problems which beset the people or to exclude from the airways anything but their own views of fundamental questions. The statute, long administrative practice, and cases are to this effect.

Licenses to broadcast do not confer ownership of designated frequencies, but only the temporary privilege of using them . . . The statute mandates the issuance of licenses if the "public convenience, interest, or necessity will be served thereby."

We need not and do not now ratify every past and future decision by the FCC with regard to programming. There is no question here of the Commission's refusal to permit the broadcaster to carry a particular program or to publish his own views; of a discriminatory refusal to require the licensee to broadcast certain views which have been denied access to the airwaves; of government censorship of a particular program contrary to or of the official government view dominating public broadcasting. Such questions would raise more serious First Amendment issues. But we do hold that the Congress and the Commission do not violate the First Amendment when they require a radio or television station to give reply time to answer personal attacks and political editorials.

It is so ordered.

DISCUSSION POINTS

1   Do you agree with the Court's ruling in this case? Do you agree with its rationale? Why or why not?

2   The Court refers to a difference between the old (print) and new (electronic) media. What are these differences? Should they matter in the Court's calculus?

3 If airwaves became less scarce or demand for licenses dropped, should that matter?

4 Was the station correct that some self-censorship might occur?

5 The Fairness Doctrine has since been discontinued by the FCC in the 1980s as part of a trend toward deregulation. Should it be re-adopted? Why or why not?

6 We do not require liberal or conservative publications to print different sides. How can we justify requiring conservative or liberal radio stations to do so?

39

New York Times Co. v. United States
403 U.S. 713 (1971)

In 1964, President Lyndon Baines Johnson decided to escalate American military involvement in an armed conflict between North Vietnam, which was pro-communist, and our allies in South Vietnam, which was anti-communist. The Administration asserted that the war would both be quick and successful and that it could be fought without major economic sacrifice on the part of the American people. These predictions proved inaccurate, and by the mid-1960s, there was tremendous public protest aimed at the War in Vietnam. These protests contributed to Johnson's decision not to seek re-election and the election to the presidency in 1968 of Richard Nixon. Despite strong opposition to the War from the public, Nixon continued the war, even escalating it.

In 1971, Daniel Ellsberg, a former Marine and military analyst, provided the New York Times *with a secret Pentagon study of decision making in Vietnam. This study, which came to be known as the* Pentagon Papers, *was made up of 47 volumes and numbered 7,000 pages in length. The* Pentagon Papers *did not contain materials related to current or even future military activities. Rather, it contained a series of cables and memorandum, some of which were classified. This material was potentially embarrassing to the United States both because it revealed a pattern of deception on the part of American officials and because it called into question the wisdom of a number of policy decisions made by past America presidents with respect to Vietnam.*

The New York Times, *after reviewing the leaked materials for a period of three months, began publishing excerpts of the* Papers. *Immediately, the United States charged the paper with espionage contending that the paper had communicated classified materials to the enemy. The Government obtained a court injunction halting further publications by the* New York Times. *Simultaneous to this* court order, Ellsberg leaked a portion of the study to the Washington Post. The Post, within a few days, analyzed and published portions of the study. The United States again obtained an injunction halting further publications. The newspapers appealed to the United States Supreme Court. The Court, in light of the importance of the case, accepted the case and immediately scheduled it for oral argument.

The request by the United States for the judiciary to forbid the New York Times *and the* Washington Post *from publishing from the* Pentagon Papers *is the first and only such federal request in American history. To forbid the press to report on a story is to levy what is known as a prior restraint. That the First Amendment forbids prior restraints with respect to expressions that are critical of the state and its leaders is a bedrock principle of American law. Whether prior restraints are allowed when national security concerns are implicated is a different matter. The decision to charge the papers with espionage meant that the newspapers's owners were charged with a felony. Felons cannot own newspapers or television or radio stations. The publishers of both the* New York Times *and the* Washington Post *owned all three. If convicted, the publishers of both newspapers would have lost a fortune.*

Again, due to the importance of the case, the Court's verdict in New York Times vs. U.S. *(1971), was issued a mere four days after arguments were heard. The vote was 6–3 in favor of the newspapers. The Court moved so quickly at least in part because the majority felt that everyday that passed was a kind of victory for the United States. Because its decision was issued so quickly, the majority did not produce more than the single paragraph printed below. The majority opinion was issued as a* Per Curiam *opinion (an opinion without any signed authorship). The* Per Curiam *opinion appeared first and was followed by the Justices' individual opinions. Because Justice Black's opinion appears first, there is a tendency to view it as the opinion of the Court. The fact, however, is that the Justices' individual opinions were published in order of seniority and Black was the senior member. If anything, Justice Brennan's concurrence, which alludes to four possible instances when prior restraint might be justified, is likely the view that attracted the most support given the views of the other members of the majority and of the three dissenters. Because the dissents did not focus on matters related to the First Amendment they are summarized rather than excerpted.*

Per Curiam.

We granted certiorari in these cases in which the United States seeks to enjoin the *New York Times* and the *Washington Post* from publishing the contents of a classified study entitled "History of U.S. Decision-Making Process on Viet Nam Policy."

"Any system of prior restraints of expression comes to this Court bearing a heavy presumption against its constitutional validity." *Bantam Books, Inc. v. Sullivan,* (1963); see also *Near v. Minnesota,* (1931). The Government "thus carries a heavy burden of showing justification for the imposition of such a restraint." *Organization for a Better Austin v. Keefe,* (1971). The District Court for the Southern District of New York in the *New York Times* case and the District Court for the District of Columbia and the Court of Appeals for the District of Columbia Circuit in the *Washington Post* case held that the Government had not met that burden. We agree.

The judgment of the Court of Appeals for the District of Columbia Circuit is . . . affirmed . . . The stays entered June 25, 1971, by the Court are vacated.

Justice BLACK, with whom Justice DOUGLAS joins, concurring.

I believe that every moment's continuance of the injunctions against these newspapers amounts to a flagrant, indefensible, and continuing violation of the First Amendment.

[F]or the first time . . . since the founding of the Republic, the federal courts are asked to hold that the First Amendment does not mean what it says, but rather means that the Government can halt the publication of current news of vital importance to the people of this country.

In seeking injunctions against these newspapers and in its presentation to the Court, the Executive Branch seems to have forgotten the essential purpose and history of the First Amendment. When the Constitution was adopted, many people strongly opposed it because [they feared that] the new powers granted to a central government might be interpreted to permit the government to curtail freedom of religion, press, assembly, and speech . . . The Bill of Rights changed the original Constitution into a new charter under which no branch of government could abridge the people's freedoms of press, speech, religion, and assembly. Yet the Solicitor General argues and some members of the Court appear to agree that the general powers of the Government adopted in the original Constitution should be interpreted to limit and restrict the specific and emphatic guarantees of the Bill of Rights adopted later. I can imagine no greater perversion of history . . . Both the history and language of the First Amendment support the view that the press must be left free to publish news, whatever the source, without censorship, injunctions, or prior restraints.

In the First Amendment . . . [t]he press was protected so that it could bare the secrets of government and inform the people. Only a free and unrestrained press can effectively expose deception in government. And paramount among the responsibilities of a free press is the duty to prevent any part of the government from deceiving the people and sending them off to distant lands to die of foreign fevers and foreign shot and shell. In my view, far from deserving condemnation for their courageous reporting, the *New York Times,* the *Washington Post,* and other newspapers should be commended for serving the purpose that the Founding Fathers saw so clearly. In revealing the workings of government that led to the Vietnam war, the newspapers nobly did precisely that which the Founders hoped and trusted they would do.

The Government's case here is based on premises entirely different from those that guided the Framers of the First Amendment. The Solicitor General has carefully and emphatically stated:

> "Now, Mr. Justice [BLACK], your construction of . . . [the First Amendment] is well known, and I certainly respect it. You say that no law means no law, and that should be obvious. I can only say, Mr. Justice, that to me it is equally obvious that 'no law' does not mean 'no law', and I would seek to persuade the Court that is true. . . . [T]here are other parts of the Constitution that grant powers and responsibilities to the Executive, and . . . the First Amendment was not intended to make it impossible for the Executive to function or to protect the security of the United States."

And the Government argues in its brief that in spite of the First Amendment, "[t]he authority of the Executive Department to protect the nation against publication of information whose disclosure would endanger the national security stems from two interrelated sources: the constitutional power of the President over the conduct of foreign affairs and his authority as Commander-in-Chief."

In other words, we are asked to hold that despite the First Amendment's emphatic command, the Executive Branch, the Congress, and the Judiciary can make laws enjoining publication of current news and abridging freedom of the press in the name of "national security." . . . To find that the President has "inherent power" to halt the publication of news by resort to the courts would wipe out the First Amendment and destroy the fundamental liberty and security of the very people the Government hopes to make "secure."

Justice BRENNAN, concurring.

Our cases . . . have indicated that there is a single, extremely narrow class of cases in which the First Amendment's ban on prior judicial restraint may be overridden. Our cases have thus far indicated that such cases may arise only when the Nation "is at war," *Schenck v. United States*, (1919), during which times "[n]o one would question but that a government might prevent actual obstruction to its recruiting service or the publication of the sailing dates of transports or the number and location of troops." *Near v. Minnesota*, (1931). Even if the present world situation were assumed to be tantamount to a time of war, or if the power of presently available armaments would justify even in peacetime the suppression of information that would set in motion a nuclear holocaust, in neither of these actions has the Government presented or even alleged that publication of items from or based upon the material at issue would cause the happening of an event of that nature."

Justice STEWART, with whom Justice WHITE joins, concurring.

In the governmental structure created by our Constitution, the Executive is endowed with enormous power in the two related areas of national defense and international relations. This power, largely unchecked by the Legislative and Judicial branches, has been pressed to the very hilt since the advent of the nuclear missile age ... [T]he only effective restraint upon executive policy and power in the areas of national defense and international affairs may lie in an enlightened citizenry—in an informed and critical public opinion which alone can here protect the values of democratic government ... [W]ithout an informed and free press there cannot be an enlightened people.

If the Constitution gives the Executive a large degree of unshared power in the conduct of foreign affairs and the maintenance of our national defense, then under the Constitution the Executive must have the largely unshared duty to determine and preserve the degree of internal security necessary to exercise that power successfully. It is an awesome responsibility, requiring judgment and wisdom of a high order. I should suppose that moral, political, and practical considerations would dictate that a very first principle of that wisdom would be an insistence upon avoiding secrecy for its own sake. For when everything is classified, then nothing is classified, and the system becomes one to be disregarded by the cynical or the careless, and to be manipulated by those intent on self-protection or self-promotion. [T]he hallmark of a truly effective internal security system would be the maximum possible disclosure, recognizing that secrecy can best be preserved only when credibility is truly maintained.

Justice WHITE, with whom Justice STEWART joins, concurring.

I do not say that in no circumstances would the First Amendment permit an injunction against publishing information about government plans or operation ... [However] the United States has not satisfied the very heavy burden that it must meet to warrant an injunction against publication in these cases, at least in the absence of express and appropriately limited congressional authorization for prior restraints in circumstances such as these ...

I am not, of course, saying that either of these newspapers has yet committed a crime or that either would commit a crime if it published all the material now in its possession. That matter must await resolution in the context of a criminal proceeding if one is instituted by the United States.

Justice MARSHALL, concurring.

The Government contends that the only issue in these cases is whether in a suit by the United States, "the First Amendment bars a court from prohibiting a newspaper from publishing material whose disclosure would pose a 'grave and immediate danger to the security of the United States.'"... I believe the ultimate issue in these cases is even more basic than the one posed by the Solicitor General. The issue is whether this Court or the Congress has the power to make law.

The problem here is whether in these particular cases the Executive Branch has authority to invoke the equity jurisdiction of the courts to protect what it believes to be the national interest.

It would, however, be utterly inconsistent with the concept of separation of powers for this Court to use its power of contempt to prevent behavior that Congress has specifically declined to prohibit... The Constitution provides that Congress shall make laws, the President execute laws, and courts interpret laws. *Youngstown Sheet & Tube Co. v. Sawyer*, (1952). It did not provide for government by injunction in which the courts and the Executive Branch can "make law" without regard to the action of Congress. It may be more convenient for the Executive Branch if it need only convince a judge to prohibit conduct rather than ask the Congress to pass a law, and it may be more convenient to enforce a contempt order than to seek a criminal conviction in a jury trial. Moreover, it may be considered politically wise to get a court to share the responsibility for arresting those who the Executive Branch has probable cause to believe are violating the law. But convenience and political considerations of the moment do not justify a basic departure from the principles of our system of government.

Chief Justice BURGER, dissenting.

[The Chief Justice's dissent focused a great deal on how unfair it was to the Court and the Government that the case was expedited in the manner in which it was. He charged that the Justices "literally do not know what we are acting on" and that "when judges are pressured as in these cases the result is a parody of the judicial function." In addition, the Chief Justice complained that the papers had published the papers rather than return them to the Government.].

Justice HARLAN, with whom The Chief Justice and Justice BLACKMUN join, dissenting.

[Justice HARLAN focused largely on what he termed an "almost irresponsibly feverish [pace] in dealing with these cases." In addition, Justice HARLAN questioned if under the doctrine of separate powers the Court had the authority to act in this matter in what he might have termed an unilateral fashion. He advocated giving greater weigh to the president's claims of authority and favored seeking the advice of the Secretaries of State and Defense in the matter].

Justice BLACKMUN, dissenting.

[Like the other dissenters, Justice BLACKMUN voiced distress over the handling of the case. He opined that "[t]he First Amendment . . . is only one part of an entire Constitution" and that as such he did not view it as automatically superceding other provisions. In an uniquely personal way, Justice BLACKMUN wrote that, "If . . . damage has been done" by the publications ar bar to America and its troops that the American people then the newspapers would be at fault for such "damage."]

DISCUSSION POINTS

1 What do you think of the Court's decision in this case?

2 Which of the concurrences do you find most or least persuasive and why?

3 Justice Black was famous for his absolutist position that "no law" meant "no law." Is this a reasonable view of the First Amendment or one that is naive?

4 What does Justice Stewart mean when he writes: "when everything is classified, then nothing is classified, and the system becomes one to be disregarded by the cynical or the careless, and to be manipulated by those intent on self-protection or self-promotion. [T]he hallmark of a truly effective internal security system would be the maximum possible disclosure, recognizing that secrecy can best be preserved only when credibility is truly maintained."?

5 Justice Marshall, known for his ability to get to the heart of a case, wrote "[t]he issue is whether this Court or the Congress has the power to make law." What did he mean?

6 In his autobiography, *A Good Life: Newspapering and Other Adventures*, the *Washington Post*'s Managing Editor, Ben Bradlee, wrote, "We had won—sort of." What did he mean? Are there clear winners and losers in this case? If so, who are they and why?

40

Branzburg v. Hayes
408 U.S. 665 (1972)

Branzburg v. Hayes *(1972) held that the First Amendment allows the state to compel journalists to reveal the identity of secret sources. Over thirty years later, a series of events, most famously an investigation into a White House leak of the identity of a secret CIA operative (who happened to be the wife of a critic of President George W. Bush) and rumors of a possible investigation into the leak of a classified domestic spying program, have revived concerns about the propriety of compelling the press to reveal its sources. As a result, the issue of whether the press has a right to refuse to reveal its sources has emerged as one of the first major free press questions of the twenty-first century. In fact, it may only be a matter of time before the courts reexamine* Branzburg v. Hayes *(1972). It is within this framework and sense of history that students are encouraged to place and consider the facts and opinion that ensues.*

A number of states have what are known as "shield laws." Shield laws protect the media from having to reveal to the state the identity of secret sources. Usually such revelations would be made to a grand jury. Some states provide the media with an absolute protection; while others may provide the media a more qualified protection. There is no federal shield law. In 1969, Paul Branzburg, a reporter in Kentucky, refused to testify before a criminal grand jury about the identities of more than a dozen individuals whom he had watched both use and synthesize narcotics. Grand juries are used to decide if there is enough evidence to bring criminal charges and have a criminal trial in an investigation. Branzburg argued that Kentucky law and the First Amendment to the United States Constitution protected him from being made to reveal his sources. The judge, John Hayes, rejected Branzburg's claims of privilege. Branzburg appealed to the Supreme Court.

Justice WHITE wrote the opinion of the Court.

The issue in these cases is whether requiring newsmen to appear and testify before state or federal grand juries abridges the freedom of speech and press guaranteed by the First Amendment. We hold that it does not.

Branzburg . . . [argues] that to gather news it is often necessary to agree either not to identify the source of information published or to publish only part of the facts revealed, or both; that if the reporter is nevertheless forced to reveal these confidences to a grand jury, the source so identified and other confidential sources of other reporters will be measurably deterred from furnishing publishable information, all to the detriment of the free flow of information protected by the First Amendment. Although the newsmen in these cases do not claim an absolute privilege against official interrogation in all circumstances, they assert that the reporter should not be forced either to appear or to testify before a grand jury or at trial until and unless sufficient grounds are shown for believing that the reporter possesses information relevant to a crime the grand jury is investigating, that the information the reporter has is unavailable from other sources, and that the need for the information is sufficiently compelling to override the claimed invasion of First Amendment interests occasioned by the disclosure.

We do not question the significance of free speech, press, or assembly to the country's welfare. Nor is it suggested that news gathering does not qualify for First Amendment protection; without some protection for seeking out the news, freedom of the press could be eviscerated. But these cases involve no intrusions upon speech or assembly, no prior restraint or restriction on what the press may publish, and no express or implied command that the press publish what it prefers to withhold. No exaction or tax for the privilege of publishing, and no penalty, civil or criminal, related to the content of published material is at issue here. The use of confidential sources by the press is not forbidden or restricted; reporters remain free to seek news from any source by means within the law. No attempt is made to require the press to publish its sources of information or indiscriminately to disclose them on request.

The sole issue before us is the obligation of reporters to respond to grand jury subpoenas as other citizens do and to answer questions relevant to an investigation into the commission of crime. Citizens generally are not constitutionally immune from grand jury subpoenas; and neither the First Amendment nor any other constitutional provision protects the average citizen from disclosing to a grand jury information that he has received in confidence . . .

[T]he great weight of authority is that newsmen are not exempt from the normal duty of appearing before a grand jury and answering questions relevant to a criminal investigation. At common law, courts consistently refused to recognize the existence of any privilege authorizing a newsman to refuse to reveal confidential information to a grand jury . . .

A number of States have provided newsmen a statutory privilege of varying breadth, but the majority have not done so, and none has been provided by federal statute. Until now the only testimonial privilege for unofficial witnesses that is rooted in the Federal Constitution is the Fifth Amendment privilege against compelled self-incrimination. We are asked to create another by interpreting the First Amendment to grant newsmen a testimonial privilege that other citizens do not enjoy. This we decline to do. Fair and effective law enforcement aimed at providing security for the person and property of the individual is a fundamental function of government, and the grand jury plays an important, constitutionally mandated role in this process.

[W]e cannot seriously entertain the notion that the First Amendment protects a newsman's agreement to conceal the criminal conduct of his source, or evidence thereof, on the theory that it is better to write about crime than to do something about it. Insofar as any reporter in these cases undertook not to reveal or testify about the crime he witnessed, his claim of privilege under the First Amendment presents no substantial question. The crimes of news sources are no less reprehensible and threatening to the public interest when witnessed by a reporter than when they are not. There remain those situations where a source is not engaged in criminal conduct but has information suggesting illegal conduct by others. Newsmen frequently receive information from such sources pursuant to a tacit or express agreement to withhold the source's name and suppress any information that the source wishes not published. Such informants presumably desire anonymity in order to avoid being entangled as a witness in a criminal trial or grand jury investigation. They may fear that disclosure will threaten their job security or personal safety or that it will simply result in dishonor or embarrassment.

The argument that the flow of news will be diminished by compelling reporters to aid the grand jury in a criminal investigation is not irrational, nor are the records before us silent on the matter. But we remain unclear how often and to what extent informers are actually deterred from furnishing information when newsmen are forced to testify before a grand jury. The available data indicate that some newsmen rely a great deal on confidential sources and that some informants are particularly sensitive to the threat of exposure and may be silenced if it is held by this Court that, ordinarily, newsmen must testify pursuant to subpoenas, but the evidence fails to demonstrate that there would be a significant constriction of the flow of news to the public if this Court reaffirms the prior common-law and constitutional rule regarding the testimonial obligations of newsmen. Estimates of the inhibiting effect of such subpoenas on the willingness of informants to make disclosures to newsmen are widely divergent and to a great extent speculative.

Accepting the fact, however, that an undetermined number of informants not themselves implicated in crime will nevertheless, for whatever reason, refuse to talk to newsmen if they fear identification by a reporter in an official investigation, we cannot accept the argument that the public interest in possible future news about crime from undisclosed, unverified sources must take precedence over the public interest in pursuing and prosecuting those crimes reported to the press by informants and in thus deterring the commission of such crimes in the future.

We are admonished that refusal to provide a First Amendment reporter's privilege will undermine the freedom of the press to collect and disseminate news. But this is not the lesson history teaches us. As noted previously, the common law recognized no such privilege, and the constitutional argument was not even asserted until 1958. From the beginning of our country the press has operated without constitutional protection for press informants, and the press has flourished. The existing constitutional rules have not been a serious obstacle to either the development or retention of confidential news sources by the press.

It is said that currently press subpoenas have multiplied, that mutual distrust and tension between press and officialdom have increased, that reporting styles have changed, and that there is now more need for confidential sources, particularly where the press seeks news about minority cultural and political groups or dissident organizations suspicious of the law and public officials. These developments, even if true, are treacherous grounds for a far-reaching interpretation of the First Amendment fastening a nationwide rule on courts, grand juries, and prosecuting officials everywhere. The obligation to testify in response to grand jury subpoenas will not threaten these sources not involved with criminal conduct and without information relevant to grand jury investigations, and we cannot hold that the Constitution places the sources in these two categories either above the law or beyond its reach.

We are unwilling to embark the judiciary on a long and difficult journey to such an uncertain destination. The administration of a constitutional newsman's privilege would present practical and conceptual difficulties of a high order. Sooner or later, it would be necessary to define those categories of newsmen who qualified for the privilege, a questionable procedure in light of the traditional doctrine that liberty of the press is the right of the lonely pamphleteer who uses carbon paper or a mimeograph just as much as of the large metropolitan publisher who utilizes the latest photocomposition methods. Freedom of the press is a "fundamental personal right" which "is not confined to newspapers and periodicals. It necessarily embraces pamphlets and leaflets. . . . The press in its historic connotation comprehends every sort of publication which affords a vehicle of information and opinion." The informative function asserted by representatives of the organized press in the present cases is also performed by lecturers, political pollsters, novelists, academic researchers, and dramatists. Almost any author may quite accurately assert that he is contributing to the flow of information to the public, that he relies on confidential sources of information, and that these sources will be silenced if he is forced to make disclosures before a grand jury.

In each instance where a reporter is subpoenaed to testify, the courts would also be embroiled in preliminary factual and legal determinations with respect to whether the proper predicate had been laid for the reporter's appearance: Is there probable cause to believe a crime has been committed? Is it likely that the reporter has useful information gained in confidence? Could the grand jury obtain the information elsewhere? Is the official interest sufficient to outweigh the claimed privilege?

Thus, in the end, by considering whether enforcement of a particular law served a "compelling" governmental interest, the courts would be inextricably involved in distinguishing between the value of enforcing different criminal laws. By requiring testimony from a reporter in investigations involving some crimes but not in others, they would be making a value judgment that a legislature had declined to make, since in each case the criminal law involved would represent a considered legislative judgment, not constitutionally suspect, of what conduct is liable to criminal prosecution. The task of judges, like other officials outside the legislative branch, is not to make the law but to uphold it in accordance with their oaths.

At the federal level, Congress has freedom to determine whether a statutory newsman's privilege is necessary and desirable and to fashion standards and rules as narrow or broad as deemed necessary to deal with the evil discerned and, equally important, to refashion those rules as experience from time to time may dictate. There is also merit in leaving state legislatures free, within First Amendment limits, to fashion their own standards in light of the conditions and problems with respect to the relations between law enforcement officials and press in their own areas. It goes without saying, of course, that we are powerless to bar state courts from responding in their own way and construing their own constitutions so as to recognize a newsman's privilege, either qualified or absolute.

Justice POWELL, concurring.

I add this brief statement to emphasize what seems to me to be the limited nature of the Court's holding. The Court does not hold that newsmen, subpoenaed to testify before a grand jury, are without constitutional rights with respect to the gathering of news or in safeguarding their sources. Certainly, we do not hold, as suggested in Mr. Justice STEWART's dissenting opinion, that state and federal authorities are free to "annex" the news media as "an investigative arm of government."

Justice STEWART dissenting.

The Court's crabbed view of the First Amendment reflects a disturbing insensitivity to the critical role of an independent press in our society . . . The Court . . . invites state and federal authorities to undermine the historic independence of the press by attempting to annex the journalistic profession as an investigative arm of government. Not only will this decision impair performance of the press' constitutionally protected functions, but it will, I am convinced, in the long run harm rather than help the administration of justice.

The reporter's constitutional right to a confidential relationship with his source stems from the broad societal interest in a full and free flow of information to the public. It is this basic concern that underlies the Constitution's protection of a free press . . .

Enlightened choice by an informed citizenry is the basic ideal upon which an open society is premised, and a free press is thus indispensable to a free society. Not only does the press enhance personal self-fulfillment by providing the people with the widest possible range of fact and opinion, but it also is an incontestable precondition of self-government . . . As private and public aggregations of power burgeon in size and the pressures for conformity necessarily mount, there is obviously a continuing need for an independent press to disseminate a robust variety of information and opinion through reportage, investigation, and criticism, if we are to preserve our constitutional tradition of maximizing freedom of choice by encouraging diversity of expression.

[W]hen a reporter is asked to appear before a grand jury and reveal confidences, I would hold that the government must (1) show that there is probable cause to believe that the newsman has information that is clearly relevant to a specific probable violation of law; (2) demonstrate that the information sought cannot be obtained by alternative means less destructive of First Amendment rights; and (3) demonstrate a compelling and overriding interest in the information.

DISCUSSION POINTS

1   Do you agree with the Court's ruling? Why or why not?

2   Both Justices White and Stewart believed that the state could compel journalists to testify before grand juries about secret sources. They arrived at that conclusion as the result of different sets of reasoning and, consequently, they viewed Branzburg's situation differently. Which Justice do you think offers a stronger rationale for arriving at the conclusion that journalists may be compelled to reveal their sources? Why do you favor that Justice's justification?

3   What is the potential harm to the media, if not the nation, from the majority's opinion?

4   The majority was unwilling to issue a ruling in favor of the media based on potential damage to the media's ability to cover public issues. Yet, when it comes to publications that it believes would pose a "clear and present danger" to the public, the Court has proven willing to act to avoid potential damage to society. Why is the majority unwilling to issue a ruling based on such possible damage to the media's ability to cover public issues? Does this distinction make sense? Why or why not?

5   Justice Stewart suggests a three-tier test for judging similar cases in the future. This has essentially become the law of the land as it has been the test that has been applied to future cases. What is this standard? How does it differ from the majority's reasoning in *Branzburg*?

Miami Herald Publishing Co. v. Tornillo
418 U.S. 241 (1974)

Florida's legislature, concerned that its cities tended to be dominated by single newspapers and, as a result, its citizens were not exposed to multiple points of view on public issues, enacted a "right of reply" law. Under the law, if a political candidate for election or re-election has his or her personal character or official record assailed by any newspaper, he or she had a right to demand, free of charge, that the newspaper print a reply. The reply had to appear in a conspicuous place and in the same type as the original charges. Failure to comply with the statute constituted a first-degree misdemeanor.

The Miami Herald *published a pair of editorials that were critical of Pat Tornillo, a candidate for the state house of representatives. Tornillo requested that the paper print his replies as per Florida's "right of reply" law. A Florida Circuit Court found the law in violation of the First Amendment. Florida's Supreme Court reversed the lower court. The* Miami Herald *appealed to the U.S. Supreme Court.*

Chief Justice BURGER delivered the opinion of the Court.

The issue in this case is whether a state statute granting a political candidate a right to equal space to reply to criticism and attacks on his record by a newspaper violates the guarantees of a free press.

The challenged statute creates a right to reply to press criticism of a candidate for nomination or election. The statute was enacted in 1913, and this is only the second recorded case decided under its provisions.

Appellant contends the statute is void on its face because it purports to regulate the content of a newspaper in violation of the First Amendment. Alternatively it is urged that the statute is void for vagueness since no editor could know exactly what words would call the statute into operation. It is also contended that the statute fails to distinguish between critical comment which is and which is not defamatory.

The appellee and supporting advocates of an enforceable right of access to the press vigorously argue that government has an obligation to ensure that a wide variety of views reach the public ... It is urged that at the time the First Amendment to the Constitution was ratified ... the press was broadly representative of the people it was serving. While many of the newspapers were intensely partisan and narrow in their views, the press collectively presented a broad range of opinions to readers. Entry into publishing was inexpensive; pamphlets and books provided meaningful alternatives to the organized press for the expression of unpopular ideas and often treated events and expressed views not covered by conventional newspapers. A true marketplace of ideas existed in which there was relatively easy access to the channels of communication.

Access advocates submit that although newspapers of the present are superficially similar to those of 1791 the press of today is in reality very different from that known in the early years of our national existence ... Newspapers have become big business and there are far fewer of them to serve a larger literate population. Chains of newspapers, national newspapers, national wire and news services, and one-newspaper towns, are the dominant features of a press that has become noncompetitive and enormously powerful and influential in its capacity to manipulate popular opinion and change the course of events ... the elimination of competing newspapers in most of our large cities, and the concentration of control of media that results from the only newspaper's being owned by the same interests which own a television station and a radio station, are important components of this trend toward concentration of control of outlets to inform the public.

The result of these vast changes has been to place in a few hands the power to inform the American people and shape public opinion. Much of the editorial opinion and commentary that is printed is that of syndicated columnists distributed nationwide and, as a result, we are told, on national and world issues there tends to be a homogeneity of editorial opinion, commentary, and interpretive analysis. The abuses of bias and manipulative reportage are, likewise, said to be the result of the vast accumulations of unreviewable power in the modern media empires. In effect, it is claimed, the public has lost any ability to respond or to contribute in a meaningful way to the debate on issues.

The monopoly of the means of communication allows for little or no critical analysis of the media except in professional journals of very limited readership . . .

The obvious solution, which was available to dissidents at an earlier time when entry into publishing was relatively inexpensive, today would be to have additional newspapers. But the same economic factors which have caused the disappearance of vast numbers of metropolitan newspapers, have made entry into the marketplace of ideas served by the print media almost impossible. It is urged that the claim of newspapers to be "surrogates for the public" carries with it a concomitant fiduciary obligation to account for that stewardship. From this premise it is reasoned that the only effective way to insure fairness and accuracy and to provide for some accountability is for government to take affirmative action. The First Amendment interest of the public in being informed is said to be in peril because the "marketplace of ideas" is today a monopoly controlled by the owners of the market.

Proponents of enforced access to the press take comfort from language in several of this Court's decisions which suggests that the First Amendment acts as a sword as well as a shield, that it imposes obligations on the owners of the press in addition to protecting the press from government regulation . . .

They also claim the qualified support of Professor Thomas I. Emerson, who has written that "[a] limited right of access to the press can be safely enforced," although he believes that "[g]overnment measures to encourage a multiplicity of outlets, rather than compelling a few outlets to represent everybody, seems a preferable course of action."

However much validity may be found in these arguments, at each point the implementation of a remedy such as an enforceable right of access necessarily calls for some mechanism, either governmental or consensual. If it is governmental coercion, this at once brings about a confrontation with the express provisions of the First Amendment and the judicial gloss on that Amendment developed over the years.

A responsible press is an undoubtedly desirable goal, but press responsibility is not mandated by the Constitution and like many other virtues it cannot be legislated.

Appellee's argument that the Florida statute does not amount to a restriction of appellant's right to speak because "the statute in question here has not prevented the *Miami Herald* from saying anything it wished" begs the core question. Compelling editors or publishers to publish that which "'reason' tells them should not be published" is what is at issue in this case. The Florida statute operates as a command in the same sense as a statute or regulation forbidding appellant to publish specified matter. Governmental restraint on publishing need not fall into familiar or traditional patterns to be subject to constitutional limitations on governmental powers. *Grosjean v. American Press Co.* (1936). The Florida statute exacts a penalty on the basis of the content of a newspaper. The first phase of the penalty resulting from the compelled printing of a reply is exacted in terms of the cost in printing and composing time and materials and in taking up space that could be devoted to other material the newspaper may have preferred to print.

Faced with the penalties that would accrue to any newspaper that published news or commentary arguably within the reach of the right-of-access statute, editors might well conclude that the safe course is to avoid controversy. Therefore, under the operation of the Florida statute, political and electoral coverage would be blunted or reduced. Government-enforced right of access inescapably "dampens the vigor and limits the variety of public debate," *New York Times Co. v. Sullivan* (1964).

Even if a newspaper would face no additional costs to comply with a compulsory access law and would not be forced to forgo publication of news or opinion by the inclusion of a reply, the Florida statute fails to clear the barriers of the First Amendment because of its intrusion into the function of editors. A newspaper is more than a passive receptacle or conduit for news, comment, and advertising. The choice of material to go into a newspaper, and the decisions made as to limitations on the size and content of the paper, and treatment of public issues and public officials—whether fair or unfair—constitute the exercise of editorial control and judgment. It has yet to be demonstrated how governmental regulation of this crucial process can be exercised consistent with First Amendment guarantees of a free press as they have evolved to this time. Accordingly, the judgment of the Supreme Court of Florida is reversed.

Justice BRENNAN, with whom Justice REHNQUIST joins, concurring.

I join the Court's opinion which, as I understand it, addresses only "right of reply" statutes and implies no view upon the constitutionality of "retraction" statutes affording plaintiffs able to prove defamatory falsehoods a statutory action to require publication of a retraction.

Justice WHITE, concurring.

According to our accepted jurisprudence, the First Amendment erects a virtually insurmountable barrier between government and the print media so far as government tampering, in advance of publication, with news and editorial content is concerned. *New York Times Co. v. United States*, (1971). A newspaper or magazine is not a public utility subject to "reasonable" governmental regulation in matters affecting the exercise of journalistic judgment as to what shall be printed. *Mills v. Alabama* (1966). We have learned, and continue to learn, from what we view as the unhappy experiences of other nations where government has been allowed to meddle in the internal editorial affairs of newspapers. Regardless of how beneficent-sounding the purposes of controlling the press might be, we prefer "the power of reason as applied through public discussion" and remain intensely skeptical about those measures that would allow government to insinuate itself into the editorial rooms of this Nation's press.

Of course, the press is not always accurate, or even responsible, and may not present full and fair debate on important public issues. But the balance struck by the First Amendment with respect to the press is that society must take the risk that occasionally debate on vital matters will not be comprehensive and that all viewpoints may not be expressed.

DISCUSSION POINTS

1   What do you think of the Court's opinion in this case? Does your answer depend at all on whether a city is a one- or multiple-paper town? Why or why not?

2   If the press serves the public by informing it, and if by virtue of this responsibility the press gains certain rights, does it have a responsibility to tell both sides?

3   Is there is a difference in legal doctrine between *stopping* the press from printing something (which is conceivable as in the case of government secrets) and *requiring* that the press publish something (also conceivable at least as far as defamation law goes)?

4   What is it about the print media that makes it different from the electronic media, and, as a result, insulates it from most government attempts at regulation?

5   How does one distinguish a case like *Red Lion* from *Tornillo*?

42

Richmond Newspapers, Inc. v. Virginia
448 U.S. 555 (1980)

In the 1970s, the Supreme Court heard a series of cases that explored how far judges could go to seek to ensure fair trials. One of the issues was whether judges, for the purposes of keeping the jury pool untainted, could bar the press from trial or pre-trial proceedings. In Gannett Co. v. DePasquale, *(1979), the Court held that judges could exclude the public and the press from certain pretrial proceedings.* Gannett *included language to the effect that such exclusions could only be applied to pre-trial proceedings and that judges were not empowered to seal their courtroom off to the press carte blanche. Yet, that is essentially what happened. In response, four sitting Justices of the United States Supreme Court "took the unusual step of telling audiences around the country that* Gannett *had been 'misread' to place unacceptable restraints on the press."* The next year, the Court, in* Richmond Newspapers, Inc. v. Virginia *(1980), sought to clarify its position in* Gannett Co. *(1979).*

In 1976 a Virginia trial court in Richmond convicted a Virginia man of murder. The state supreme court reversed his conviction. Several trials ensued—each resulting in a mistrial. In 1978, as a fourth trial was commencing, the defense asked the judge to close the court off to the public and the press during the trial so that jurors would not read inaccurate news summaries or undue speculation about the case. The prosecution did not object and the judge ordered the courtroom closed. Richmond Newspapers, Inc., filed suit on First Amendment grounds. It lost and appealed to the Supreme Court. During oral argument, Virginia asserted that because the Constitution contains no explicit language

---

* Louis Fisher, *American Constitutional Law.* 2nd Edition. New York: McGraw-Hill, 1995: 666).

recognizing a right of the press to attend judicial proceedings the states are free to close off their courtrooms if they so choose. Note how Chief Justice Burger relies on historical inquiry to set aside Virginia's argument and, in doing so, to blaze new trials in the interpretation of the Ninth Amendment.

Chief Justice BURGER announced the judgment of the Court and delivered an opinion, in which Justice WHITE and Justice STEVENS joined.

We begin consideration of this case by noting that the precise issue presented here has not previously been before this Court for decision. In *Gannett Co. v. DePasquale*, [1979] the Court was not required to decide whether a right of access to trials, as distinguished from hearings on pretrial motions, was constitutionally guaranteed. The Court held that the Sixth Amendment's guarantee to the accused of a public trial gave neither the public nor the press an enforceable right of access to a pretrial suppression hearing. One concurring opinion specifically emphasized that "a hearing on a motion before trial to suppress evidence is not a trial. . . ." (Burger, C. J., concurring).

[T]hroughout its evolution, the trial has been open to all who cared to observe . . . In the days before the Norman Conquest, cases in England were generally brought before moots, such as the local court of the hundred or the county court, which were attended by the freemen of the community . . . From these early times, although great changes in courts and procedure took place, one thing remained constant: the public character of the trial at which guilt or innocence was decided. . . . We have found nothing to suggest that the presumptive openness of the trial, which English courts were later to call "one of the essential qualities of a court of justice," was not also an attribute of the judicial systems of colonial America. In Virginia, for example, such records as there are of early criminal trials indicate that they were open, and nothing to the contrary has been cited. Indeed, when in the mid-1600's the Virginia Assembly felt that the respect due the courts was "by the clamorous unmannerlynes of the people lost, and order, gravity and decorum which should manifest the authority of a court in the court it selfe neglected," the response was not to restrict the openness of the trials to the public, but instead to prescribe rules for the conduct of those attending them . . . In some instances, the openness of trials was explicitly recognized as part of the fundamental law of the Colony . . .

As we have shown, and as was shown in both the Court's opinion and the dissent in *Gannett*, the historical evidence demonstrates conclusively that at the time when our organic laws were adopted, criminal trials both here and in England had long been presumptively open.

This is no quirk of history; rather, it has long been recognized as an indispensable attribute of an Anglo-American trial . . . From this unbroken, uncontradicted history, supported by reasons as valid today as in centuries past, we are bound to conclude that a presumption of openness inheres in the very nature of a criminal trial under our system of justice. This conclusion is hardly novel; without a direct holding on the issue, the Court has voiced its recognition of it in a variety of contexts over the years. Even while holding, in *Levine v. United States* (1960), that a criminal contempt proceeding was not a "criminal prosecution" within the meaning of the Sixth Amendment, the Court was careful to note that more than the Sixth Amendment was involved:

> "[D]ue process demands appropriate regard for the requirements of a public proceeding in cases of criminal contempt . . . as it does for all adjudications through the exercise of the judicial power, barring narrowly limited categories of exceptions. . . ."

And recently in *Gannett Co. v. DePasquale*, (1979), both the majority, and dissenting opinion, *id.*, at 423, agreed that open trials were part of the common-law tradition.

Despite the history of criminal trials being presumptively open since long before the Constitution, the State presses its contention that neither the Constitution nor the Bill of Rights contains any provision which by its terms guarantees to the public the right to attend criminal trials. Standing alone, this is correct, but there remains the question whether, absent an explicit provision, the Constitution affords protection against exclusion of the public from criminal trials.

The First Amendment, in conjunction with the Fourteenth, prohibits governments from "abridging the freedom of speech, or of the press; or the right of the people peaceably to assemble, and to petition the Government for a redress of grievances." These expressly guaranteed freedoms share a common core purpose of assuring freedom of communication on matters relating to the functioning of government. Plainly it would be difficult to single out any aspect of government of higher concern and importance to the people than the manner in which criminal trials are conducted; as we have shown, recognition of this pervades the centuries-old history of open trials and the opinions of this Court . . . The explicit, guaranteed rights to speak and to publish concerning what takes place at a trial would lose much meaning if access to observe the trial could, as it was here, be foreclosed arbitrarily.

The State argues that the Constitution nowhere spells out a guarantee for the right of the public to attend trials, and that accordingly no such right is protected. The possibility that such a contention could be made did not escape the notice of the Constitution's draftsmen;

they were concerned that some important rights might be thought disparaged because not specifically guaranteed. It was even argued that because of this danger no Bill of Rights should be adopted. See, e. g., *The Federalist* No. 84 (A. Hamilton). In a letter to Thomas Jefferson in October 1788, James Madison explained why he, although "in favor of a bill of rights," had "not viewed it in an important light" up to that time: "I conceive that in a certain degree . . . the rights in question are reserved by the manner in which the federal powers are granted." He went on to state that "there is great reason to fear that a positive declaration of some of the most essential rights could not be obtained in the requisite latitude." 5 *Writings of James Madison* 271 (G. Hunt ed. 1904).*

[T]he Court has acknowledged that certain unarticulated rights are implicit in enumerated guarantees. For example, the rights of association and of privacy, the right to be presumed innocent, and the right to be judged by a standard of proof beyond a reasonable doubt in a criminal trial, as well as the right to travel, appear nowhere in the Constitution or Bill of Rights. Yet these important but unarticulated rights have nonetheless been found to share constitutional protection in common with explicit guarantees . . . We hold that the right to attend criminal trials is implicit in the guarantees of the First Amendment; without the freedom to attend such trials, which people have exercised for centuries, important aspects of freedom of speech and "of the press could be eviscerated." *Branzburg*. [1972].

Having concluded there was a guaranteed right of the public under the First and Fourteenth Amendments to attend the trial of Stevenson's case, we return to the closure order challenged by appellants. Absent an overriding interest articulated in findings, the trial of a criminal case must be open to the public.† Accordingly, the judgment under review is Reversed.

---

* It was here that the Chief Justice inserted the following: [Footnote 15] Madison's comments in Congress also reveal the perceived need for some sort of constitutional "saving clause," which, among other things, would serve to foreclose application to the Bill of Rights of the maxim that the affirmation of particular rights implies a negation of those not expressly defined. See 1 *Annals of Cong.* 438–440 (1789). See also, e. g., J. Story, *Commentaries on the Constitution of the United States* (5th ed. 1891). Madison's efforts, culminating in the Ninth Amendment, served to allay the fears of those who were concerned that expressing certain guarantees could be read as excluding others.

† It was here that the Chief Justice inserted the following: [Footnote 18] We have no occasion here to define the circumstances in which all or parts of a criminal trial may be closed to the public, but our holding today does not mean that the First Amendment rights of the public and representatives of the press are absolute. Just as a government may impose reasonable time, place, and manner restrictions upon the use of its streets in the interest of such objectives as the free flow of traffic, see, e. g., *Cox v. New Hampshire*, (1941), so may a trial judge, in the interest of the fair administration of justice, impose reasonable limitations on ac-

Justice BRENNAN, with whom Justice MARSHALL joins, concurring in the judgment.

The instant case raises the question whether the First Amendment, of its own force and as applied to the States through the Fourteenth Amendment, secures the public an independent right of access to trial proceedings . . . I believe that the First Amendment—of itself and as applied to the States through the Fourteenth Amendment—secures such a public right of access . . .

[T]he Court has not ruled out a public access component to the First Amendment in every circumstance. Read with care and in context, our decisions must therefore be understood as holding only that any privilege of access to governmental information is subject to a degree of restraint dictated by the nature of the information and countervailing interests in security or confidentiality. These cases neither comprehensively nor absolutely deny that public access to information may at times be implied by the First Amendment and the principles which animate it.

The Court's approach in right-of-access cases simply reflects the special nature of a claim of First Amendment right to gather information. Customarily, First Amendment guarantees are interposed to protect communication between speaker and listener. When so employed against prior restraints, free speech protections are almost insurmountable . . . But the First Amendment embodies more than a commitment to free expression and communicative interchange for their own sakes; it has a structural role to play in securing and fostering our republican system of self-government. Implicit in this structural role is not only "the principle that debate on public issues should be uninhibited, robust, and wide-open," *New York Times Co. v. Sullivan*, (1964), but also the antecedent assumption that valuable public debate—as well as other civic behavior—must be informed. The structural model links the First Amendment to that process of communication necessary for a democracy to survive, and thus entails solicitude not only for communication itself, but also for the indispensable conditions of meaningful communication.

---

cess to a trial. "[T]he question in a particular case is whether that control is exerted so as not to deny or unwarrantedly abridge . . . the opportunities for the communication of thought and the discussion of public questions immemorially associated with resort to public places." It is far more important that trials be conducted in a quiet and orderly setting than it is to preserve that atmosphere on city streets. Compare, e. g., *Kovacs v. Cooper*, with *Illinois v. Allen*, (1970), and *Estes v. Texas*, (1965). Moreover, since courtrooms have limited capacity, there may be occasions when not every person who wishes to attend can be accommodated. In such situations, reasonable restrictions on general access are traditionally imposed, including preferential seating for media representatives.

Justice STEWART, concurring in the judgment.

[T]he First and Fourteenth Amendments clearly give the press and the public a right of access to trials themselves, civil as well as criminal . . . But this does not mean that the First Amendment right of members of the public and representatives of the press to attend civil and criminal trials is absolute. Just as a legislature may impose reasonable time, place, and manner restrictions upon the exercise of First Amendment freedoms, so may a trial judge impose reasonable limitations upon the unrestricted occupation of a courtroom by representatives of the press and members of the public . . . Since in the present case the trial judge appears to have given no recognition to the right of representatives of the press and members of the public to be present at the Virginia murder trial over which he was presiding, the judgment under review must be reversed.

Justice BLACKMUN, concurring in the judgment.

The Court's ultimate ruling in *Gannett*, with such clarification as is provided by the opinions in this case today, apparently is now to the effect that there is no Sixth Amendment right on the part of the public—or the press—to an open hearing on a motion to suppress. I, of course, continue to believe that *Gannett* was in error, both in its interpretation of the Sixth Amendment generally, and in its application to the suppression hearing, for I remain convinced that the right to a public trial is to be found where the Constitution explicitly placed it—in the Sixth Amendment.

The Court, however, has eschewed the Sixth Amendment route. The plurality turns to other possible constitutional sources and invokes a veritable potpourri of them—the Speech Clause of the First Amendment, the Press Clause, the Assembly Clause, the Ninth Amendment, and a cluster of penumbral guarantees recognized in past decisions. This course is troublesome, but it is the route that has been selected and, at least for now, we must live with it. No purpose would be served by my spelling out at length here the reasons for my saying that the course is troublesome. I need do no more than observe that uncertainty marks the nature—and strictness—of the standard of closure the Court adopts.

Justice REHNQUIST, dissenting.

In the Gilbert and Sullivan operetta "Iolanthe," the Lord Chancellor recites:

> "The Law is the true embodiment of everything that's excellent,
> It has no kind of fault or flaw,
> And I, my Lords, embody the Law."

It is difficult not to derive more than a little of this flavor from the various opinions supporting the judgment in this case. The opinion of The Chief Justice states:

> "[H]ere for the first time the Court is asked to decide whether a criminal trial itself may be closed to the public upon the unopposed request of a defendant, without any demonstration that closure is required to protect the defendant's superior right to a fair trial, or that some other overriding consideration requires closure."

The opinion of Justice BRENNAN states:

> "Read with care and in context, our decisions must therefore be understood as holding only that any privilege of access to governmental information is subject to a degree of restraint dictated by the nature of the information and countervailing interests in security or confidentiality."

I do not believe that either the First or Sixth Amendment, as made applicable to the States by the Fourteenth, requires that a State's reasons for denying public access to a trial, where both the prosecuting attorney and the defendant have consented to an order of closure approved by the judge, are subject to any additional constitutional review at our hands. And I most certainly do not believe that the Ninth Amendment confers upon us any such power to review orders of state trial judges closing trials in such situations.

The issue here is not whether the "right" to freedom of the press conferred by the First Amendment to the Constitution overrides the defendant's "right" to a fair trial conferred by other Amendments to the Constitution; it is instead whether any provision in the Constitution may fairly be read to prohibit what the trial judge in the Virginia state-court system did in this case. Being unable to find any such prohibition in the First, Sixth, Ninth, or any other Amendment to the United States Constitution, or in the Constitution itself, I dissent.

DISCUSSION POINTS

1 In your opinion, was this case decided correctly? Why or why not?

2 Does the distinction between pre-trial and trial proceedings make sense as far as a judge's ability to bar the public or the press from a courtroom?

3 What are the differences between the arguments in favor of opening courtrooms during trials? Whose do you favor? Chief Justice Burger's? Justice Brennan's? Justice Blackmun's?

4   Can you envision instances when the press should be excluded from a trial? What are they?

5   The Court's opinion left open the idea that trials could be closed to the media. The Court did not state how this would be done. [See Footnote †, page 273 (Footnote 18) from the Chief Justice.] In subsequent cases, the Court has tried to refine or clarify its doctrine. The leading approach, articulated in subsequent cases, has been to ask if: (1) the judicial proceeding is historically open and, if so, (2) if the basic fairness of a trial is enhanced by letting the press attend, and, again, if so, (3) if closure is essential to preserve some higher values and, if so, (4) if the closure is narrowly tailored to serve that interest. See *Press-Enterprise v. Riverside County Supervisor Court* (1984) and *In Press-Enterprise v. Riverside County Supervisor Court II* (1986).

6   What point about the law and the proper role of judges was Justice Rehnquist making when he invoked Gilbert and Sullivan's *Iolanthe*?

CREDITS AND COPYRIGHTS

1. From Thomas Emerson, *Toward a General Theory of the First Amendment*. Reprinted by permission of The Yale Law Journal Company and Henry S. Hein Company from *The Yale Law Journal*, Vol. 72, (April, 1963), pages *877–956*.

2. From Vincent Blasi, *The Checking Value in the First Amendment,* Law & Social Inquiry, Vol. 2:3, pages 521–538. Copyright © 1977 by Blackwell Publishing. Reprinted by permission of the publisher.

3. From *Protecting the Best Men: An Interpretive History of The Law of Libel*, by Norman L. Rosenberg. Copyright © 1986 by the University of North Carolina Press. Used by permission of the publisher.

4. Reprinted with the permission of Simon & Schuster Adult Publishing Group from *All the President's Men*, by Carl Bernstein and Bob Woodward. Copyright © 1974 by Carl Bernstein and Bob Woodward.

5. From *See How They Run*, by Paul Taylor, copyright © 1990 by Paul Taylor. Used by permission of Alfred A. Knopf, a division of Random House, Inc.

6. From Larry J. Sabato, *Feeding Frenzy: Attack Journalism and American Politics*. Copyright © 2000 by Larry J. Sabato. Reprinted by Permission of LANAHAN PUBLISHERS, INC., Baltimore, MD.

7. Abridged from *A Good Life: Newspapering and Other Adventures*, by Ben Bradlee. Copyright © 1995 by Benjamin C. Bradlee. Used with the permission of Simon & Schuster Adult Publishing Group.

8. Reprinted from *White House Studies 4*, No. 2 (2004): pages 217–220, 225–229 [with cuts], "September 11th and the Bush Presidency: Rally Around the Rubble" by Stephen E. Frantzich. Copyright © 2004 by Nova Science Publishers, Inc. Used with the permission from Nova Science Publishers, Inc.

9. From Daniel Shea and John Michael Burton, *Campaign Craft: The Strategies, Tactics, and Art of Political Campaign Management*. Copyright © 2001 by Daniel M. Shea and John Michael Burton. Reproduced with permission of Greenwood Publishing Group, Inc., Westport, CT.

10. From Katherine Q. Seelye, "Making of the Digital Press Corps" in *The New York Times*. [Jan. 29, 2004] Copyright © 2004 by The New York Times Co. Reprinted with permission.

11. From Richard Davis, *Electing Justice: Fixing the Supreme Court Nomination Process*. Copyright © 2005 by Richard Davis. By permission of Oxford University Press.

12. Abridged from *A Good Life: Newspapering and Other Adventures*, by Ben Bradlee. Copyright © 1995 by Benjamin C. Bradlee. Used with the permission of Simon & Schuster Adult Publishing Group.

13. From Danny Schechter, "Information Warriors: From the News Dissector's Weblog" in *Media Wars: News at a Time or Terror*, by Danny Schechter. Copyright © 2003 by Danny Schechter. Used with permission from Rowman & Littlefield Publishing Group.

14. From Jake Lynch "Tips for Covering Conflict" in *Media Wars: News at a Time or Terror*, by Danny Schechter. Copyright © 2003 by Danny Schechter. Used with permission from Rowman & Littlefield Publishing Group.

15. From Irwin Sonny Fox "Using Soap Operas to Confront the World's Population Problem" in *Advocacy Groups and the Entertainment Industry*, edited by Michael Suman and Gabriel Rossman. Copyright © 2000 by Center for Communication Policy. Reproduced with permission of Greenwood Publishing Group, Inc., Westport, CT.

16. From Emily Nussbaum, "When a TV Network Could Be Cynical About a War" in *The New York Times* [April 27, 2003]. Copyright © 2003 by The New York Times Co. Reprinted by permission.

17. From Elizabeth Jensen, *Public Broadcasting and Political Balance: A New Twist* in *The New York Times* [June 29, 2005]. Copyright © 2005 by The New York Times Co. Reprinted by permission.

18. From César G. Soriano, *Politics Creates a Disturbance in the Force* [May 18, 2005]. Copyright © 2005 by USA Today. Reprinted with permission.

19. From *Operation Hollywood: How the Pentagon Shapes and Censors the Movies* "A Commercial for Us" by David L. Robb, pages 33–38, 47–48. (Amherst, NY: Prometheus Books). Copyright © 2004 by David L. Robb. Reprinted with permission of the publisher.

20. From Ray Bradbury, *Fahrenheit 451*. Reprinted by permission of Don Congdon Associates, Inc. Copyright © 1979 by Ray Bradbury.

21. From Alessandra Stanley, "No Jokes or Spin. It's Time (Gasp) to Talk" in *The New York Times* [Oct. 20, 2004, Arts & Culture Section, page 7]. Copyright © 2004 by The New York Times. All Rights Reserved. Used by permission and protected by the Copyright Laws of the United States. The printing, copying, redistribution, or retransmission of the Material without express written permission is prohibited.

22. From Sheryl Gay Stolberg, "Laugh and the Voters Laugh with You, or at Least at You" in *The New York Times* [Feb. 26, 2006]. Copyright © 2006 by The New York Times Co. Reprinted with permission.

23. From John Borland, "Bloggers Drive Hoax Probe into Bush Memos" in CNET.com [Sept. 10, 2004]. Copyright © 2004 by CNET Neworks, Inc. Reprinted by permission.

24. From Jim VandeHei, "Blogs Attack From Left as Democrats Reach for Center" in *The Washington Post* [Jan. 28, 2006, page A6]. Copyright © 2006 by The Washington Post. Reprinted with permission.

25. From Eugene Volokh, "You Can Blog, But You Can't Hide" in *The New York Times* [Dec. 2, 2004, Op-Ed page]. Copyright © 2004 by The New York Times Co. Reprinted by permission.

26. From *Inventing Reality* by Michael Parenti. Copyright © 1985 by Michael Parenti, and reprinted by permission of St. Martin's Press, LLC.

27. Excerpts from pages 33–43 and 67–70 from *News: The Politics of Illusion*, 6th Edition, by W. Lance Bennett. Copyright © 2005 by Pearson Education. Reprinted by permission.

28. From Ted Koppel, "And Now, a Word for our Demographic" in *The New York Times* [Jan. 29, 2006, Op-Ed page]. Copyright © 2006 by The New York Times Co. Reprinted by permission.

29. From Michael Schudson, "The Social Origins of Press Cynicism in Portraying Politics" in *Is Journalism Hopelessly Cynical?* edited by Laura Lawrie, *American Behavioral Scientist*, Vol. 42 No. 6, March 1999, 999–1008. Copyright © 1999 by Sage Publications, Inc. Reprinted by permission of the publisher.

30. Reprinted with the permission of Simon & Schuster Adult Publishing Group from *All the President's Men*, by Carl Bernstein and Bob Woodward. Copyright © 1974 by Carl Bernstein and Bob Woodward.

31. From David Brinkley, "On Being an Anchorman" in *The New York Times* [June 14, 2003, Op-Ed page]. Copyright © 2003 by The New York Times Co. Reprinted by permission.

32–42. Excerpted from *United States Reports*, published by the United States Government Printing Office, Washington, D.C. [A note on case location: In the full title of the case, the number to the left of "U.S." refers to the volume number; the number to the right indicates the page number. The date in parentheses is the year the case was handed down by the United States Supreme Court.]